Key Perspectives in Crimino

Key Perspectives in Criminology

John Tierney

 Open University Press

Open University Press
McGraw-Hill Education
McGraw-Hill House
Shoppenhangers Road
Maidenhead
Berkshire
England
SL6 2QL

email: enquiries@openup.co.uk
world wide web: www.openup.co.uk

and Two Penn Plaza, New York, NY 10121–2289, USA

First published 2009

A catalogue record of this book is available from the British Library

ISBN-13: 978-0-335-229147 (pb) 978-0-335-22913-0 (hb)
ISBN-10: 0-33-522914-X (pb) 0-33-522913-1 (hb)

Typeset by Kerrypress, Luton, Bedfordshire
Printed and bound in the UK by Bell and Bain Ltd., Glasgow

The *McGraw·Hill* Companies

Contents

This book is dedicated to my mother, Mary

Introduction

Criminology, in common with all academic disciplines, incorporates a variety of theoretical perspectives that have emerged and developed over the years. Students of criminology are, of course, expected to become familiar with these perspectives, together with the ideas, concepts, agendas and traditions with which they are associated. This includes an appreciation of their place and influence within the history of criminology, the debates and theoretical refinements stimulated by them, points of convergence and divergence between one and another, and their continuing relevance to contemporary criminological theory and practice. This book is designed to provide students with a critical and accessible introduction to the major perspectives and traditions found in criminology. As the title indicates, the book does not attempt to provide an exhaustive, dictionary-style list of every conceivable perspective one might be able to identify. Rather, what follows are detailed discussions of the *key* theoretical perspectives within criminology. As such, decisions regarding what to include and what to omit were guided by the author's assessment of a perspective's historical significance and continuing relevance, or, in the case of more recent developments, the influence of a particular perspective on contemporary criminological thought.

The discussion of each of these perspectives also provides a context within which to examine a range of key criminological terms and concepts. This is important in that while these terms and concepts could obviously be formally defined and discussed in their own right, it is argued here that they only become 'alive' when placed within the different conceptual and theoretical frameworks associated with the various perspectives. Thus the chapter on labelling theory, for instance, 'naturally' includes a discussion of such things as interactionism, the social construction of deviance, moral panics, folk devils, deviancy amplification and primary and secondary deviation. In addition, a cross-referencing system to every chapter allows the reader to explore further particular terms, concepts, themes and debates within the context of other perspectives.

In short, the intention has been to provide the reader with detailed knowledge and understanding of the key theoretical perspectives and traditions within criminology, along with the relevant conceptual language. It is hoped that the book will provide a strong foundation for those interested in getting to grips with, and developing a serious interest in, the discipline of criminology.

1 Abolitionism

The origins of contemporary forms of abolitionism lie in the penal reform movements that emerged in the Scandinavian countries during the 1960s; by the 1980s abolitionism had developed into an important perspective within critical criminology. Subsequently, it became part of the so-called 'new European criminology' that developed during the second half of the 1990s (Ruggiero et al. 1998; Taylor 1999). This Europeanized criminology turned its attention to issues of crime and control within the context of the European Community, the 'European dream', and the deregulated neo-liberal market that by then provided its economic foundation. Attention focused on such things as transnational policing and the increasing cooperation among the police forces of Europe (Sheptycki 1995); pan-European surveillance and security, involving the exchange of information and the movement of the security services around Europe (Sheptycki 1997); transnational organized crime (Ruggiero 2000); and, in the case of abolitionism, systems of punishment and exclusion.

The most influential figures associated with abolitionism are: Bianchi and van Swaaningen 1986; Hulsman 1986; Mathiesen 1990; Christie 1993. Abolitionism is both a theoretical perspective and a political movement oriented towards radical change in the spheres of criminal justice and penal policy. At the core of abolitionism is a critique of the criminal justice and penal systems of Europe (and by implication elsewhere), with particular attention being given to the use of imprisonment. It is an expression of what Cohen (1985) calls the 'deconstructionist impulse' in the sociology of deviance: a desire to expose and challenge official, conventional thinking on matters of crime and justice and ultimately to see the abolition of extant state mechanisms of control and domination. From this perspective, these systems are both ineffective and counterproductive. They are ineffective because they do not deter or rehabilitate offenders, and counterproductive because they create more problems than they solve. Imprisonment may satisfy the demand for retribution – an 'eye for an eye' – and through incapacitation prevent an individual from offending, yet, according to abolitionists, the overall effect is to create harm and increase amounts of offending. Thus, abolitionists argue that imprisonment:

- is a punitive response that deflects attention away from the social circumstances and experiences that lead to offending in the first place;

- is the culmination of social control and judicial processes that discriminate on the bases of class and 'race'. The criminal justice system concentrates on the crimes of the powerless rather than the crimes of the powerful;
- does not provide an appropriate setting for rehabilitation, or as abolitionists put it, dispute settlement and the integration of the offender into society. On the contrary, imprisonment exacerbates social exclusion and reduces the likelihood of successful re-integration into society. This is reflected in high rates of recidivism;
- may remove an individual from society and thus the opportunity to offend, but only in terms of the 'outside world'. A great deal of offending, for example, violence and illicit drug use, occurs in prisons;
- places the offender into a brutal and brutalizing enclosed society, one where there are countless opportunities to learn new criminal skills and join new criminal networks;
- increases, rather than reduces, feelings of anger, resentment, humiliation, frustration and alienation.

A distinction between the abolitionism found in continental Europe and the 'neo-abolitionism' found in Britain can be noted. In the case of the latter, there has been greater involvement in grass-roots movements involving such things as prisoners' rights and miscarriages of justice (see, for example, Sim 1994).

As indicated above, abolitionism is not concerned with the liberal reform of prisons, rather, it is oriented towards dismantling the criminal justice and penal systems as presently constituted in Europe and North America, and replacing them with radically different approaches to criminalized problems. There are two key dimensions to this. First, abolitionists argue for the development of a new 'replacement discourse': a new conceptual language pertaining to 'crime', 'criminals', and so on aimed at challenging and undermining existing, taken-for-granted understandings. This is a strategy that to some extent aligns them with constitutive criminology, as well as other critical perspectives (see Chapter 7). Hulsman (1986), for instance, argues that the category of 'crime' should be replaced by 'problematic situations', making the point that there is: 'nothing which distinguishes those (conventionally understood) "criminal" events intrinsically from other difficult or unpleasant situations' (p. 65). Thus 'crime' would be defined by reference to problematic situations rather than criminal law. In a similar vein, Pepinsky and Quinney (1991) wish to reconceptualize criminology as peacemaking, an approach to dealing with crime and criminals based upon reconciliation and healing, as opposed to one based on a punitive 'war against crime'. This takes us to the second key dimension, which is a commitment to replacing current criminal justice and penal systems with more humane, life-affirming and effective modes of conflict resolution such as community participation in processes of adjudication, mediation schemes, and forms of restorative justice.

Versions of restorative justice have been tried in Britain, the United States and other parts of the world, though historically it was mainly found in small societies, such as the Maori society in New Zealand. It represents an alternative to justice systems based upon retribution and deterrence, which are seen as alienating an offender from the community and increasing anger, resentment and conflict. Restorative justice involves discussions among all relevant parties as part of a process aimed at healing the harm done to the victim and the community by some form of reparation. The major theoretical work on restorative justice is associated with Braithwaite (1989), who introduced the notion of 'reintegrative shaming', a process meant to prevent the stigmatization and marginalization that normally arise from conventional criminal justice processes. The basic idea is that offenders acknowledge the wrongfulness of their offending; that is, experience shame, and agree to repair the damage done. More recently, Braithwaite and colleagues (Ahmed et al. 2001) have added the concepts of 'ethical identity' and 'shame management' to their theoretical model. The former describes a situation where an offender accepts the wrongfulness of their behaviour and that there is an aspect of self-identity that must change, while at the same time understanding that they are not fundamentally 'bad' and have the capacity to change. The latter describes an element of the process of reintegrative shaming whereby an offender is helped to develop a 'self-regulating conscience'.

Abolitionism has been criticized for its Utopianism and 'idealism', and what appears to be an all or nothing commitment to radical change, 'mere' reform seen by proponents as liberal tinkering with the system (thus attitudes towards, say, restorative justice programmes are likely to be somewhat ambivalent). There is also the question of whether or not there is a place for prisons of any sort in an 'ideal' future society, and if there is, what would they look like? Feminist writers in particular have queried the idea of dismantling the prison system in view of the extent of male violence towards women.

Evidence from attempts to evaluate the success of restorative justice programmes is inconclusive (see, for example, Crawford and Newburn 2002). On a more theoretical level, Pavlich (2005) argues that, while the rhetoric of restorative justice promises something totally different to traditional approaches, in practice it continues to use the same sort of vocabulary and conceptual framework. Thus instead of offering a replacement discourse as advocated by abolitionists, it recycles taken-for-granted concepts such as 'crime' and 'offender'. In addition, 'crime', as conventionally understood, takes centre stage and, therefore, there is an implicit assumption that criminal law definitions of 'harm' or 'problematic situations' will suffice. In Pavlich's view, this dilution of its radicalism was an inevitable precondition for the (even limited) incorporation of restorative justice into the traditional criminal justice process.

Further reading

Good discussions of the abolitionist approach by some of the major figures are Bianchi, H. and van Swaaningen, R. (eds) (1986) *Abolitionism: Towards a Non-repressive Approach to Crime*. Amsterdam: Free University Press; Mathiesen, T. (1990) *Prison on Trial*. London: Sage Publications; and Christie, N. (1993) *Crime Control as Industry: Towards Gulags Western Style*. London: Routledge. A collection of readings that gives particular attention to the issue of 'race' and ethnicity is James, J. (ed.) (1991) *The Angela Y. Davies Reader*. Oxford: Blackwell Publishing. On European critical criminology, see van Swaaningen, R. (1997) *Critical Criminology: Visions from Europe*, London: Sage Publications.

2 Administrative Criminology

Administrative criminology comprises two kindred perspectives – routine activity theory and rational choice theory – and is sometimes referred to as opportunity theory or environmental criminology. A more recent development, crime science, has similar concerns and this will be discussed at the end of this chapter. Although administrative criminologists acknowledge that criminality (i.e. offending behaviour) does not appear 'out of the blue', but will be linked to various causal factors, their approach to the study of crime in effect makes these causal factors irrelevant. It is thus an approach that can be placed within the classical tradition in criminology (see Chapter 5). There is, however, a key difference between the two: while administrative criminology concentrates on the situational prevention of crime, classical criminology was fundamentally concerned with creating a more efficient and effective criminal justice system in order to deter the individual from offending. There are similarities too between control theory (also part of the classical tradition – see Chapter 6) and administrative criminology, though the key difference here is that while the former links the notion of control to criminal motivations, the latter ignores such motivations, and seeks to control already motivated individuals through situational crime prevention.

Instead of focusing on the criminal, administrative criminology focuses on the crime. Particular emphasis is placed on notions of opportunity and decision-making, with offenders seen as 'rationally' weighing up the costs and benefits prior to committing a crime (similar to classical criminology's pleasure–pain principle). By seeing offenders as making rational choices, it follows that they are also seen as blameworthy; in no sense can their behaviour be excused. Thus in terms of policy, it challenged, and then replaced, a previously dominant liberal positivist paradigm, which had emphasized analyses of causal factors; for example, an offender's social background and, on this basis, the development of policy interventions aimed at 'correcting' the behaviour of individual offenders.

Although it would be simplistic to characterize administrative criminology as necessarily politically conservative, because of their nature, the ideas associated with this type of criminology found a favourable audience among conservative politicians, on both sides of the Atlantic, during the 1980s. As Young (who first used the term 'administrative criminology') puts it, it became 'the major paradigm in establishment approaches to crime' (Young 1994: 91). This influence on criminal justice policy has continued right up to the present day. It is also worth noting that one of the two criminologists credited with playing a key role in the genesis and subsequent development of administrative criminology is the American neo-conservative James Q. Wilson (see Chapter 15). The other criminologist is Ron Clarke, also an American, who helped set up a major power base for administrative criminology at the Home Office, where he worked in the 1980s.

Rational choice theory

Rational choice theory works on the assumption that there are lots of potential offenders 'out there' in society. The task then becomes one of exploring the specific circumstances under which an individual decides to go ahead and commit a crime. Once this has been established, then suitable interventions designed to alter these circumstances, in other words situational crime prevention, can be devised. Perhaps unsurprisingly the chief focus is on 'conventional' crime such as burglary and criminal damage. Although the need for detailed research into the nature of these circumstances can be readily appreciated, the view that offenders take them into consideration when deciding whether or not to commit an offence may, to an outside observer, seem commonsensical to a fault. Clearly, it would not be unusual for, say, an intending burglar to select a particular property at a particular time of day, ascertain if the property is occupied, and check out any security system. Likewise, an intending street robber is likely to consider such things as type of victim, possible prying eyes and escape routes. However, as we shall see, the issue of 'weighing up' the circumstances and attendant decision-making processes on the part of an individual are not as straightforward as one might first think.

Clarke and other proponents of rational choice theory are fundamentally concerned with reducing the opportunities and temptations available to the potential offender. The aim is to reduce these opportunities and temptations, and in the process make crime, against a person or property, 'irrational'. According to Clarke (1995, then updated by Cornish and Clarke 2003) there are a number of interrelated ways in which this can be achieved (and based on a summary provided by Crawford 2007: 874).

Increasing the perceived effort involved in carrying out the crime

- *Target hardening* – protection provided for a potential target, for example, bolts on doors and security devices on cars.
- *Access control* – making it difficult to get to the target, for example, b electronic cards to access premises.

- *Screen exits* – for example, electronics screening of tagged goods at the exits to stores.
- *Deflecting offenders* – offering non-offending alternatives, such as litter bins, or physically separating individuals from the opportunity to offend, for example, rival football supporters.
- *Controlling means/facilitators* – preventing access to goods and services that lead to offending, for example, controls on the sale of alcohol.

Increasing the perceived risks of being caught

- *Extend guardianship* – providing another line of defence, for instance screening baggage in airports.
- *Formal surveillance* – surveillance provided by dedicated personnel, such as police officers, or technologies such as speed cameras and CCTV systems.
- *Employee surveillance* – surveillance provided by an organization's employees, such as school janitors and bus drivers.
- *Natural surveillance* – a more general improvement in surveillance involving, for example, reducing environmental or architectural features that provide cover for an offender, better street lighting or the use of neighbourhood watch schemes.
- *Reduce anonymity* – providing people with some form of identity.

Reducing the anticipated rewards of crime

- *Target concealment* – this involves keeping valuables in a place of safety; for example, a car in a secure garage.
- *Target removal* – for example, minimizing the amount of cash carried by, say, a taxi driver, or providing secure transport for vulnerable people.
- *Property identification* – for example, a security code etching on a car windscreen, or a post code etching on household goods.
- *Disruption of markets* – this refers to markets that may be used for the sale of stolen or illegal goods, for example, car boot sales, or pubs trading in smuggled cigarettes.
- *Deny benefits* – taking actions that negate the benefits associated with the offending, for example, automatic disabling of electronic goods.

Reducing provocation

- *Decreasing stress and frustration* – for example, the proper management of potential 'pressure points' such as late night taxi ranks, or ensuring polite service in bars and clubs.

- *Minimizing the possibility of disputes* – an attempt to pre-empt conflict by measures such as clear and agreed taxi fares, or ensuring that places of entertainment are not overcrowded.
- *Reducing temptation and arousal* – this focuses on the control of factors that may influence offending; for example, incitement to racial hatred in the media.
- *Neutralizing peer pressure* – such things as education programmes aimed at under-age drinking, which are intended to insulate individuals from any negative influences from peer groups.
- *Discourage imitation* – removing 'invitations' to commit crime by, for example (and as right realists – see Chapter 15 – would put it), 'mending broken windows'.

Removing excuses

- *Rule setting* – providing official paperwork, such as a tax return or tenancy agreement, establishing a clear set of rules.
- *Posting instructions* – ensuring good signage relating to, for example, 'no smoking', or warnings about the action that will be taken against rule-breakers.
- *Stimulating conscience* – efforts made to get people to appreciate the moral dimensions to offending; for example, road safety information on the highway.
- *Facilitating compliance* – the provision of such things as ample public toilets in order to encourage non-offending behaviour.
- *Controlling disinhibitors* – this includes a wide range of possibilities aimed at hindering the temptation to offend; for instance, parental control of the ease of access to alcohol in the home by their children, or making breathalysers available in pubs.

Critical analyses of rational choice theory can be pitched on three different levels: technical, qualitative and theoretical. The first two focus on crime prevention as discussed above, while the third is concerned with rational choice theory as a whole. On a technical level, analyses are directed at practical application (can it be done?) and effectiveness (does it work?). From the point of view of practical application, analyses look at, for instance, the costs involved in implementing a particular crime initiative, or the quality of CCTV images. The issue of effectiveness is more complex, and usually involves the use of evaluative studies that draw upon statistical data relating to various types of offending, with the ultimate goal of measuring the impact of specific crime prevention initiatives on crime and victimization rates. Leaving aside problems associated with gathering together reliable data and attempting to plot trends, the complexities surrounding the issue of effectiveness can be illustrated by looking at the notion of 'displacement'. Many critics have argued that, rather than preventing or reducing crime, situational crime prevention initiatives often lead to the displacement or deflection of crime. Hakim and Rengert (1981) outline five different ways in which this can occur:

1   *Spatial displacement* – the crime takes place, but in an alternative, less protected location.
2   *Temporal displacement* – the crime takes place, but at a different time of day.
3   *Tactical displacement* – the crime takes place, but the methods employed to commit it are modified.
4   *Target displacement* – the crime takes place in that location, but the crime target shifts.
5   *Type of crime displacement* – a crime takes place in that location, but the nature of the crime alters.

Over the years, many studies have attempted to gauge the extent to which crime displacement occurs, though in terms of a general picture results are inconclusive. This is hardly surprising, given the vast range of crime prevention measures and offences towards which they are directed. Obviously, it is inevitable that some displacement will occur; however, rational choice theorists have made the point that this does not necessarily represent a failure on the part of particular measures. Some (e.g. Barr and Pease 1990) have argued (controversially) that crime displacement may be beneficial if it leads to a more equal distribution of victimization rates. In addition, it has been argued that, with regard to certain sorts of crime, displacing their location from residential to non-residential areas can be beneficial for a neighbourhood. Matthews (1992b), for instance, describes how this occurred following a clampdown on street prostitution in an area of London (with the added bonus that it also led to a reduction in other types of offence previously linked to the prostitution in that area). Cultural criminologists are highly critical of the above models of crime prevention, arguing that they fail to take into account the fact that many crimes are motivated by a desire for thrill, excitement and protest (see Chapter 8), rather than instrumental gain. This, they say, means that increasing the risks attached to offending may be counterproductive in that in such cases, the increased risks will make the offending even more attractive.

Critical analyses pitched at a qualitative level focus on the implications of different forms of situational crime prevention in terms of quality of life issues. Clearly, the fact that particular initiatives may 'work', in the sense that they achieve significant reductions in crime, does not in itself justify their use, as the gains may be offset by unacceptable costs. These can be wide ranging; for example:

- The financial expenditure required is too great.
- The inconvenience to the public is unacceptable. Consider the length of time currently taken for a traveller to progress through the various security checks in an airport when leaving and entering a country. Although people may grumble, a degree of inconvenience has become part of the routine of air travel and, given concerns about terrorist threats, for most of the public attendant delays are acceptable. However, the extent to which delays will be tolerated is not limitless.
- So-called 'designing out' crime initiatives may have a highly negative impact on the aesthetics of urban space.
- Various forms of surveillance, for instance, by the police, the use of CCTV, or simply 'nosey' neighbours, may be judged to be unwelcome intrusions into personal privacy.
- Surveillance may also incorporate discriminatory practices based upon the use of misleading stereotypes, for example, as with institutional and personal forms of racism.
- Some crime prevention initiatives may raise human rights issues. One current example is the use of the so-called *Mosquito*, a device that emits a high-pitched whine, loud enough to be heard by teenagers, but inaudible to older people. The device has been increasingly used by shopkeepers, local councils and householders in an effort to deter young people from 'hanging around'. It was described by the human rights organization Liberty as: 'a degrading and indiscriminate weapon that targets children in a way that would provoke uproar if it were used against other groups' (Hinsliff 2008: 5).

The above raises a further important issue. Those involved in introducing crime prevention initiatives, from the government down, will be at pains to point out that their primary goal is to protect the public, who in large measure understand and are concerned about these risks. Clearly, from a political standpoint, the consent of the public is crucial. However, it should be noted that governments and the media play an active role in generating or encouraging specific concerns or fears among the public – perhaps in the form of moral panics (see Chapter 10). If this occurs, and regardless of the actual nature of the threat, or its seriousness compared to other threats, the task of convincing the public that stronger measures are required is made somewhat easier.

Critical analyses pitched at a theoretical level are directed at rational choice theory as a whole. To begin with (and this is particularly associated with cultural criminology and sections of critical criminology – see Chapters 1 and 8), there are those who question the idea that policy-oriented research should be the primary task of criminology. For these critics, the key problem is that research of this kind is necessarily constrained by the demands and agendas of the public or private organization (e.g. the Home Office) that is funding it. From this perspective, the parameters and possibilities of such research are severely restricted by political ideologies and the need to produce 'practical' and 'relevant' outcomes – those holding the purse strings will have little time for abstract theory. Having said that, there are some types of policy-oriented research towards which critical theorists have always been more favourably inclined, specifically, research directed at the crimes of the powerful.

Criticisms of the theoretical underpinnings of rational choice theory have focused their attention on the central argument that offenders employ cost–benefit judgements as rational decision-makers within the context of opportunity. Rock (2007: 16) sums this up as 'the convenient fiction of economic man':

> Economic man in his (or her) criminal guise does not have a past, complex motives, rich social life, or, indeed, a recognizable social identity (a 'disposition' is how Ron Clarke would put it) ... He or she needs no such complexity, because what weighs ... is the piecemeal theoretical analysis of discrete instances of disembodied offending behaviour conducted by people making decisions around the issues of risk, effort, and reward.

> (Rock 2007: 16)

Thus it is argued, rational choice theory ignores much that is (or should be) of interest to the criminologist: the links between criminal motivations and prior social and cultural experiences; social identities and understandings of self; and the social structural contexts within which criminal motivations are shaped. With rational choice theory, there is no interest in the development of criminal motivations or dispositions, they are simply assumed to exist. Furthermore, critics argue that understandings of crime and criminality are severely handicapped because of a lack of interest in conducting qualitative, ethnographic research. The focus is on the criminal event and the immediate, situationally based decision-making processes leading to an individual choosing to offend. Thus critics have emphasized the point that although individuals make decisions, in this case to offend, they do so (and to paraphrase Marx) under circumstances that are not of their own choosing. These circumstances will include issues associated with social class, ethnicity and gender, peer group pressure, relative deprivation (see Chapter 3), drug and alcohol dependency, and so on. Mullins (2006), in a study based in St Louis in the United States, for instance, analyses serious male violence within the context of specific understandings of masculinity conceptualized in terms of its existence as both a structural feature of society (and as manifested within the culture of lower-class streetlife in particular) and a perceptual preoccupation. It then becomes a concern embedded in situational experiences, for example, when someone believes that they are being disrespected.

Similarly, and also in the United States, Wright and Decker (1994) explain how the street culture characterizing certain socially deprived and disorganized neighbourhoods helps shape the offending behaviour of the young men concerned. The problem with rational choice theory, say its critics, is that it fails to address these sorts of background factors, factors that explain why the motivation and decision to offend are not randomly distributed, as if any individual is as likely as another to commit burglary, rape, street robbery or serious violent crime.

The notion of *rational* choice has also attracted the attention of critics. While rational choice theorists accept that offenders do not always act in perfectly rational ways when weighing up whether or not to offend, their ideas, especially when translated into practical measures aimed at preventing crime, are based upon an assumption that offenders do make rational decisions. This raises a fundamental issue regarding precisely what is meant by 'rational', and takes us back to the economists' concept of 'economic man' who, as an ideal type, will act in a perfectly rational manner (while 'flawed' economic man will act in a partly, or even wholly, non-rational manner). Rational choice theorists though seem to be saying that regardless of whether an action is perfectly rational, partly rational, or wholly non-rational, it is always rational from the perspective of the offender (and reflects social background and immediate circumstance). This raises two issues. First, it ignores the possibility that an individual may engage in offending behaviour in spite of perceiving the behaviour to be irrational (say, because of a high risk of apprehension). In this situation, measures aimed at deterring crime will hardly be effective. Second, within rational choice theory there is an implicit assumption that while potential offenders will make choices that are rational for them, these choices are not always 'really' rational, which suggests that an objective yardstick – devised by rational choice theorists – exists against which rationality can ultimately be judged. It is this that informs crime prevention measures aimed at making offending irrational. However, if offenders are only acting rationally from their perspective, then crime prevention measures informed by some 'outside', and apparently objective, perspective regarding what is rational become highly problematic from the point of view of functioning as a deterrent.

Critics have also made the point that there is an absence of any engagement with deeper analytical debates relating to the conceptual language of criminology. One outcome of this is that current state definitions and understandings of 'crime' and the 'crime problem' are simply taken as given.

Routine activity theory

Routine activity theory is principally associated with the American criminologist Marcus Felson (Cohen and Felson 1979; Felson 1986, 1987, 1998, 2000). As with administrative criminology in general, the theory ignores the aetiology of criminal behaviour as normally understood, and concentrates instead on crime events and their sources within the 'routine activity' constituting everyday social life. The assumption is that there will always be individuals in society who, for whatever reasons, are in varying degrees motivated to commit crime. Whether or not these motivated individuals go ahead and engage in criminal behaviour, it is argued, depends on opportunities and a rational assessment of the attendant risks and rewards. The focus is on predatory crime and the aim is to devise pragmatic policies based on increasing the risks and reducing the rewards of crime, in order to prevent such crime occurring. Thus routine activity theory has much in common with rational choice theory, the major distinction being that the former steps back and analyses crime events on a societal level, while the latter is interested in crime events that are specific and situational.

An interesting and crucial dimension to the theory is that the bulk of crime is conceptualized as mundane and ordinary, not spectacular and novel. From this perspective, crime occurs as a result of the opportunities arising from the routines of ordinary, everyday life: work, school, family life, leisure activities, and so on. However, crime is not seen as occurring in a random fashion; rather, it results from the opportunities provided by the convergence of three key factors: a motivated offender, a suitable target and the lack of a capable guardian (e.g. an adult in charge of a child, or the presence of a security system). Routine activity theorists have used this model as a basis for analysing variations in crime rates over time (the primary focus has been on the United States, though the theory makes claims for universal application). According to the model, increases in crime rates since the mid-twentieth century did not occur because of more motivated offenders, in the sense that the 'pool' of individuals with criminal dispositions increased. Rather, these increases resulted from the greater opportunities to commit crime provided by changes in people's routine activities within the context of a more affluent society. Thus greater affluence increased the range of portable and expensive consumer goods available to a potential offender, while at the same time an increase in working families meant that more houses were left unattended during the day, as well as during the evening because of increasing participation in leisure activities.

Furthermore, individuals became more vulnerable because they tended to make a greater number of trips alone. As a consequence, there was a significant increase in the number of suitable targets, coupled with a significant decrease in the number of suitable guardians. The growth in criminal opportunities, therefore, created a situation where committing crime was accompanied by fewer risks and greater rewards, hence the increases in crime rates. From the perspective of routine activity theory, this led to an increase in the number of motivated offenders (thus analytically combining the three elements: motivated offender, suitable targets and lack of capable guardians) though, and importantly, 'motivated offender' has a very specific meaning in this context. As stated above, there is no suggestion that the 'pool' of criminally disposed individuals increased; rather, there were more 'motivated offenders' only in the sense that the expansion of (low risk/high reward) criminal opportunities encouraged and 'triggered' a decision to commit crime among more individuals. However, given that such individuals have 'tried their hand' at crime, and the range of possibilities in terms of subsequent social experiences; for instance, peer group pressure, it could very well follow that they do swell the 'pool' of motivated offenders as normally understood.

More recently, Felson (2000) has added the lack of an 'intimate handler' to his original three elements, while at the time addressing four additional types of crime that he labels 'exploitative' (e.g. rape, street robbery); 'mutualistic' (prostitution, drug dealing); 'competitive' (fighting); and 'individualistic' (drug use). An intimate handler is someone close to, and respected by, a potential offender, who is in a position to restrain the latter's behaviour.

Some time ago, Garofalo (1987) echoed some of the ideas found in routine activity theory, though he preferred the term 'lifestyle'. Drawing on the results of surveys of victimization, Garofalo argues that the uneven distribution of victimization is associated with different lifestyles (in effect, routine activities); some people are more at risk than others. Social class is an important factor here, for example, those who have to rely on late night public transport because they cannot afford to use taxis are significantly more likely to face the threat of violent assault.

Again, as with rational choice theory, routine activity theory has been criticized for ignoring broader social, economic and cultural factors in shaping criminal motivations. Therefore, say critics, a major weakness in the theory is that it fails to take such things as unemployment, inequality, urban decline, racism and the deregulation of financial markets (relevant to corporate crime) into consideration. All of these factors have important implications in terms of 1) explaining why some, but certainly not all, individuals decide to exploit the criminal opportunities that are made available and 2) developing analyses that acknowledge the possibility that the 'pool' of motivated offenders may increase or decrease over given time periods. Furthermore, and again echoing criticisms of rational choice theory, attention has been drawn to routine activity theory's lack of interest in white collar and corporate crime. However, Alvesalo et al. (2006) utilize the basic tenets of routine activity theory and argue that situational crime prevention can be usefully applied to corporate crime specifically. Indeed, in their view, it does not necessarily follow that situational crime prevention with respect to this type of crime, as opposed to conventional crime, will deflect the development of more radical interventions directed at social and economic factors. Rather, they argue that situational crime prevention in this context will have the benefit of making monitoring and control processes more public, encourage local populations to become involved, and strengthen the links among various social movements oriented towards issues of justice and equality.

Finally, and unsurprisingly, cultural criminologists (see Chapter 8) are as critical of routine activity theory as they are of rational choice theory, and again it is the absence of any reference to the visceral and emotional, as opposed to purely instrumental, dimension to crime that is highlighted. The critique is well put by Young:

> Cultural criminology reveals almost exactly the opposite of Felson's world of mundane crime stressing the sensual nature of crime, the adrenaline rushes of edgework – voluntary illicit risk-taking and the dialectic of fear and pleasure. The existential motivational structure they explore inverts the very basis of routine activities, opportunities and control theory. Here the motivation to commit crime is not mundane but the revolt against the mundane – rules transgressed because they are there, risk is a challenge not a deterrent.
>
> (Young 2007: 19)

Crime science

Described by proponents as a 'new discipline', crime science gained formal recognition in 2001, with the establishment of the Jill Dando Institute of Crime Science at University College, London. Jill Dando, a television broadcaster, was murdered in London in 1999 and the Institute was founded in her memory. Crime science rejects many of the traditional, especially theoretical, concerns of criminology and is instead explicitly committed to the employment of 'scientific' methods in order to prevent crime and detect offenders. Focusing on offences rather than offenders, the work seeks to develop practical solutions to problems of crime and disorder, guided by 'hard', 'objective', quantitative data and scientific processes. It is multidisciplinary in character, with contributions coming from, for instance, geography, forensic science, economics, engineering and certain cognate areas in criminology, such as administrative criminology. Thus crime science research involves such things as the mapping of crime hot spots, 'designing out' crime, scenes of crime evidence, crime management and policing practices, and improving the technology employed by the security industry. It is a hybrid approach to 'doing criminology', where the classical tradition found in administrative criminology is underpinned by a strong commitment to the employment of positivist methodologies and frames of reference.

Many academic criminologists are, for various reasons, highly critical of crime science and what it purports to offer (to a larger extent criticisms replicate those aimed at rational choice theory and routine activity theory). Some critics question whether crime science can be properly described as criminology. Interestingly, for many people outside of the discipline, crime science conforms exactly with their perception of what 'criminology' is. As someone once said to me when I mentioned what I did for a living: 'Hmm, you must have seen some grisly murders over the years'. Some intending students of criminology have this 'crime-busting' perception of criminology, stimulated by television programmes such as *CSI*, and in their mind's eye there are, perhaps, future scenarios where they discover that little bit of DNA that brings a murderer to justice. In response, undergraduate degree pro-grammes in crime science have begun to appear. Whether or not it is criminology depends, of course, on how one defines criminology. What we can say is that crime science represents a particular understanding of the 'criminological project'. This project takes us into a world of computer modelling, statistical data, graphs, charts and DNA, but it is a world that denies access to social theory and ethnographic and other types of qualitative research. This is totally at variance with the criminological project as understood by, for instance, cultural criminologists (see Chapter 8):

> Techniques designed to generate objective, quantifiable, comparative data, and survey methods are of little use to cultural criminology; their illusions of precise objectivity mask an inherent and imposed imprecision, and inability (and an unwillingness) to explore particular meanings of legal authority, situated symbolism, and interpersonal style in the lived experiences of everyday criminality.

> (Ferrell and Sanders 1995: 305)

There is another, implicitly political, dimension to this, and one that draws attention to the relationship between competing claims to, on the one hand (scientific), knowledge and, on the other, governance. As Hope says in a review of one recent crime science text:

> Practical demands come to dominate scientific discourse, placing in the hands of those that make them opportunities to choose within the scientific marketplace; and different purveyors of useful knowledge emerge to compete among each other to supply diagnoses and solutions to the practical problems posed by political managers.

> (Hope 2006: 245)

Hope begins the review with a comment attributed to Travis Hirschi: 'There are two kinds of theory – theory, and grant-theory'. And, in a recent and highly critical discussion of crime science, Walters argues:

> Such work is more suited to the commercial world of corporate research than to academic institutions. Yet the income-generation policies of contemporary university managers and politicians will ensure that the menial and the mundane prevails over the creative and the critical.

(Walters 2007: 20)

Further reading

In the case of rational choice theory, major original sources are Clarke, R.V. (1995) Situational crime prevention, *Crime and Justice*, 19: 91–150; Cornish, D.B. and Clarke, R.V. (eds) (1986) *The Reasoning Criminal: Rational Choice Perspectives on Offending*. New York: Springer-Verlag; and Cornish, D.B. and Clarke, R.V. (2003) Opportunities, precipitators and criminal decision, *Crime Prevention Studies*, 16: 41–96.

In the case of routine activities theory, major sources are Felson, M. (1986) Routine activities, social controls, rational decisions and criminal outcomes, in D.B. Cornish and R.V. Clarke (eds) Situational crime prevention, *Crime and Justice*, 19: 91–150; Felson, M. (1987) Routine activities and crime prevention in the developing metropolis, *Criminology*, 25: 911–31; Felson, M. (1998) *Crime and Everyday Life*, 2nd edn. Thousand Oaks, CA: Pine Forge Press; and Felson, M. (2000) The routine activity approach as a general social theory, in S.S. Simpson (ed.) *Of Crime and Criminality: The Use of Theory in Everyday Life*. Thousand Oaks, CA: Pine Forge Press.

The case for crime science is put by Ekblom, P. (1997) Gearing up against crime: a dynamic framework to help designers keep up with the adaptive criminal in a changing world, *International Journal of Risk, Security and Crime Prevention*, 2(4): 249–65; Pawson, R. and Tilley, N. (1997) *Realistic Evaluation*. London: Sage Publications; and Smith, M.J. and Tilley, N. (eds) (2005) *Crime Science: New Approaches to Preventing and Detecting Crime*. Cullompton: Willan Publishing.

Good, general discussions of the field of crime prevention and community safety (with references to the work above) are Crawford, A. (1998) *Crime Prevention and Community Safety; Politics, Policies and Practice*. London: Longman; Crawford, A. (2007) Crime prevention and community safety, in M. Maguire, R. Morgan and R. Reiner (eds) *The Oxford Handbook of Criminology*, 4th edn. Oxford: Oxford University Press; and Hughes, G. (1998) *Understand-

ing Crime Prevention. Buckingham: Open University Press. Good overviews from strong supporters of this field are: Pease, K. (2002) Crime reduction, in M. Maguire, R. Morgan and R. Reiner (eds) *The Oxford Handbook of Criminology*, 3rd edn. Oxford: Oxford University Press; and Tilley, N. (ed.) (2005) *Handbook of Crime Prevention and Community Safety.* Cullompton: Willan Publishing.

A succinct and critical discussion will be found in Lilly, J.R., Cullen, F.T. and Ball, R.A. (2007) *Criminological Theory: Context and Consequences.* Thousand Oaks, CA: Sage Publications. The critical review of Smith, M.J. and Tilley, N. (2005) *Crime Science: New Approaches to Preventing and Detecting Crime.* Cullompton: Willan Publishing by Hope, T. (2006) in *Theoretical Criminology,* 10 (2) is well-worth reading.

3 Anomie Theory

The word anomie comes from *anomia*, the Greek word for lawless. In general English usage, it refers to a lack of moral standards among members of a group or on the part of an individual and, not surprisingly, over the centuries various writers have drawn on the concept (though not necessarily referring to the word 'anomie' explicitly) when discussing crime and criminals. However, the first systematic sociological use of the concept of anomie is associated with the French positivist sociologist Emile Durkheim (1858–1917). Since then, it has had a chequered though enduring history. Within the context of criminological theorizing, discussions of the concept of anomie have usually been referenced against the version of anomie theory developed by R.K. Merton, who was strongly influenced by Durkheim, later on in the middle of the last century (this is discussed below). Durkheim discusses anomie in *The Division of Labour in Society* ([1893] 1964) and *Suicide* ([1897] 1970). For Durkheim, anomie denoted a social, rather than a psychological, condition, though he acknowledged that there were psychological implications for those experiencing an anomic society, and this dimension was explored further in his study of suicide. Anomie describes a condition of normlessness, where the regulatory power of norms and values has been severely weakened. When this occurs, people are in effect freed from traditional or conventional constraints, thereby increasing the likelihood of deviant or criminal behaviour.

Along with other writers and thinkers in the late nineteenth century, Durkheim was especially concerned with the social implications of the transition from an agrarian to an industrial economy in France and other European countries, in particular, the implications for social cohesion and solidarity. His work was aimed at developing an understanding of modernity, and its impact on social life. He argued that in pre-modern societies, social order derived from what he called 'mechanical solidarity'. Such societies lacked the complex social institutions of modernity and were held together by a largely homogeneous and stable collective conscience; that is, a shared agreement regarding norms and values. Although this moral force regulating people's behaviour was internalized through socialization processes, for Durkheim it existed as an independent, structural feature of society, as a 'social fact'.

> A social fact is every way of acting, fixed or not, capable of exercising on the individual, an influence or an external constraint;

or again, every way of acting which is general throughout a given society, while at the same time existing in its own right independent of its individual manifestations.

(Durkheim 1982: 59)

His basic premise was that human desires are essentially unlimited. The general acceptance of conventional norms and values – a collective conscience resulting from socialization processes – in pre-industrial societies held these desires in check; it was the key mechanism of social control. In practice, of course, these 'desires' were never kept in check in any complete sense; crime (along with periodic insurrections on the part of the rural poor, for example) was a permanent feature of life in agrarian Europe, and as Durkheim acknowledges, social control also required a Draconian penal code. However, for Durkheim, a certain amount of rule-breaking, regardless of the nature of the society, is not only inevitable, it is also functionally necessary. Rule-breaking/crime is necessary, he said, because, first, it introduces new ideas, thereby preventing society from stagnating (an 'adaptive' function) and, second, reactions to it reaffirm notions of right and wrong among the populace (a 'boundary maintenance' function).

However, the rapid social change associated with industrialization altered irrevocably the traditional sources of social solidarity. Over a short period old norms and values were no longer appropriate for the developing modern society, and the social institutions responsible for the socialization of society's members were unable to adjust swiftly enough to these new conditions. In particular, industrialization brought with it rising aspirations – increasingly people set their sights on a significant improvement in their material standard of life. It also brought with it a shift towards what Durkheim called 'individuation': an increasing stress on individualism and a self-seeking egoism. For Durkheim, new and appropriate mechanisms of social control were required if society was to constrain the potentially limitless desires of its members, for modernism had freed people from the traditional normative constraints on these desires. He described this situation during the period of transition from agrarian to industrial society as one of anomie. Thus an anomic society is one that lacks regulatory power.

One crucial dimension to this, argued Durkheim, is an individual's subjective feelings regarding their lot in life. For him, a well-ordered society was one where people felt that what they had achieved or acquired was commensurate with what they deserved or could reasonably expect. They may not be thrilled by their situation and possessions, but if that is all that can be expected, given the circumstances as they see them, so be it. Clearly, because it is a subjective assessment on the part of an individual, it does not necessarily correspond with an 'objective' reading of the situation. People living in abject poverty in a grossly exploitative society may accept their situation by rationalizing it in terms of, for instance, the natural order of things, or their own lack of talent or enterprise. The alternative situation, that is, one where people subjectively feel that they have less than they deserve is referred to as 'relative deprivation'. Although Durkheim did not use the term, it emerged later on in the twentieth century among some theorists (notably R.K. Merton) as a key concept in analyses of criminal and deviant behaviour, and has a continuing presence in criminological theorizing.

While the basis of social order in an agrarian society was organic solidarity, as described above, in an industrial society social order is based upon what Durkheim referred to as 'organic solidarity'. In other words, industrialization requires organic solidarity as the panacea for anomie. The term was used to describe a society where social integration and order derive from the establishment of functionally interdependent institutions. Of primary importance, as the title of his book suggests, is the division of labour – unlike pre-industrial society, modern, industrial society is characterized by an increasingly specialized set of work tasks. At the same time, as already mentioned, there was an increasing stress on individualism, rather than the all-encompassing collectivism associated with agrarian society. The eradication of anomie was, for Durkheim, predicated upon the establishment of a fully integrated network of social institutions (e.g. educational institutions), in effect supporting the division of labour, by providing appropriate modes of socialization, coupled with a 'natural' or 'spontaneous' division of labour. Durkheim described a society where this did not occur as 'unhealthy' or 'pathological'. A natural division of labour is one based upon meritocratic principles; that is, where work tasks are allocated on the basis of ability and equal opportunities. Although Durkheim warned of the dangers of unfettered individualism, he welcomed the increasing individualism associated with modernity, providing that socialization processes functioned appropriately. Thus a collective conscience was still necessary within a modern, industrial society. However, unlike in a pre-industrial society, this collective conscience, while clustering around certain core norms and values, would allow people a degree of leeway, which would provide spaces for diversity and the development of individual identities.

Durkheim returned to the concept of anomie in his study of suicide, though here he spends more time than he did in *The Division of Labour in Society* addressing the social psychological implications of an 'unhealthy' society. However, even this study illustrates how he endeavours to utilize the concepts and methods of sociology, by analysing suicide as a social, rather than a psychological phenomenon. Thus instead of restricting his study to the level of the individual and, say, their personal problems, he focused on a comparison of suicide *rates* among different societies and among different groups (e.g. according to religious affiliation) within the same society. In this way people were dealt with as aggregates, not individuals. A key argument in his analysis is that while the people involved obviously changed over time, the respective suicide rates remained more or less constant; in this formulation the source of suicide, as manifested in differential suicides rates, lies in a social reality external to the individual.

In fact, he identified four different types of suicide, though each results from a different type of 'pathological' society. *Altruistic* suicide results when social integration is too strong, and the individual is 'lost' within a wider collective. An example would be individuals who take their own lives because of some shameful episode. *Fatalistic* suicide occurs when social regulation is too strong; for example, in the case of a suicide bomber. *Egoistic* suicide occurs when social integration is too weak; that is, a commitment to the group has been replaced by self-seeking individualism, and the individual lacks the normative support such a group would provide in a healthy society. This extends the discussion of 'individuation' introduced earlier. Likewise, *anomic* suicide extends the discussion of the concept of anomie. Durkheim argued that anomic suicide manifests itself during periods of economic crises, when forces regulating people's behaviour become severely weakened; that is, normlessness ensues. This idea is clearly congruent with his discussion of anomie in *The Division of Labour in Society*, and his argument that the deregulation brought about by economic crises removes the constraints on people's desires, which, as discussed earlier, he views as unlimited, unless normatively controlled.

Anomie has had remarkable longevity as a theoretical concept within criminology. Some have embraced what they see as its continuing explanatory power, while modifying or reworking its meaning and implications; others have rejected it in a blaze of intense criticism. As mentioned earlier, more recent analyses of anomie have revisited not just Durkheim, but also, and notably, the work of the American sociologist R.K. Merton. To make matters more complicated, these analyses have stimulated intense debate regarding both how Merton defined and used anomie, and its usefulness in terms of explaining criminal and deviant behaviour. In particular, as we shall see, that his analysis seems to operate on two levels: a macro level involving cultural and social structures and their impact on members of society viewed as aggregates (in a similar fashion to Durkheim), and a micro level, in the sense of addressing the impact of disjunctions in these structures on individual members of society.

Merton was not a criminologist *per se*; rather, he was a grand theorist of the functionalist school, whose writings in general had a huge influence on American sociology in the middle years of the twentieth century. He turned his attention to crime and deviance specifically in an article – 'Social structure and anomie' – first published in 1938 in his book *Social Theory and Social Structure*. Modified versions – clarifications rather than substantial revisions – subsequently appeared in 1949, 1957, 1964 and 1968. The article has been widely cited within criminology and some suggest that it is the most commonly cited work in the literature of criminology.

Along with Durkheim, Merton rejects the idea that deviant and criminal behaviour can be explained in terms of individual psychology or biology. For him, the causes of crime and deviance lie in the nature of American society itself, a society built upon the promise of equality of opportunity, where citizens are socialized into believing that, providing they work hard and have the right attitudes, everyone can achieve success. As a number of commentators have pointed out (e.g. Stinchcombe 1975), the irony is that the roots of deviance lie in the ideology of the American Dream.

Merton's theory is based upon the relationship between social structure and culture (the latter being internalized through processes of socialization). The social structure contains various institutions, such as the education system, that provide the legitimate means – the institutionalized means – for achieving cultural goals. Certain goals are seen as highly desirable; in particular, and the one that Merton concentrates on, the goal of material success. The promise of equal opportunities raises people's expectations regarding the achievement of this goal. The problem, says Merton, is that a disjunction exists between culture and social structure, a lack of fit between, on the one hand, the heavily stressed goal of material success and, on the other, the legitimate means available for achieving this goal. Thus Merton paints a picture of a society where there is an extremely heavy emphasis on the goal of pecuniary success, inherent limitations on the achievement of the goal and, none the less, an ideology that stresses opportunities for all. For Merton, this is a source of anomie and attendant deviant behaviour. As Cullen and Messner put it:

> In this situation, there is structural strain on the institutional norms, which lose their legitimacy and regulatory power. When this attenuation of normative regulation transpires, 'anomie' is said to occur.
>
> (Cullen and Messner 2007: 11)

However, according to Merton, different individuals respond or adapt in different ways. He illustrates this by using Table 3.1 based upon 'ideal type' categories, four of which are forms of deviance. The pluses and minuses represent, respectively, acceptance or rejection of the cultural goal (of material success) and the institutionalized (i.e. legitimate) means available for achieving this goal. A plus and a minus represent rejection of institutionalized goals/means, and their replacement with new goals/means.

Table 3.1   A typology of modes of individual adaptation

Modes of adaptation	Cultural goals	Institutionalized means
I. Conformity	+	+
II. Innovation	+	−
III. Ritualism	−	+
IV. Retreatism	−	−
V. Rebellion	−/+	−/+

'Conformists' are individuals who, regardless of their own level of achievement, accept the goals and, the means and therefore, are in a non-deviant category; all the rest are examples of deviance. 'Innovators' are individuals who have internalized and accepted the desirability of material success, but because of blocked opportunities reject the institutionalized means and resort to alternative, illegitimate means. According to this formulation, innovators are associated with property crime. 'Ritualists' have abandoned the goal of material success (and hence for Merton are deviant), yet accept the means, and in a ritualistic manner simply go through the motions. Merton gives as an example a lowly clerical worker who has given up on promotion, but none the less continues to dutifully abide by the rules. 'Retreatists' reject both the goal and the means and thus 'retreat' from normal society. Merton points to hobos and drug addicts as examples. 'Rebels' are political revolutionaries. The plus *and* a minus in each column signifies a rejection of both the cultural goals and the institutionalized means while at the same time substituting their own alternative goals and means.

Various commentators on his work have taken a leaf out of Merton's original article and, in order to illustrate his argument, have drawn an analogy between American society and playing some sort of game. Taking one of Merton's examples (and embellishing it slightly), it is as if people in the United States are all participating in a game of poker, where the enormous stress on winning (a product of *normal* socialization) is not accompanied by a universal commitment to playing by the rules. In addition, and to make matters worse, there is an unequal distribution of chips when the game begins, giving some players a powerful advantage. Conformists adhere to the rules and make the best of a bad job. Innovators are card sharps who cheat to win. Ritualists play on according to the rules, but have no interest in actually winning. And, finally, rebels argue for an alternative game with different rules. Thus both Merton and Durkheim see anomie as a condition where the power of societal norms to regulate behaviour is significantly weakened. In Merton's formulation it derives from the excessive emphasis placed on winning, combined with relative deprivation (as defined earlier) arising from a lack of equal opportunities, and this contradicts the promises held out by the American Dream.

The poker analogy can be used to indicate the social policy implications of this situation, as Merton saw them. His assumption is that the creation of equal opportunities, that is, a meritocracy, where achievement is based on ability, will eradicate, or at least reduce, relative deprivation, because individuals will appreciate that what they achieve reflects what they justly deserve, making deviant behaviour much less likely. However, realizing the meritocractic ideal would not mean that the players in the game of poker would each begin with the same stack of chips (that would represent a society based upon *equality*), rather, some would still have more chips than others, but all players would accept this as fair, that is, relative deprivation would no longer exist. Again, there are strong echoes of Durkheim here, though for him it was the functional interdependence of a natural division of labour (i.e. one based upon meritocratic principles), rather than a reduction in relative deprivation, which would shift society away from an anomic condition.

Interestingly, not long after Merton first published his ideas on anomie, when America had entered the Second World War, political leaders and social commentators wanted to suspend the American Dream. As part of the wartime effort, Americans were encouraged to view 'consumerism as selfish and decadent' (Samuel 2001: xi). When the war ended, however, commercial television was seen by its proponents as the way to revive the 'national mythology of the American Dream' (Ibid p.x).

Although Merton bases his work on Durkheim, and each sees anomie as a result of the societal norms lacking regulatory power, some key differences emerged as Merton developed his analysis. Crucially, and as noted by Box (1981), in the early part of his article Merton follows Durkheim and discusses anomie as something affecting the whole of society. However, later on when discussing the deviant behaviour arising from anomie, such behaviour is linked to certain sections of society; specifically, the poorer, lower classes. This resulted from his theoretical understanding of the sources of anomie coupled with the empirical evidence from crime statistics, apparently showing the greater criminality of the lower classes.

> Of those located in the lower reaches of the social structure, the culture makes incompatible demands. On the one hand, they are asked to orient their conduct toward the prospect of large wealth ... and on the other, they are largely denied effective opportunities to do so institutionally.

> (Merton 1993: 259)

Remaining with the Durkheimian model would have meant seeing anomie (and therefore deviance) in existence throughout the whole of society, among all social classes. There is a further point of departure between the theories of Durkheim and Merton. Durkheim argued that anomie arose out of rapid social change, when a weakening of normative regulation set free unlimited and uncontrolled desires. Merton, however, treats these desires as *expectations* deriving from people internalizing, via socialization processes, the ideology of the American Dream. From the perspective of the individuals concerned, therefore, these are realistic expectations regarding the material rewards that will come their way. Here desires are limited in the sense that they are in line with certain expectations, the nature and magnitude of which will be determined by the reference groups that people look to and choose to emulate. However, deviant behaviour arises because even these limited expectations are, for certain poorer sections of society, likely to remain unmet. Therefore, while Durkheim and Merton agree on what anomie is, they differ in terms of its distribution and its source. For Merton, its source was inequality of opportunity and the resultant relative deprivation; for Durkheim, its source was rapid social change or, in the case of anomic suicide, economic crises.

Many texts on criminological theory (including my own; see Tierney 2006) refer to Merton's analysis in *Social Theory and Social Structure* as an example of 'strain theory'. There are varieties of strain theory, but, as the name suggests, in very broad terms they all see criminal and/or deviant behaviour as the result of something 'going wrong' that places pressure on people to engage in transgressive behaviour. In 1987 two American criminologists (Cullen and Messner 2007) conducted an interview with Merton, who was then in his seventies. Interestingly, during the course of this interview Merton disputed the view that his was an example of strain theory. Here he was defining strain theory as an approach that focused on the individual and sought to identify 'a psychological variable of the internal emotional or other psychic (strain) that individuals caught up in such situations experience' (Ibid:21), adding that he, on the other hand, was 'dealing with rates of deviant behavior in the purely Durkheimian sense' (Ibid:21). Debates about what Merton 'really' meant, and even if he realized the full ramifications of his analysis, have rumbled on since his article first appeared. As Baumer (2007) indicates, contributors to these debates have interpreted Merton's work in three different ways.

Some argue that Merton's analysis *is* an example of the sort of strain theory that he distances himself from in the 1987 interview. Guided by a social psychological perspective, they have examined the ways in which the strains experienced by an individual, because of a lack of opportunities to achieve cultural goals, leads to deviant behaviour (e.g. Kornhauser 1978; Agnew 1987). Others, rejecting this focus on the strain experienced by the individual, have opted for a macro level of analysis, and address the strains resulting from a disjunction between culture and social structure (and manifested in a weakening of normative controls) then linking these strains to different *rates* of deviance among different sections of society (Bernard 1987; Messner and Rosenfeld 2001). This approach seems to correspond with the comments made by Merton in the interview and, although not based on social psychology, it can none the less be seen as a version of strain theory. Furthermore, and illustrating just how divided opinion is within academic criminology, others have argued that Merton's work incorporates each of these dimensions, though as two separate theoretical models. Baumer (2007) himself enriches these debates further by developing a multilevel theory that seeks to synthesize these different levels of analysis into one, integrated paradigm.

A number of criminologists have sought to show the relevance of Merton's theory to an explanation of deviant behaviour among all sections of society, rich or poor; for example, white collar and corporate crime (Menard 1995; Passas and Agnew 1997; Parnaby and Sacco 2004). In fact, Merton (1957) himself explored this theme in an article on deviance within the scientific community, acknowledging that deviant behaviour arose among all social classes. The argument here is that anyone can experience a gap between expectations or aspirations and opportunities with the resultant strain towards deviance. However, it is useful to distinguish between expectations and aspirations. The latter are perceived by an individual to be desired outcomes that may *possibly* be realized. Expectations, on the other hand, are desired outcomes that an individual feels are *likely* to be realized. This has particular saliency within the context of Mertonian anomie theory because of the notion of relative deprivation – to reiterate: a subjective feeling of being treated unjustly in terms of material achievement (with the irony that the culture in that society has been instrumental in creating these expectations). However, aspirations, and other terms such as 'wants' or 'desires', are important, in that deviant/criminal behaviour is not only, or necessarily, a function of relative deprivation. Returning to the game of poker analogy, an unequal distribution of chips at the start means that even some of the 'well off' have fewer chips than others and, regardless of their feelings about fairness, they may very well covet these extra chips.

Over the years Merton's article has stimulated a huge amount of empirical research and theoretical analysis on the theme of anomie and crime and deviance. Agnew (1992), for instance, has put forward what he calls general strain theory. Focusing on the notion of strain in a social psychological sense, he adds a further dimension to Merton's ideas by looking at non-economic sources of strain (though, as already stated, Merton was aware of other sources). Agnew explores the strain resulting from, first, the 'removal of positively valued stimuli' and, second, the 'presentation of negative stimuli'. The former refers to some personal loss in someone's life, for instance, a divorce or death of a friend; the latter refers to distressing personal experiences, such as being a victim of crime. Each is said to trigger anger and resentment and eventually engagement in deviant behaviour. Messner and Rosenfeld (2001) have developed what they call 'institutional anomie theory'. They agree with Merton that American society is inherently criminogenic – crime producing – because of the excessive emphasis placed on material success coupled with a limited opportunity structure. However, their subsequent analysis differs from that put forward by Merton.

To begin with, they argue that in comparison with other developed societies, American society is characterized by particularly high rates of homicide and, indeed, serious crime in general (for a critique of this premise, see Chamlin and Cochran 2007). Their explanation for this is based upon a trenchant critique of the American economic system, and they are highly sceptical of the view that an increase in economic growth and opportunities will lead to a corresponding reduction in anomie and, hence, criminality. This, they argue, is because a thriving economy is likely to intensify even further the cultural value placed on material success. They add to this dystopian view of America's future by arguing that the social institutions expected to provide a counterbalance to this obsession with material success, for example, in areas of education, religion and family, will fail to do so. This, the authors argue, is because such institutions will themselves absorb, and be increasingly committed to, the dominant economic values.

Inevitably, given its length of service, Merton's anomie theory has stimulated a large amount of criticism, as well as support, modification and theoretical development (as indicated above). This final section provides a brief overview of some of the major critical arguments.

- Although Merton acknowledged that the relative deprivation result-ing from anomie will be found throughout society, he did believe that it and corresponding deviant behaviour was more likely to occur among poorer people. For him, this understanding was based upon the message from official crime statistics combined with his interpretation of the logic of his theoretical model. Critics, however, have argued that this reflected too much faith in crime statistics, which, they say, under-represent amounts of white collar and corporate crime. In addition, as mentioned above, it has been argued that Merton's model is quite capable of explaining deviant behav-iour among the better off. In this context, it is important to note that while relative deprivation is a product of social and cultural structures, it involves individuals' subjective understanding of whether or not they are being treated fairly, with rewards matching what they see as reasonable expectations; hence the argument that it is not wealth and material possessions *per se* that are at issue.

- Even if we accept the validity of Merton's formulation, there is no explanation of the dynamics at work whereby some people opt for a specific mode of adaptation (conformity, innovation, ritualism, retreatism or rebellion). In spite of ostensibly being socialized into the American Dream, many citizens opt for 'conformity'. Among these will, of course, be many who are relatively poor and, in this context, we need to consider such things as the degree to which the Dream is internalized or perceived as credible, the ways in which people shape their own understandings of realistic expectations and what is thought to be morally acceptable behaviour. Similarly, we need to consider the factors lying behind a decision to opt for one or other of the deviant modes of adaptation.
- Cultural criminologists in particular have argued that much criminal behaviour is expressive in nature, and motivated by a desire for risk-taking, excitement and thrill, and so on as opposed to the material rewards highlighted by Merton: brawling and so-called joy-riding are good examples (see Chapter 8). In America, A.K. Cohen (1955), who developed his own version of strain theory, argued that juvenile delinquency tended to be non-instrumental in nature (see Chapter 16). In Britain, Jock Young, who drew on Merton's concept of relative deprivation as part of a left realist approach to crime (see Chapter 11), has more recently, and in line with cultural criminology, stressed the emotional dimension to much transgressive behaviour – 'Merton with energy', as well as social structure, as he puts it. Even predatory crime, such as street robbery, for instance, may be motivated as much by emotion (e.g. exercising power over someone) as by the possibility of financial gain.
- A.K. Cohen also made the point that adaptations to 'strain' – in his case on the part of juvenile delinquents – should be seen as collective, in the shape of subcultural formations. This is clearly at variance with Merton's formulation, which is based upon *individual* modes of adaptation.

Further reading

As always, readers are encouraged to read original sources. In the case of Durkheim: Durkheim, E. ([1893] 1964) *The Division of Labour in Society*. New York: Free Press. Durkhein, E. ([1897] 1970) *Suicide: A Study in Sociology*. London: Routledge & Kegan Paul. For a critique of Durkheim's functions of crime argument, see Roshier, B. (1977), The functions of crime myth, *Sociological Review*, May. In the case of Merton: Merton, R.K. ([1938] 1993) Social structure and anomie, in C. Lemert (ed.) *Social Theory: The Multicultural Readings*. Boulder, CO: Westview Press.

In addition to the texts already mentioned, useful discussions of anomie can be found in Adler, F. and Laufer, W.S. (eds) (1995) *Advances in Criminological Theory: Volume 10, The Legacy of Anomie Theory*, New Brunswick, NJ: Transaction; Farnworth, M. and Leiber, M.J. (1989) Strain theory revisited: economic goals, educational means, and delinquency, *American Sociological Review*, 54(2): 263–74; Featherstone, R. and Deflem, M. (2003) Anomie and strain: context and consequences of Merton's two theories, *Sociological Inquiry*, 73(4): 471–89; Orru, M. (1987) *Anomie: History and Meanings*. Boston, MA: Allen & Unwin. Volume 11, No. 1, February 2007, is a special edition of the journal *Theoretical Criminology* that is devoted (largely) to Merton's anomie theory and the concept of relative deprivation.

4 Chicago School

The Chicago School came to prominence during the 1920s and 1930s, and was based in the Department of Sociology at the University of Chicago. The themes, ideas and research methodologies that grew out of the School have had an enduring influence on urban sociology and on sociological studies of crime and delinquency. In the United States, the late nineteenth and early twentieth centuries had seen the rapid growth of major urban centres such as Chicago and, among the general public, politicians and various reformers, increasing concerns about the social problems (especially crime and immorality) seen as accompanying this growth. By the time that the Chicago School came into being, 'the city' had become a major social issue. Indeed, Chicago itself had become a sprawling, archetypal example, thus providing researchers at the University with a ready-made social laboratory right on their doorstep. As opportunities for employment expanded, so did the city; by the early 1930s its population had reached three million. People arrived from all over Europe, as well as from the southern states in America.

Similar concerns about city life, particularly when it involved the poor (sometimes as victims, sometimes as threats), had arisen in Europe earlier on in the nineteenth century, leading to the growth of various philanthropic and reformist movements targeting such things as child labour, alcohol consumption and 'fallen' women. These concerns also stimulated early social scientific investigations into the lifestyles and experiences of the urban poor (e.g. in England by Mayhew ([1861] 1967); Booth ([1902] 1967). Novelists too got involved. Focusing on the meat packing industry, Sinclair's (1905) classic novel *The Jungle* provides a powerful insight into the brutal social worlds of those who had emigrated to Chicago from Europe in search of a better life. Two years previously, another American novelist, Jack London ([1903] 1995), published *The People of the Abyss*, a documentary account of life among London's poor. The titles themselves are highly evocative of contemporaneous images of the urban landscape (corresponding images still abound today, of course; 'sink estates', 'dangerous places', 'no-go areas', etc.).

Robert Park (1926; Park et al. 1925), who had worked as a journalist before turning to sociology, played a major role in the establishment and early development of the Chicago School. Park, who had studied sociology in Germany, and his colleagues, were influenced by the work of European positivist sociologists, notably Emile Durkheim (see Chapter 3). Of particular importance here is that although a significant number of writers in Europe, and especially in Britain, during the mid-nineteenth century identified what they saw as the social causes of criminality, by the end of that century positivist explanations based upon the individual and their biology or psychology were becoming increasingly influential. However, and following Durkheim, the Chicago School located the causes of crime in social factors, rather than in the individual. In fact, their work offers a fascinating glimpse into early attempts to develop, within an American context, an academically credible *sociology* of crime and delinquency. This sociological positivism was though supplemented by another approach based upon ethnographies and 'life histories'. In other words, encouraged by Park, researchers went out into Chicago's neighbourhoods to observe what was taking place and to talk to those involved. In effect, while sociological positivism was used to explain the causal factors leading to the structure of urban social life – especially when it involved crime and delinquency – ethnographic research was used to illuminate the implications in terms of biography, culture and social interaction, in a sense breathing life into the structural models.

Under the guidance of Park, the Chicago School developed a social ecological model of the city – nowadays, members of the School are often referred to as the Chicago ecologists. The term 'ecology' is used in the biological sciences to describe the interrelationships among organisms, and between these organisms and their physical environment. Ecological systems are in a constant state of flux, involving periods of equilibrium and disequilibrium, and over time an evolutionary process is set in motion as organisms adapt or fail to adapt to changing circumstances (a process based upon, as Darwin famously put it, the 'survival of the fittest'). For the Chicago School, a comparable process, though social rather than biological in nature, occurred within an urban environment (their approach is sometimes described as social Darwinism). Thus the Chicago ecologists sought to analyse the interrelationships among different groups, and between these groups and the specific areas of the city in which they lived. As was commonplace then (and today for that matter), there was a basic, and apparently self-evident, assumption that crime was a product of 'something going wrong'; in other words, it resulted from pathological situations and circumstances. This was an assumption shared with biological and psychological positivists, who attempted to locate the pathological sources of criminality within the individual (Lombroso, for example, believed that some people were born with 'criminal' genes – see Chapter 13).

The Chicago ecologists, however, looked for the sources of criminality within an individual's social environment. From their perspective, criminal behaviour was not distributed randomly around the city, but was concentrated in specific 'criminal areas'. These areas were characterized by relative poverty, transient, often disreputable, populations, overcrowding, heterogeneous communities, and conflicting norms and values. These were the areas where less well-off newcomers to the city, such as migrants from Europe, would usually head for when they first arrived in Chicago. Burgess (1925) produced a 'social map' of the city that purported to show the location of the different areas, including the criminal area, created by the social evolutionary processes referred to above. Basically, his map showed five concentric circles, each representing a particular zone. At the core was Zone One: the central business district (made up mainly of offices) surrounded by factories. Around this were, in turn: the zone of transition (which equates with the criminal area); a respectable working-class zone; a middle-class zone; and a semi-rural upper middle-class commuter zone. For most of those living in the zone of transition, moving to the respectable working-class zone was the primary goal, representing as it did a major step towards realizing the American Dream.

The Chicago ecologists argued that while on a general level a consensus regarding norms and values ensured that American society was well organized and orderly, areas such as Burgess's zone of transition were characterized by conflict over norms and values and a condition of social disorganization. According to their social ecological model, different types of social life evolve in different geographical areas through a 'natural' process of adaptation, and as with, say, plant and animal life in a forest, an area can move from equilibrium to disequilibrium. Potentially, many factors can contribute to this process: increases in the number of migrants placing pressure on housing markets, instability arising from conflict over norms and values, changes to employment opportunities in response to market forces, and so on. However, in some areas, such as the zone of transition, these pressures are sometimes so intense and protracted that adaptation is extremely difficult, and they experience a sustained period of decline, in the process becoming increasingly disorganized. As a consequence, these areas are characterized by high crime rates, significant physical and mental health problems among the population, drug and alcohol abuse, and so on.

Social disorganization was the key explanatory concept for the Chicago ecologists. Essentially, it describes a situation where community bonds are transitory and weak, norms and values are in conflict, and informal social controls are relatively ineffective. In this context, particular attention was given to the many different ethnic communities clustered together in different areas of the zone of transition. Not only was there conflict over housing and jobs between one ethnic community and another, there was also conflict between first- and second-generation immigrants as the latter absorb more of the dominant American culture, thus finding themselves 'caught between two cultures'. Furthermore, it was argued that joining a gang and engaging in delinquency provided youngsters from the various ethnic groups with an opportunity to create their own, alternative 'community'.

In a highly detailed study, Shaw and McKay (1931, 1942) used court records to map the residential distribution of (10–16-year-old) juvenile delinquents in Chicago. These data were then used to determine delinquency rates in different parts of the city. Note that 'delinquency rates' were based upon where a known offender resided, rather than on the location of the offence. Their conclusion was that, while there was some variation within specific zones, delinquency rates were highest in the inner city/zone of transition, and that the further away an area was from the inner city, the lower the rate. The spatial distribution of delinquency rates, they discovered, had conformed to this basic pattern for 40 years. They also sought to link these high rates of delinquency to the zone of transition as a site of social disorganization, and to this end analysed in detail a range of social and economic factors that, as they saw it, acted as indicators of social disorganization in a neighbourhood. Thus they documented relatively high levels of such things as ethnic heterogeneity, ill health, truancy, overcrowding, suicide and welfare benefit recipients.

Endorsing the work of earlier Chicago ecologists, Shaw and McKay argued that the causes of crime and delinquency lay not in the individual, but in the social environment. In other words, some areas were criminogenic. Their research strongly supported the view that because crime was a consequence of place, rather than individuals, when people moved out of high crime areas, they left their criminality behind. If correct, this would have enormous implications from the point of view of social policy interventions, in that it questions the idea that some individuals and families are inherently and irretrievably a 'problem' and, therefore, likely to continue their criminal behaviour and 'pollute' those around them regardless of where they live.

The Chicago School's interest in qualitative research – ethnography and in-depth interviews – as well as quantitative research was referred to earlier. Shaw and McKay (who incidentally were researchers in a child guidance clinic in Chicago, though they worked closely with the university) also went into the city to carry out qualitative research aimed at illuminating the processes involved in the transmission of delinquent values from one person to another. For them, these processes were captured in the concept of cultural transmission, a version of social learning theory derived in large part from an earlier, and now famous, ethnographic study of delinquent gangs by Thrasher ([1927] 1963), who saw these gangs as providing a viable, alternative source of social integration and support for its members, qualities largely absent within the wider, disorganized community of the criminal area. Shaw and McKay's concept of cultural transmission describes the process whereby the delinquent norms and values entrenched in these areas (norms and values at odds with those of mainstream American society) are internalized by each new generation. This idea was to influence subsequent crimino-logical work that concentrated on deviance and culture (see Chapter 16).

Another major figure of the Chicago School during the 1930s was Edwin Sutherland, and he introduced the concept of differential association. This is similar to the notion of cultural transmission; however, it incorporates learning processes conducive to conformity as well as non-conformity. He argues that, depending on the nature of the social environment, the cultural influences acting on an individual can encourage conformity as well as non-conformity; in other words, these influences can make us free or unfree to break the law: 'a person becomes delinquent because of an excess of definitions favourable to violation of law over definitions unfavourable to violation of law' (Sutherland quoted in Taylor et al. 1973: 126). This is clearly a precursor of Hirschi's (1969) control theory (see Chapter 6). Sutherland made another important contribution to the work of the Chicago School, though this involved a major shift in how the so-called 'criminal area' was conceptualized. Unlike the earlier theorists, Sutherland argued that it was highly misleading to view the criminal area as socially disorganized. For him, different areas of the city were *differentially* socially organized, and criminal behaviour need not be a product of a disorganized – that is, pathological – area (Sutherland 1937). This reflected a further dimension to Sutherland's work, one that was to have a significant influence on subsequent crimino-logical theory. He was critical of the widely accepted view among sociologists at the time that, apart from 'pathological' areas, American society functioned on the basis of a general consensus regarding norms and values, conceived of as conformist mainstream culture. In his view, American society was made up of a plurality of many different cultures, depending on class, ethnicity, region, and so on. It was this view that eventually led him to undertake research into criminality among middle and upper-middle-class white-collar workers – apparently highly respectable members of 'mainstream' society.

The Chicago School produced a very large amount of work (supported by copious statistical data) on crime and delinquency and its urban context, and it created the foundations for much criminology that was to follow in its wake. It was, in many respects, trailblazing work, which partly explains why there are some inconsistencies, contradictions and changes of direction. There was, too, a tension between the positivism that informed a social ecological approach, and the symbolic interactionism that informed an ethnographic approach. It is interesting to compare the criminology of the Chicago School with that of the subcultural strain theorists, whose ideas gained influence during the 1950s and 1960s (see Chapter 16). While the Chicago School saw delinquency as resulting from the norms and values associated with socially disorganized areas, subcultural strain theory sees delinquency as a reaction to the 'strains' experienced by some young people because they have failed to achieve success as judged by middle-class standards (see also Merton's strain theory in Chapter 3).

By the time sociological criminology began to develop in Britain in the late 1950s, of these two major approaches, it was the Chicago School, rather than subcultural strain theory, which had the most influence. Although these pioneering British criminologists (notably Mays 1954; Morris 1957) did not accept the ideas from the Chicago School whole cloth – there were, for instance, doubts about the social ecological model – they did focus on socially deprived 'criminal areas', seeing them as the main source of delinquent subcultures. Rather than arising as reactions to a failure to 'make it' according to middle-class standards, such subcultures, they argued, were formed 'naturally' through the members being socialized into the (delinquent) norms and values of the area. However, Morris disagreed with the Chicago School's argument that delinquency resulted from the criminal area being socially disorganized. In this context, it is important to note that there was an important difference between British and American housing markets, especially in the 1950s and 1960s, in that Britain had a substantial number of municipally owned council houses. In Morris's view, rather than social disorganization, it was the housing policies of the local authority interacting with the social class of council tenants that created a criminal area, in that there was a tendency to house so-called 'problem families' together on the same estate. Furthermore, and contradicting the argument of the Chicago School, the implication of this is that moving problem families and delinquent individuals into more salubrious social environments would not lead to a reduction in delinquent behaviour. Indeed, Morris edged towards the view that such people would 'pollute' others around them; for instance, he compares the spread of delinquency to the spread of cholera.

More recently, a number of researchers in Britain and the United States, using much more advanced research techniques than were available in the 1920s and 1930s, have carried out empirical studies in order to reassess the ideas of the Chicago School. One important study that used data from the first (1982) British Crime Survey was carried out by Sampson and Groves (1989). The British Crime Survey, which is now conducted annually, is a large-sweep victim survey, and data are based on the accounts of victims of crime; therefore, Sampson and Groves used an alternative definition of 'crime rates' to that used by Shaw and McKay. To a large extent their findings vindicated the work of the Chicago School. The research, which focused on 238 different localities, involved assessing a variety of structural variables – deprivation, social class, ethnic heterogeneity, broken families, and so on – associated with each locality, as well as measuring the degree to which a locality was socially disorganized. Three key dimensions to social life in these localities were used as a tool for measuring social disorganization. First, the extent to which people interacted and cooperated on the basis of informal friendships. Second, and more formally, the extent to which people inter-acted and cooperated on the basis of community organizations and projects. And third, the extent to which younger people were supervised by parents or other older residents. The researchers found that the highest crime rates occurred in the most socially disorganized localities.

In subsequent research along these lines, though in an American context, by Sampson, particular emphasis is given to what he calls the 'collective efficacy' found in different localities, a concept used to describe the strength or weakness of the informal control networks. Seen as reflecting the degree of social organization in a locality, collective efficacy is manifested in the extent to which residents actively engage in informal social control activities, especially in relation to youngsters, for example, through chastise-ment, informing parents or calling the police (Sampson 2006). Collective efficacy was found to be at its weakest in localities where there were high levels of social deprivation and transient populations. In a recent overview of research into the links between social disorganization and crime, Pratt and Cullen (2005) come to the conclusion that in broad terms this research does support the findings of Shaw and McKay. They do, however, make the point that one of the problems surrounding such an assessment is that the research tends to concentrate on structural factors, as indices of social disorganiza-tion, rather than on conceptualizing and measuring social disorganization *per se*. Sampson's research thus provides an important exception.

Criticisms of the Chicago School

Inevitably, with the passage of time the work of the Chicago School has come under intense critical scrutiny.

- One of the chief criticisms, which first surfaced in an analysis by Alihan (1938), strikes at the heart of the social ecological approach to crime. By basing their research on an analogy between plant and animal life and the social life of human beings, the Chicago ecologists necessarily produced statistical data on the behaviour of people as *groups*, rather than *individuals* (in the same way that biologists would, for instance, produce data on all the daffodils in a forest). The use of aggregated data leads to what critics call the 'ecological fallacy'. This, the argument runs, is because of an erroneous assumption that the actions of the individual (in this case of a criminal nature) can be explained by statistical data pertaining to groups of people.
- A second set of criticisms relate to the types of crime data collected by the Chicago School, and the types of people identified as the source of the 'crime problem'. Researchers drew on official crime

statistics (from police or court records), and (in addition to the issue of accuracy) these would over-represent 'conventional' crime, such as street robbery, theft, burglary and criminal damage, while at the same time under-representing white-collar and corporate crime. This would have drawn the Chicago School ineluctably towards the zone of transition given that, first, conventional crime tends to be associated with lower-class young males and, second, that middle-class young males carrying out the same offences are less likely to be apprehended and/or prosecuted. This does raise important questions regarding perceptions of the crime problem, though Sutherland's ([1949] 1983) ground-breaking work on white-collar crime in the 1940s has to be acknowledged. In this context, the lack of research into the problem of organized crime is particularly noticeable.

Between 1920 and 1930, there was a legal ban on the manufacture, transportation and sale of alcohol throughout the United States: the era of Prohibition. During this period, Chicago became notorious for its organized crime networks and powerful 'mob' figures such as Al Capone and Bugs Moran, whose activities were, to a large extent, directed at contravening the Prohibition laws. These activities included murder, protection rackets, smuggling and illegal drinking establishments known as speakeasies (by 1930 Al Capone controlled all of the 10,000 speakeasies in Chicago). However, these criminal networks stretched well beyond the 'underworld'. Bribery and corruption drew police officers, politicians, business leaders and other 'respectable' members of society into the highly lucrative world of 'organized' crime. As the Commissioner of Prohibition, then based in Chicago, noted:

> ... the fruitless efforts at enforcement are creating public disregard not only for this law but for all laws. Public corruption through the purchase of official protection of this illegal traffic is widespread and notorious.
>
> (Anderson 1931: 90)

Why was none of this studied by the Chicago School? Perhaps the best answer is found in this comment by the British criminologist Colin Sumner (1994: 51):

As Harold Finestone, a doctoral student there in the 1930s, once told me in conversation, in response to my query about the lack of studies on the mob itself: 'the mob was the government at that time, and you don't do fieldwork on the government, do you?'

• The third criticism concerns the concept of social organization and the factors or indices used to measure it. As we have seen, for the

Chicago School, crime resulted from the social disorganization found in certain areas. However, this formulation has been criticized for being tautological, in that crime can be viewed as one of the factors contributing to a state of social disorganization. Taking the example of Shaw and McKay, their basic argument was that socially disorganized areas were characterized by an absence of informal social controls on youngsters and an existing delinquent culture into which they are socialized. At the very least we might pose the question: to what extent does the existence of delinquency in an area actually produce social disorganization and a lack of informal controls?

- Fourth, because of the nature of their data, what was described by Shaw and McKay as a 'criminal/delinquent area' was the area in which adjudicated delinquent youths lived. These data in themselves, then, provide no information on the areas in which the delinquent acts occurred.
- Fifth, many subsequent developments in empirical research and criminological theory have exposed the Chicago School to critical questions relating to:
  - the determinism of a social ecological model, suggesting that individuals are relatively passive products of their social environments;
  - why it is that not everyone living in a socially disorganized area turns to crime;
  - (following labelling theory) the lack of attention paid to agents of social control in the construction of crime and delinquency rates;
  - (following feminist theory) the lack of attention paid to the issue of gender.

- Finally, by viewing the evolution of different areas of the city as a 'natural' process, the Chicago ecologists failed to recognize broader social and economic influences – the actions of capitalist entrepreneurs, owners of land and property, and local and federal government, for instance – which contributed to the nature of social life across the city of Chicago.

Further reading

In addition to Thrasher's ([1927] 1963) study referred to above, other enthographic studies from that period worth reading are: Anderson, N. ([1923] 1975) *The Hobo: The Story of Chicago's Prohibition Era*. London: Hutchinson; Shaw, C.R. (1930) *The Jack-roller: A Delinquent Boy's Own Story*.

Chicago, IL: Chicago University Press; and Shaw, C.R. and Moore, M.E. (1931) *The Natural History of a Delinquent Career*. Chicago, IL: University of Chicago Press.

For examples of the Chicago School's social ecological approach to crime and the city, see Park, R.E., Burgess, E.W. and McKenzie, R.D. (eds) (1925) *The City*. Chicago, IL: University of Chicago Press; Shaw, C.R. (1929) *Delinquency Areas*. Chicago, IL: University of Chicago Press; Shaw, C.R. and McKay, H.D. (1942) *Juvenile Delinquency and Urban Areas*. Chicago, IL: University of Chicago Press.

An excellent, up-to-date review of socio-spatial approaches to crime and delinquency is provided by Bottoms, A.E. (2007) Place, space, crime and disorder, in M. Maguire, R. Morgan and R. Reiner (eds) *The Oxford Handbook of Criminology*, 4th edn. Oxford: Oxford University Press.

5 Classical Criminology

All theoretical perspectives, or 'schools of thought', in criminology (together with the policies and practices based upon the theories), emerge and develop within particular social, economic and political contexts. As a consequence, they incorporate various assumptions, understandings and agendas regarding 'human nature' and the nature of the social order. Classical criminology, or classicism, emerged in Europe during the second part of the eighteenth century, and reflected the philosophical and political thought associated with the Enlightenment, the 'Age of Reason'. Spanning the seventeenth and eighteenth centuries, the Enlightenment coincided with a period of massive social, economic and political change across Europe and in the colonies of North America. There was the transition from feudalism to capitalism, and with it the growth in power of a capitalist class. At the same time, the power of the *ancien régime* – the old system of order and government, based upon an absolute monarch, an aristocracy and the Church – was being increasingly challenged.

Enlightenment philosophers and thinkers, such as Voltaire, Montesquieu, Rousseau and Locke, spoke of 'natural' rights, citizenship and equality, ideas that were to create a basis for the subsequent development of social democracy. The ideas also underpinned violent struggles to overturn the old order, notably, the French Revolution and the American War of Independence in the late eighteenth century, and were embodied in the French Declaration of Man and Citizen and the American Declaration of Independence. Utilitarian philosophy was one of the cornerstones of Enlightenment thinking. According to utilitarianism, people and social institutions should be useful and make a positive contribution to the well-being of society – 'the greatest good for the greatest number'. From this perspective, the *ancien régime* was not useful. Enlightenment thinkers, then, saw ahead of them a brave new world founded on democratic principles and scientific knowledge, and based upon a principle of progress. A world, they believed, where even nature would be controlled for the benefit of society. It was, therefore, the beginning of modernism.

Turning to assumptions about human nature, at the core of Enlightenment thinking was the view that individuals are motivated primarily by a desire for pleasure (coupled with a desire to avoid pain). However, although they are essentially selfish and self-seeking, *men* are also rational. The word 'men' is used here because at the time writers referred explicitly to men rather than women, or human beings – this is returned to below. This led philosophers to argue that if a suitable mechanism for maintaining social order was established, men would act rationally and control their passions, recognizing that to do otherwise would lead inevitably to social chaos. Thus the philosophers Locke and Hobbes in the seventeenth century, and Rousseau in the eighteenth century, put forward the idea of the social contract as the mechanism for achieving social order. According to social contract theory, all men, using reason, will enter into an accord whereby they will agree to give up some of their freedoms in return for a well-ordered, tranquil society. This will also entail the universal acceptance of the legitimate authority of the state to introduce and enforce laws and, if necessary, administer punishment. Hobbes called this authority *Leviathan*, arguing that such an arrangement would prevent a 'war of all against all'. The social contract, therefore, appeals to the individual's desire for pleasure, in the sense that it would provide a well-ordered society of benefit to everyone. Such a system, however, would only 'work', said Enlightenment philosophers, if there was mutual agreement that men are born equal and should share the same fundamental human rights. Hence the importance of creating a society founded upon notions of citizenship, rights, equality, and so on, as discussed above.

Before turning to classical criminology itself, it is worth looking through a critical lens at the Enlightenment and the ideas associated with it. From a contemporary vantage point, and especially one imbued with late-modern sensibilities, it is no surprise that criticisms are many and varied. While Enlightenment thinkers laid great stress on equality, it was by no means a rallying call for the creation of an egalitarian society beyond that of formal equality in terms of the law. There might have been a jaundiced view of absolute monarchs and the landed aristocracy, but the existence of social divisions rooted in wealth and power was never questioned, and the right to own private property was taken as sacrosanct. During the eighteenth century, and indeed well into the nineteenth century, private property included the ownership of slaves. For over 300 years, many millions of black Africans were shipped across the Atlantic to the colonies. In fact, black people, along with indigenous people in the colonies established by the European powers, were described as 'savages'. For such people, deemed to lack intelligence and rationality, so-called 'universal' human rights were of no relevance (e.g. those relating to citizenship and the right to vote). They were thus excluded from the social contract. By way of illustration, the philosopher Hume observed, in the middle of the eighteenth century:

> I am apt to suspect the Negroes, and in general all the other species of men ... to be naturally inferior to the whites. There never was a civilized nation of any complexion than white, nor even any

individual eminent in action or speculation. No ingenious manufactures amongst them, no arts, no sciences.

(Quoted by Hartmann and Husband 1974: 24)

It is also important to note, and returning to the earlier comment regarding the word 'men', that women were seen as lacking the ability to think and act in a rational manner. Although respected as wives and mothers, they too were denied full citizenship rights and participation in the social contract. In the vast literature of the Enlightenment all those references to 'men' were literal references; the inclusion of women in public affairs was simply seen as an irrelevance. It was also seen as an irrelevance in relation to the poor. Thus all citizens would enter into the social contract, providing that they were white, male and owners of property.

Clearly, these are harsh criticisms of Enlightenment thought, and further criticisms linked specifically to classical criminology are outlined below. However, valid as they are, those features of the Enlightenment being criticized have, of course, to be situated within the context of that historical period. Post-modernist writers in particular have criticized the 'march of progress' view of social development subscribed to by Enlightenment thinkers. For them, the modernist project is a failed project. It is true that 'rational' bureaucracy eventually gave the world the Holocaust, and 'rational' scientific knowledge gave it the bombs that fell on Hiroshima and Nagasaki, but the attributes of modernism also took social life in other more positive directions. In spite of its inequalities, sexism and racism, few would see the Enlightenment as a step backwards. The stress on rationality and the discourses surrounding notions of democracy, personal liberty, human rights and equality before the law, may have been severely truncated and contradicted by contemporary social arrangements, but they did lay the foundations for a range of subsequent and inexorable processes that led to these discourses having a significant, and global, substantive reality.

This, then, provided the context within which the classical school of criminology emerged and developed during the eighteenth century. Classical criminology is usually seen as the first 'real' criminology (see, for example, Taylor et al. 1973; Roshier 1989). Some, however, have questioned this on the grounds that it was 'pre-scientific' (Vold 1958) and narrowly concerned with the administration of justice, rather than, for instance, exploring the causes of crime and criminal motivations. Whether or not it is seen as 'real' criminology obviously depends on how one conceptualizes the business of 'doing criminology', though the general view among contemporary criminologists is that, regardless of one's feelings regarding its theoretical status and relevance, its qualities are such that it should be admitted into the academy. Importantly, it was the first significant attempt to develop systematic theorizing of issues of crime and punishment. In addition, it is worth noting that the ideas associated with classical criminology have influenced many subsequent criminologists, right up to the present day (see, for instance, Chapters 2 and 6).

The most influential figure in eighteenth-century classical criminology was the Italian Cesare Beccaria (1963). In 1764 he published *An Essay On Crimes and Punishments*, which had an enormous impact on Enlightenment thinkers across Europe and in North America. This short book was in effect a manifesto, comparable, in terms of its highly charged polemical message, to *The Communist Manifesto*, written two centuries later by Marx and Engels. Along with many other Enlightenment figures, Beccaria was highly critical of the system of justice in operation in Europe at that time, a system that reflected its origins in feudal society. It was attacked for being arbitrary, corrupt, barbaric and, in particular, inefficient – the latter especially offending utilitarian principles – it was, therefore, not rational. A legal procedure known as *Lettres de cachet* illustrates how arbitrary and corrupt the criminal justice system was at that time:

> A *lettre de cachet* was a sealed administrative order signed by the monarch containing a command that an individual be detained. It was to be executed swiftly, secretly and with no recourse to the courts. The order gave no explanation, there was no trial and no legal mechanism for appeal, and release was dependent upon the monarch's pleasure. A *lettre de cachet* could be granted to a private person for action on another individual.

> (Valier 2002: 8)

A rational system of justice, argued Beccaria, would actually 'work', meaning that it would prevent crime. Beccaria's essay also reflected Enlightenment ideas pertaining to notions of justice and human rights. Notably, that the law and the judicial process should treat all citizens equally and fairly, thus no advantage should accrue from rank or 'connections'; legal rights should be universal; judges should act neutrally and in accordance with the dictates of the law; punishment should be set at an appropriate minimum level of severity; all accusations should be made public and the accuser identified (so as to guard against malicious or mischievous indictment); and the law itself should be clear, and formulated in such as way that it minimizes as much as possible the restrictions on a citizen's freedom. Given the nature of criminal justice in Europe at that time, this was a tall order, but one that received strong approval among those who saw themselves as 'progressive' and literally 'enlightened'.

As mentioned earlier, Enlightenment thinkers believed that a law-abiding, well-ordered society could be achieved through the social contract. In theory, it was rational for citizens to adhere to the contract and forgo certain freedoms, because they would recognize the benefits in the shape of a peaceful and tranquil society. It is, therefore, a theory based upon the assumption that individuals are motivated by a desire for pleasure; in other words, that they are essentially selfish. However, writers such as Beccaria also understood that in practice some individuals will not abide by the rules – sometimes the contract will be broken, or not accepted at all. Therefore, he argued that a disincentive, or deterrent, in the form of punishment was necessary. He reasoned that because they are rational, people would accept as fair and legitimate an arrangement where the state had the power to punish transgressors, as they would appreciate the benefits that would accrue to themselves and rest of society: 'the greatest happiness to the greatest number'. For Beccaria, the creation of a criminal justice system based on equality and fairness, as discussed above, was a necessary precondition, otherwise there would be no consensus regarding the social contract. He argued that punishment should not be based upon revenge or retribution, as it was at the time. Punishment, he said, should have one purpose – to deter people from breaking the law – and if it is to be effective, then it must be swift and certain.

Furthermore, Beccaria believed that the nature of the punishment should reflect the nature of the offence and its harmfulness to society, but the severity of the punishment should only be sufficient to act as a deterrent; excessive punishment would be inefficient. Beccaria's approach to punishment is the application of the pleasure–pain principle – the pleasure of crime should be outweighed by the pain of punishment. This was a cornerstone of classical thinking. The punishment should be proportional to the social harm of the crime, rather than the harm to individual victims *per se*. Revenge or retribution, on the other hand, is based upon the principle that the punishment should be proportional to the harm done to the victim in individual cases; that is, it is what the offender deserves. Beccaria strongly rejected the death penalty and the use of torture, both of which were commonplace during that period of history. There were two reasons why he argued against the death penalty: first, that the state would breach the social contract by taking someone's life, thereby jeopardizing its existence and, second, that it did not actually deter people from committing capital offences. Similarly, he argued against the use of torture on the grounds of inefficiency, rather than morality. The authorities used torture to extract confessions from alleged offenders, however, as Beccaria observed, this simply resulted in guilt or innocence being determined according to whether the accused was weak or strong.

In Britain, Beccaria's ideas were picked up and popularized by the philosopher Jeremy Bentham. Although he was critical of some of the ideas of the earlier Enlightenment thinkers (e.g. those relating to natural rights), he was interested in issues of law, social order and penal reform, and was a major figure in the classical criminological tradition. He greatly admired

Beccaria's *An Essay On Crimes and Punishments*, seeing it as a supreme example of utilitarian philosophy, with which he is particularly associated. In line with Beccaria and other Enlightenment thinkers, he conceived of individuals as rational beings who apply a pleasure–pain principle when assessing whether or not to commit a crime. Thus he too argued that swift and certain punishment, proportional to the harm inflicted on society by the crime, would act as a deterrent. He strongly believed, however, that the system would only be successful if the law itself were to be codified and logically structured, so that people would be clearly aware of what the rules were.

Bentham was much more enthusiastic about the use of imprisonment as a form of punishment for wrongdoers than was Beccaria. Indeed, he famously designed what he saw as the ideal prison, and called it Pantopticon. Its key architectural feature was a central tower occupied by guards, or 'inspectors', encircled by the prisoners' cells. The guards would be able to observe any prisoner they chose, while themselves remaining hidden from view. For Bentham, this represented the most efficient system of surveillance, in that prisoners never knew whether or not they were being watched and, therefore, it required relatively few guards. In effect, prisoners would feel themselves to be under constant surveillance. While his Panopticon was never built, the concept itself has entered the lexicon of criminological theory, being employed within the context of contemporary analyses of surveillance techniques such as closed circuit television.

In summary, classical criminology was essentially concerned with the establishment of an efficient system of justice, including the simplification and codification of the law, and the deterrent effect of punishment. Although Beccaria recognized that different 'states of mind' existed, and made reference to a link between poverty and crime, the classical criminologists concerned themselves with the prevention of crime, rather than with analysing criminal motivations. From their perspective, and on the assumption that people exercise free will, in a society organized according to the principles of the social contract, criminals are simply those pleasure-seeking individuals who have failed to grasp the irrational nature of their behaviour. A central problem with this formulation, however, is that while there is formal and universal equality before the law in such a society, the profound inequalities in the wider society are left untouched. For some people, such as the poor, the pain of non-criminal behaviour may be worse than the pain of criminal behaviour, or at least of such severity that some putative punishment cannot function as a deterrent. In addition, because all offenders would be judged according to the nature of the offence alone, no mitigating circumstances would be taken into account by the court. In fact, criminal law jurisdictions in Europe eventually developed on the basis of neo-classicism, and thus factors such as age and mental state could be taken into consideration.

Further reading

The key original sources are Beccaria, C. ([1764] 1963) *An Essay On Crimes and Punishments*. Indianapolis, NL: Bobbs-Merrill; and Bentham, J. ([1791] 1843) *Collected Works of Jeremy Bentham*. London: J. Bowring.

A recent edited collection devoted to Beccaria's work is Bellamy, R. (ed.) (1995) *Beccaria: On Crimes and Punishments and Other Writings*. Cambridge: Cambridge University Press. Very good accounts of classical criminology are provided by Roshier, B. (1989) *Controlling Crime*. Buckingham: Open University Press; and Beirne, P. (1993) *Inventing Criminology: Essays on the Rise of 'Homo Criminalis'*. Albany, NY: State University of New York Press.

The use of law as an inherent part of the Enlightenment project is explored in Carty, A. (ed.) (1990) *Post-modern Law: Enlightenment, Revolution and the Death of Man*. Edinburgh: Edinburgh University Press; and the place of women in Scott, J. (1996) *Only Paradoxes to Offer: French Feminists and the Rights of Man*. Cambridge, MA: Harvard University Press. For a general discussion of the Enlightenment, see Porter, R. (2000) *Enlightenment: Britain and the Creation of the Modern World*. London: Penguin.

6   Control Theory

In its broadest sense, various types of control theory have existed for hundreds of years, in that many philosophers and thinkers have discussed the need for effective controls to restrain human desires and passions. In this chapter though the focus is on the modern criminological versions that emerged in America in the twentieth century; in particular, the best known version associated with Hirschi (1969). Control theory can be situated within the classical tradition (see Chapter 5), in that human beings are conceptualized as rational (at least from their perspective) decision-makers, who subjectively weigh up the costs and benefits of an action. In addition, the emphasis is on those factors that act to prevent individuals from committing crime, rather than on criminal motivations and their antecedents. One difference between classicism and control theory though is that while the former assumes that individuals exercise free will when making decisions, control theory in effect makes the issue of free will irrelevant.

Instead of asking why people break the law, as criminology has traditionally done, control theory asks why do people *not* break the law? In other words, what is it that makes an individual opt for conformity rather than deviance? Writing in the 1950s, Toby (1957) introduced the term 'a stake in conformity' to describe a situation where an individual 'invests' in non-deviant behaviour because they see the benefits outweighing the costs attached to deviant behaviour. This is quite different to the approach of many other criminologists, who have sought to identify those factors that lead an individual into deviance. This can be illustrated by comparing control theory with, for instance, Cohen's (1955) subcultural strain theory (which is examined in detail in Chapter 16). For Cohen, youth delinquency results from the 'strains' experienced by lower-class boys during adolescence; specifically, an inability to achieve status in a society dominated by middle-class norms and values. Some boys, then, react by withdrawing support for these conventional norms and values, and cease to have a stake in conformity. Thus in common with much criminology, Cohen assumed that rule-breaking behaviour was a consequence of something 'going wrong'. Control theory, on the other hand, explores what 'goes right', in the sense of identifying those factors that help foster and sustain an individual's stake in conformity.

In line with classical criminology, control theorists see human beings as essentially self-seeking and, in the absence of social controls, their behaviour will be guided simply by their own needs and desires. Under these circumstances they are *free* to behave as they wish. Given that moral codes and notions of acceptable and unacceptable behaviour are cultural entities, human beings do not possess innate understandings of such things. These understandings are therefore dependent on an individual's social experiences. If these experiences result in an individual opting for conformist, non-deviant modes of behaviour, then they are in effect *unfree* to behave as they wish. Thus control theorists have concerned themselves with exploring those controls that remove the freedom to engage in deviant behaviour.

Hirschi's version of control theory is based on the results of an empirical study of 4000 American adolescents from various class and ethnic backgrounds. This included a self-report element, where respondents were asked about their delinquent behaviour. Correlations between reported offending and various factors relating to an individual's social background were then identified. One of the findings worth noting was that, from the point of view of offending, there were no significant differences between one social class and another, a finding at variance with official statistics, other research and conventional wisdom. Box (1981) has suggested that the over-representation of lower-class youth in official figures relating to delinquency is a function of discriminatory labelling processes on the part of the police and other authorities. From this perspective, Hirschi's self-report study paints a more accurate picture by bringing to light previously 'invisible' middle-class delinquency (as Box says, while official statistics provide information on 'secondary deviants', self-report studies provide information on 'primary deviants' – see Chapter 10 for a discussion of these terms). An alternative view is that Hirschi's research methodology was at fault and in consequence exaggerates the middle-class adolescents' involvement in delinquency. Downes and Rock (2007), for instance, argue that his definition of 'serious delinquency' when measuring self-reported delinquency was seriously flawed.

Hirschi argues that there are four key variables constituting the social controls influencing the extent to which an individual develops a stake in conformity. They are referred to as 'bonds'; in other words, mechanisms that tie an individual to conventional society and thus inhibit delinquent behaviour. These bonds are:

- *Attachment* – the quality of the relationships an individual has with, for example, their family, peers and school. When these relationships are strong, an individual will take into consideration and respect the feelings of those concerned. In this case, if these significant others frown on delinquency, it will deter an individual from engaging in such behaviour. Hirschi found that those with a strong attachment to parents were less likely to engage in delinquency, as were those strongly attached to teachers at school. His research also indicates that it is those who already have a reduced stake in conformity who form attachments with delinquent peers, and it is this, rather than the attachments, that correlates with delinquency (he eventually reviewed this, and admitted that he had not placed enough emphasis on attachments to delinquent peers).

- *Commitment* – the degree to which an individual recognizes the benefits accruing from conventional behaviour. A prime example is when an individual reasons that it is worth maintaining a commitment to school because of the longer-term rewards that this will bring, rewards that would be put at risk by engaging in delinquent behaviour. Research in Britain and the United States has shown a strong correlation between a lack of educational success and involvement in delinquency. It also shows a strong correlation between educational success and social class. In light of this, one might conclude that because of a weaker 'commitment', lower-class, rather than middle-class adolescents would be more likely to engage in delinquency. However, as discussed above, Hirschi argues that delinquency rates are similar for both social classes. The extent of an individual's 'commitment' is, he says, subjective, in that it reflects their perception of their ties to conventional society.

- *Involvement* – the degree to which an individual's daily life involves engaging in conventional, socially approved activities (though Hirschi subsequently felt that he had placed too much emphasis on this social bond).

- *Beliefs* – the degree to which an individual's subjective feelings regarding acceptable and unacceptable behaviour match those of conventional society. It might be thought that this variable alone would be sufficient to explain conventional behaviour. However, Hirschi did not see beliefs as a permanent, embedded component of an individual's consciousness. Rather, the nature and strength of an individual's beliefs are contingent on their attachments and, therefore, may alter significantly depending upon circumstances.

Although there is a psychological dimension to Hirschi's theoretical model, as the discussion of 'beliefs' indicates, it is primarily sociological in orientation. This distinguishes it from earlier versions of control theory, which, while identifying 'internal' and 'external' social controls, tended to place greater importance on the former than the latter when accounting for conformist behaviour. Internal (or self-) controls are those that have become an intimate part of an individual's psychological make-up, and are manifested in, for example, conscience or 'fixed' personal moral standards. Hirschi was sceptical of this view, and argued that in practice the four bonds potentially providing individuals with a stake in conformity are highly fluid, contingent and fragile. None the less, this earlier work on the reasons why some individuals are unable to bond with conventional society by, for instance, Reckless ([1950] 1973) and Nye (1958) did influence the development of his own version of control theory. In brief, Reckless described his theory as 'containment theory', and based it on the idea that the control of delinquency depended on 'outer containment' (the discipline exercised by others), and 'inner containment' (the discipline exercised by internal feelings of guilt). Nye argued that controls can be classified as 'direct' (the external threat of punishment); 'indirect' (the desire not to cause harm to significant others); and 'internal' (an internalized moral code and attendant feelings of guilt).

Since it was published, Hirschi's work has been subjected to a great deal of empirical and theoretical scrutiny. Subsequent research has tended to support aspects of his research, rather than his findings as a whole, while also indicating that although his model is useful for explaining some delinquency, it is some way short of providing a comprehensive explanation. The majority of studies aimed at testing his theory have focused on the relationship between children and parents (e.g. Johnson 1979; Poole and Regoli 1979). In general, these studies have supported Hirschi's argument that a close relationship between parents and children, where children bother about what their parents think, provides an important bond to conventional society, and hence a reduced likelihood of delinquency. The crucial factor is not that it is a 'happy family', but that it is a family where the children are aware of parental disapproval of delinquency and take this seriously. This cuts across all social classes. Wilson (1980), for example, in a British study of families living in deprived neighbourhoods, found a strong correlation between a strict, protective attitude on the part of parents and a lower incidence of delinquency on the part of children.

Criticisms of Hirschi's control theory have addressed its methodological and theoretical integrity. Some have argued that it is unable to explain why some individuals graduate from relatively minor acts of delinquency to more serious and frequent offending, or why different individuals commit different types of criminal offence (Braithwaite 1989). Drawing on the findings from a longitudinal study, Agnew (1985) has questioned the idea that delinquency is a consequence of weak bonds to the conventional order, arguing instead that it is equally likely that these weak bonds are a consequence of the delinquent behaviour itself. As well as the direction of influence in this sense, it is unclear precisely how Hirschi's social bonds interact with each other, and the relative importance of one compared to another. Others have criticized control theory for detaching the social bonds from their wider structural context; for example, inequalities due to class and ethnicity, and the nature of criminal law and processes of enforcement and criminalization (Elliot et al. 1979). Having said that, it should be noted that Hirschi argued that control theory is not intended to provide a comprehensive account and explanation of criminal behaviour in general, and is only concerned with exploring the circumstances that make delinquency possible.

These circumstances, as we have seen, create a situation where an individual is free to deviate. Using this idea as a starting point, Box (1981) developed an insightful elaboration of Hirschi's original theoretical formulation, in the process drawing on the work of labelling theorists. Although individuals may be *free* to deviate, Box argues that a complete analysis also needs to consider situations where they are *able* and *wanting* to deviate. Being free, he says, does not necessarily mean that they take up the option. Box argues that being able to deviate is contingent upon five 'issues'. First, a belief that they can conceal their actions; second, that they are skilful enough to carry them out; third, they can acquire the necessary equipment; fourth, a belief that significant others are encouraging them to carry out the actions; and fifth, moral justification from significant others. Even if they are free and able to commit a deviant act, whether or not they proceed also depends on them wanting to do so. Drawing on the work of Matza and Sykes (1961) and Matza (1964), Box (1981) suggests four potential reasons why an individual would want to go ahead and engage in deviant behaviour: thrill, confirmation of (male) gender roles, material gain, and an active and creative engagement with life.

Hirschi (together with Gottfredson) has subsequently developed a rather different version of control theory (Hirschi and Gottfredson 1995, 2000). Here, the key factor is self-control: high levels of self-control are equated with low levels of deviant behaviour. The original four bonds to conventional society are now seen as being dependent on the self-control exercised by an individual. Low levels of self-control are said to be associated with such things as impulsiveness, risk-taking behaviour and a lack of concern for victims, attributes that increase the likelihood of an individual engaging in deviance. For Hirschi and Gottfredson, the extent to which an individual is able to exercise self-control depends on their early socialization, especially in the family. However, and indicating a shift towards positivism, they introduce a deterministic dimension by arguing that the effectiveness of early socialization is partly dependent on an individual's genetic make-up. Furthermore, the authors suggest that a low level of self-control is associated with social class position, thus those of low socio-economic status are more likely to engage in deviant behaviour (in Hirschi's original formulation above, delinquency was thought to be evenly distributed among social classes).

Control balance theory

The American criminologist Charles Tittle (1995) introduced his own version of control theory in the mid-1990s, giving it the title of control balance theory – though since then he has to some extent refined his original theory (Tittle 1997, 2000, 2004). It differs from others' versions in that instead of concentrating only on the circumstances or factors that act to control an individual's behaviour, he also recognizes that individuals have the capacity to exert control over others. On this basis, he seeks to explain why some individuals develop a motivation to engage in deviant behaviour. Furthermore, and again unlike other types of control theory, he incorporates a wide range of complex and interacting factors that in combination create the conditions within which deviant motivations emerge. This is an ambitious task, especially as Tittle aims to develop a theoretical model that is relevant to all forms of deviant behaviour, stretching from minor delinquency to white-collar and corporate crime, thereby taking in both individuals and organizations. Thus it addresses the crimes of the powerful as well as those of the powerless.

It is described as control *balance* theory because it focuses on the balance between the control placed on an individual and the control that an individual has over others – the 'control ratio'. Deviance arises in situations where there is an imbalance in this ratio, that is, where there is a deficit or a surplus of control. Therefore, deviance is used to redress the balance in situations where a deficit of control exists, and to maintain or enhance the balance where there is a surplus. Tittle links this deviant response to what he sees as a fundamental human desire for autonomy, and it is most likely to occur when an individual is prevented from achieving their desired goals. Subjective understandings are important here, in that deviant behaviour is more likely to occur when individuals feel that they have been 'belittled' by others, and they believe that 'deviant behaviour can be used to strengthen their autonomy' (Tittle 2000: 320). In addition, Tittle situates an individual's decision to engage in deviance within a wider context of other contingent factors, for example: levels of self-control; risk factors; the strength of social bonds tying them to significant others; and suitable opportunities. His theory has though been criticized on a number of counts, in particular that:

- the idea that individuals are motivated primarily by a desire for autonomy;
- it is difficult to assess the relative importance of the various factors influencing deviant responses to control imbalance;
- it is difficult to establish precisely why an individual should choose a specific type of deviance;
- the huge range of complex factors involved makes the theory extremely difficult to verify empirically.

However, one of the major strengths of control balance theory:

> ... is the view that deviance can arise because an individual experiences either too much *or* too little control. It thus acts as an antidote

to the view among some policy makers that the solution to crime and deviance lies in more control.

(Tierney 2006: 333, emphasis in original)

Differential coercion theory

This theoretical perspective was introduced by the American criminologist Mark Colvin (2000). As the name suggests, the key concept is 'coercion'; specifically, the amounts and types of coercion used to make people conform with particular expectations regarding appropriate behaviour. Beginning with the family, individuals experience different sorts of coercion throughout their lives. For some, the coercion is minimal; however, for others the coercion involved is highly intensive. Thus Colvin suggests a hypothetical continuum ranging from 'non-coercion' to 'coercion', and argues that criminal behaviour is strongly associated with those who have experienced coercion at the high end of the continuum. This is not the same as, say, a 'strict upbringing'; rather, he is referring to forms of coercion that are harsh and erratic. Furthermore, he says, coercion is manifested in adverse social circumstances and pressures, such as poverty, unemployment, bad housing and racism, as well as in interpersonal relationships. As this indicates, Colvin is arguing that it is those of lower socio-economic status who are much more likely to experience harsh and erratic coercion as they go through life. These experiences in effect set in motion a series of vicious circles that operate on two levels.

First, they create what Colvin calls a 'psychological deficit' for the individuals concerned, in that they feel belittled, humiliated, angry and revengeful, and 'fight back' in kind. Second, at some stage in their lives, those concerned establish their own families, and the 'deficit' is reproduced within the context of their family relationships. Those caught up in these processes, and who routinely experience coercion of this sort are, says Colvin, much more likely to engage in serious and frequent criminal behaviour. Although more research needs to be done, some studies have supported the basic tenets of differential coercion theory (e.g. Unnever et al. 2004). However, there are some critical issues raised by the theory. While it provides a plausible explanation of criminal behaviour among poorer, more oppressed, sections of society, in what ways is the concept of coercion relevant to explanations of criminality among better-off, more powerful groups? Also, further work is required to explore the dynamics of these coercive processes among the less well-off order to explain why it is that many of them do not participate in criminal activities.

Further reading

The key original texts are Hirschi, T. (1969) *Causes of Delinquency*. Berkeley, CA: University of California Press; Hirschi, T. and Gottfredson, M.R. (1995) Control theory and the life course perspective, *Studies on Crime and Crime Prevention*, 4: 131–42; and Tittle, C.R. (1995) *Control Balance: Toward a General Theory of Deviance*. Boulder, CO: Westview (and for a recent 'refinement', see Tittle, C.R. (2004) Refining control balance theory, *Theoretical Criminology*, 8(4): 395–428.

A good and detailed overview of the various types of control theory can be found in Lilly, J.R., Cullen, F.T. and Ball, R.A. (2007) *Criminological Theory: Context and Consequences*, 4th edn. Thousand Oaks, CA: Sage; and Downes, D. and Rock, P. (2007) *Understanding Deviance*, 5th edn. Oxford: Oxford University Press.

7 Critical Criminology

Although in theory a wide range of criminological perspectives could describe themselves as 'critical', the discussion here locates critical criminology within a particular radical tradition that emerged, on the heels of labelling theory (see Chapter 10), in the late 1960s/early 1970s. Radical or critical criminology (during its early years the terms tended to be used interchangeably) developed within a theoretical framework provided by versions of conflict theory. While the early American work drew on some Marxian concepts, it was largely based upon non-Marxist conflict theory. In Britain though and reflecting a stronger European tradition of Marxist scholarship, from the outset the aim was to develop a specifically Marxist criminology. However, fairly quickly, radical criminology on both sides of the Atlantic became avowedly Marxist – or more accurately, neo-Marxist. In a nutshell, once established, the radical tradition in criminology sought to analyse phenomena of crime and deviance within the economic and political context of capitalism. Capitalist society was seen as inherently unequal and unjust (fundamentally, because it is based upon exploitative class relations), and criminogenic. Mapping the trajectories taken by this type of criminology from its early beginnings to the present day is both interesting and complex. This is because its history has in varying degrees involved ambiguity, in-fighting, reassessments, revisions and changes of heart.

The radical criminology that emerged in the late 1960s and early 1970s was to a significant extent influenced by ideas associated with labelling theory (see Chapter 10 for a fuller discussion of these ideas). In particular, we can note labelling theory's emphasis on criminalization and deviantization processes, thus making a break with the causal-corrective orientation of traditional criminology (though radical criminology was interested in the 'causes' of crime if it was the capitalist system being indicted, as well as in 'correcting' crime if it was committed by the powerful). Furthermore, some of the key themes in radical criminology directly reflected three major criticisms of labelling theory that had gathered momentum during this period. Labelling theory was criticized for:

1   failing to explore the role of the powerful in society as rule-makers, whereby the categories 'crime' and 'deviance' are defined;
2   failing to give attention to the powerful in society as major rule-breakers;
3   tending to present the deviant as a victim (of labelling processes), rather than seeing deviance as a form of resistance; that is, as political.

Three American (though at that stage non-Marxist) criminologists were particularly important in shaping the development of radical criminology in its early phase: Chambliss (1964, 1969), Quinney (1969) and Turk (1969), and each explored issues raised in point '1' above. Drawing on non-Marxist conflict theory, and in particular on Weber's concept of authority, Turk pointed to the profound inequality in American society arising from the unequal distribution of authority, and the power that went with it. Those powerful elites that possessed authority used the criminal law to protect their own interests by criminalizing the least powerful; specifically, young black males. This instrumental view of the law can be contrasted with the view that the law is a neutral instrument of universal benefit. Similar analyses were produced by Chambliss and Quinney, though both were destined to embrace an explicitly Marxist position in the 1970s (the latter following a brief dalliance with phenomenology). Chambliss (1964), for instance, used the vagrancy laws introduced in England in the fourteenth century in order to illustrate how the law was created and used by those with power; in this case, landowners, as a way of guaranteeing a plentiful supply of cheap agricultural labour.

In Britain, 1973 saw the publication of Taylor et al.'s landmark book *The New Criminology*. The title itself was significant, in that it signalled an alternative to *new deviancy* theory, and a shift towards a more politicized, 'harder' criminology. In addition, 'new' joined 'radical' and 'critical' as descriptors of this type of criminology (though the authors used the term 'radical' in the text). None the less, the focus was still on deviance (the book was subtitled *For a Social Theory of Deviance*), and elements of labelling theory were incorporated into what was intended to be a Marxist political economy of rule breaking and social control. Taylor et al.'s ambitious aim was to point to:

> the *formal* and *substantive* requirements of a fully social theory of deviance, a theory that can explain the forms assumed by social control and deviant action in 'developed' (capitalist) societies.

> (Taylor et al. 1973: 269, emphases in original)

Thus the book had both an academic (Marxist social theory) and a political (socialist) dimension, and was as much about the exploitative nature of capitalist society as about crime and deviance *per se*. Inevitably, given its polemical nature, the book stimulated a range of critical responses. The authors argued, for instance, that a future socialist society based upon equality could be free from crime. In such a society, they said, the causal factors that produce criminal behaviour (greed, self-interest, poverty, etc.) would be eradicated. At the same time, there would be no capitalist ruling class in a position to create and apply the law in order to further their own interests. This instrumental view of the law had direct links with point '1' –

the first of the three criticisms of labelling theory. However, in this formulation, 'crime-free' did not equate with stultifying conformity. On the contrary,
they used the term 'socialist diversity' to indicate the individual's freedom to
explore different behaviours and lifestyles, though the need to criminalize
these behaviours and lifestyles (on the part of 'the powerful') will have been
removed. Some critics, however, characterized Taylor et al.'s argument as
anarchist and Utopian (note how this contrasts with Durkheim's view that
crime is inevitable – see Chapter 3).

Strong links with the other two criticisms of labelling theory were also in
evidence in this text. In the case of point '2' above, the authors discussed the
criminality of those with power in society, concluding that: 'the rule-makers
are also the greatest rule-breakers' (Taylor et al. 1973: 89). The issues arising
from point '3' were particularly important in terms of the arguments
developed in the book, and subsequently among other radical criminologists.
Taylor et al. were, in line with labelling theory, highly critical of positivism
and its scientific pretensions. Therefore, when discussing deviant actions
they were keen to stress choice and voluntarism; that is, individuals are not
determined creatures propelled into deviance by factors outside of their
control; rather, they make choices. Building on Gouldner's (1968) view that
the deviant should be seen as 'man-fighting-back' (not 'on-his-back'), they
put forward the argument that 'much deviance is political', in the sense that
it is actively chosen and represents resistance to dominant; that is, bourgeois,
norms and values.

The New Criminology represented an important catalyst for future developments in radical criminology, in Britain and other parts of the world,
though these developments arose from critiques, as well as endorsements, of
Taylor et al.'s (1973) ideas. Furthermore, certain themes associated with the
three criticisms of labelling theory – 'self-interested rule-makers', 'powerful
rule-breakers' and 'deviance as politics' – continued to permeate and guide
these developments.

As stated earlier, during the 1970s, radical/critical criminologists in the
United States began to embrace an explicitly Marxist approach. Both Gordon
(1971) and Chambliss (1975) saw crime as a rational response to the
selfishness and individualism characterizing a capitalist system. The latter
also argued that crime would increase among poorer sections of American
society due to the conflict generated by increasing divisions between rich
and poor, in tandem with the imposition of an increasingly Draconian
criminal justice system by the ruling class as they attempt to control this
conflict. A similar argument was put forward by Quinney (1977), who was
then describing his (Marxist) approach as 'critical' criminology. In the late
1970s Chambliss (1978) took up the theme of powerful rule-breakers in his
study of crime and the criminal justice system in Seattle. His book was a
potent indictment of the corruption, fraud and 'turning a blind eye' inherent

in the interdependent relationships involving politicians, senior criminal justice personnel, business leaders and organized crime.

The three criticisms of labelling theory can be used as a basis for outlining the subsequent development of radical/critical criminology. It is important to note that those intent on developing a radical criminology described their analyses as 'neo-Marxist'; that is, it involved some reworking of Marxist theory. Apart from anything else, the positivistic approach of Marx and Engels when writing about crime (though they wrote relatively little on crime *per se*) and their identification of criminality with the lumpenproletariat (those who were neither members of the working nor capitalist class) did not chime well with the new deviancy-influenced sensibilities of Taylor et al., and other young Marxist scholars at the time – hence the feeling that some reworking of Marx was necessary.

Doubts about the validity of a Marxist criminology or sociology of deviance surfaced among some fellow British Marxists. Paul Hirst (1975) in particular was strongly critical of the entire project; he pejoratively described this reworking of Marxist theory as 'revisionism'. For him, Marxist analyses should be based upon the repertoire of key concepts present in the writings of Marx and his collaborator, Engels. To use a concept such as deviance, he said, was to use a bourgeois, not Marxist, concept. From this perspective, it was as if scholars were tasked with analysing 'bad' art, and assumed uncritically that this could be defined and identified in an objective way. Another Marxist protagonist was Colin Sumner (1976), though he argued that a Marxist theory of deviance was possible, providing that deviance was conceived of not as *behaviour* but as a form of bourgeois ideology. This is returned to below.

Deviance as politics

Following the publication of the *New Criminology*, a number of radical/critical criminologists began to argue that crime should be seen as a form of political action. However, unlike other work on political crime, which had focused on crimes, such as violent urban rioting, mass demonstrations, or events further back in history, such as machine smashing by the Luddites, radical criminologists were now designating a much wider range of criminal behaviour as political. Furthermore, their definition of 'political' was much broader than that found in traditional political science, and often involved terms such as 'crypto-political', 'cultural politics', 'non-ideological politics' and 'primitive rebellion'. This sort of work was clearly in tune with Taylor et al.'s (1973) argument that 'much deviance is political'. In fact, one of the authors, Taylor (1971), had already put forward the view that soccer hooliganism was political, in that it represented an attempt by some supporters to reclaim greater control of their club, this control having gradually weakened with the encroachment of commercialization and professionalization. Pearson (1976) ploughed a similar furrow when he argued that what he called a 'flood' of attacks on Asians in a Lancashire cotton town (during the mid-1960s) should be seen as 'primitive' political action. The logic for this derived from comparing those involved with the handloom weavers who, during an earlier historical period, had attempted to protect their livelihood by engaging in machine smashing (for a critique of this study, see Tierney 1980). In the United States, Quinney (1977) saw the crimes of the poor – described as 'survival crime' – as political. During the same period, a large amount of work from the Birmingham Centre for Contemporary Cultural Studies (BCCCS) explored the political status of working-class youth subcultures. Here, some young people were seen as creatively using subcultures as a form of cultural resistance; that is, challenging dominant ideas regarding acceptable behaviour and modes of dress, hairstyle, and so on (Clarke et al. 1976; Clarke and Jefferson 1976; Corrigan and Frith 1976). The same theme was addressed by other writers outside of the BCCCS; for example, Hebdige (1979), who argued that members of youth subcultures actively created their own particular 'styles' by changing the accepted cultural meanings of objects such as motor cycles and items of clothing. Again, this was seen as an act of cultural resistance (see also Willis 1978). For P. Cohen (1972, and a member of the BCCCS), working-class youth subcultures – for example, teddy boys, mods and skinheads – represented attempts, at a cultural level, to recreate for themselves a rapidly disappearing sense of community in the East End of London. Note that a contemporary reworking of these kinds of analysis has been undertaken by cultural criminologists (see Chapter 16).

The above work triggered a range of critical responses (see, for example, Hirst 1975; Hinch 1983; Tierney 1988). Many of these criticisms focused on the concept of 'political'. Although it was linked to some notion of 'resistance' – usually on the part of the least powerful members of society – it was unclear exactly where the line between political and non-political rule-breaking was to be drawn. In other words, what qualities need to be present in order for the crime or deviance to *be* political (we can also add that the term 'deviance' was often left undefined). Taylor et al.'s (1973) assertion that 'much deviance is political' – because it is the conscious infraction of dominant rules – begs the question: precisely what types of deviance are in this category, and how are they to be recognized? How important, for example, is 'a conscious intent to rebel'? (Hinch 1983: 69). We might also add a further question: what is it that makes such action 'deviant' in the first place? Other critics accused these radical criminologists of romanticizing working-class crime by interpreting it as in effect part of a revolutionary class struggle against capitalism (see, for example, Hirst 1975).

Self-interested rule-makers

This was a much more popular theme among radical criminologists than the above as the 1970s unfolded, with an emphasis on crime, and hence criminal law, as opposed to deviance. This work became increasingly complex as it moved away from an earlier, fairly simplistic instrumental view of the law, which was seen as operating directly in the interests of the ruling class: 'a means of domination, oppression and desolation' (Bankowski and Mungham 1975: 29). There was shift towards a structuralist understanding of the relationship between the ruling class, the state and the legal order (with the structuralist Marxism of Althusser 1971, and Poulantzas 1973 being particularly influential). From this perspective, the creation and enforcement of the law did not require those involved to act consciously in favour of a capitalist class, as a conspiratorial 'committee of the bourgeoisie'. However, there were clearly strong functionalist overtones in this formulation, in that regardless of the specific form that it took, in a capitalist society the law was ultimately still bourgeois law. Thus even laws that acted in the interests of the public in general, for example, in the realm of consumer protection, were seen as beneficial to 'the system' as a totality, because they functioned to manage the conflict inherent in that system, and at an ideological helped foster the view among the general public that they lived in a fair society. One problem with this is that, in theory, *any* law could be viewed as ultimately working in the interests of the ruling class.

This structural Marxist approach to crime and the legal order was well represented by the contributors to *Capitalism and the Rule of Law*, edited by Fine (1979), though they drew on a fairly eclectic range of academic sources. Foucault's writings on the links between knowledge and power – whereby public understandings of, for instance, the 'crime problem' are shaped by those with power – were becoming influential. The analysis of law and the social order in capitalist societies by the Soviet Marxist Pashukanis – and first published in the 1920s – was also drawn on by a number of contributors to this book. One of Pashukanis's arguments was that in a future communist society, state law would disappear, and social order would derive from informal social norms; in other words, a crime-free society similar to one envisioned by Taylor et al. (1973).

Powerful rule-breakers

All critical criminologists, then and now, were/are in complete unity over at least one aspect of crime and criminality: that is, state, corporate and white-collar crimes are far more harmful and costly to society than conventional crimes such as burglary and robbery. Furthermore, it is argued, such crimes are hugely under-reported and under-recorded, and therefore remain largely hidden from view. As a consequence, statistical information and media representations provide a misleading picture of the 'crime problem'. These observations stimulated a number of studies aimed at exposing the crimes of the powerful. Some examples from the period under review are: corporate crime as organized crime (Pearce 1976); 'accidents' in the mining industry (Caudill 1977); poor safety in the North Sea oil industry (Carson 1982); and financial fraud (Clinard and Yeager (1981).

Important conceptual debates relating to the ontological status of deviance and crime (already set in motion by Hirst and his argument that Marxists should have nothing to do with 'bourgeois' concepts such as deviance – see above) were now developing among radical criminologists. The British Marxist, Colin Sumner (1976) explored the concept of deviance (and crime), though his conclusion differed from that of both Hirst (1975) and Taylor et al. 1973. Sumner argued that deviance could be incorporated into a Marxist analysis, providing that it was conceptualized not as behaviour, but as an ideological social censure, or adverse judgement (similarly, crime should be seen as an ideological legal censure). This, according to Sumner, would avoid any suggestion that deviance and crime possessed some essential, inherent qualities associated with notions of harm, immorality or badness – as if they were qualitatively different to non-deviance or non-crime. It also directed attention towards the rules as well as, when appropriate, the rule-breakers. An example, albeit an extreme one, can be used to illustrate the core issues in these debates.

Imagine those in charge of a 1930s' Stalinist, or 1940s' Nazi concentration camp invited a criminologist in to carry out research for them. They were concerned about the 'criminal' behaviour of some of the prisoners, say, inciting rebellion and attempting to escape. The authorities wanted to know what caused such behaviour. Was it faulty socialization in the family? Blocked opportunities? Bad genes? Or, perhaps, artificial food colouring? It was up to the criminologist to find out. Clearly, in this example, because the behaviours under scrutiny are defined as 'criminal', it does not follow that they are inherently 'immoral' or 'bad'; indeed, the behaviour of those in charge of the camp is more obviously 'criminal'. Moreover, the authorities created the crime when they created the rules, which raises the issue of whether the criminologist should be analysing criminalization processes, rather than the behaviour defined as criminal. In other words, and to use Sumner's term, to see and study crime not as behaviour, but as an ideological social or legal censure – an adverse judgement made by those in authority. From this perspective crime/deviance exists even when no criminal/deviant *behaviour* is taking place, because it is located in the ideological rules, not in people's behaviour.

When such behaviour is judged to be occurring and is responded to, then we see the censure being applied in specific circumstances. This is not to say, however, that criminologists should *only* study criminalization processes and ignore the actual behaviour defined as criminal. In the example above, understanding and explaining why certain prisoners, say, establish a resistance movement and fight back is certainly of intellectual interest. It does though raise another important issue that has led to much debate among radical criminologists: the moral and political appropriateness of one's research. Regardless of a criminologist's motivations for carrying out such research, the key question is: who is the research being carried out for and how will it be used? As the American labelling theorist, Howard Becker, famously said: 'Whose side are we on?'

By the beginning of the 1980s some highly significant divisions were emerging within radical/critical criminology. On the one hand, were those whose views were broadly in tune with the views expressed in Taylor et al.'s (1973) *The New Criminology* and, on the other, those whose views had developed within the context of criticisms of that text. In fact, just two years after its publication, one of the authors, Young (1975), was already shifting his position, with another of the authors, Taylor (1981), following suit not long afterwards. A further indication of Young's repositioning was apparent in his chapter contribution to Fine's (1979) book mentioned earlier, in spite of the fact that in general the views of the rest of the contributors were largely in accord with those in *The New Criminology*. A collection of chapters edited by Carlen and Collison (1980) – *Radical Issues in Criminology* – brought together a number of 'radical' criminologists who were also critical of *The New Criminology* and the radical criminology with which it was associated.

Left realism and left idealism

During the first half of the 1980s these disputes coalesced around two divergent strands of radical/socialist criminology:

- On the one hand, were those who continued to work within an analytical framework derived from the ideas associated with *The New Criminology* and subsequent, neo-Marxist, theoretical developments as discussed above. Those involved saw themselves as maintaining a commitment, based upon theory and practice, to an authentic socialist criminology. They described themselves as critical criminologists. Some of the main figures were: Tony Bunyan, Paul Gilroy, Paul Gordon, Paddy Hillyard, Phil Scraton, Joe Sim, Colin Sumner and René Van Swaaningen.
- And, on the other hand, were those putting forward a revised version of socialist criminology, one that was more social democratic

in orientation. These too saw themselves as critical criminologists, though they described their approach as left realism and that of the above as left idealism. Interestingly, two of the authors of *the New Criminology* – Ian Taylor and Jock Young – were, by the early 1980s, major figures within left realism.

A detailed discussion of the latter can be found in Chapter 11; what follow summarizes some of the key disputes between the two. The term 'left idealism' was used by left realists to describe what they saw as a Utopian, and on occasion anarchist, approach to the study of crime and social control. Given that the term suggested naivety and irrelevance, the critical criminologists concerned unsurprisingly rejected the label. However, with this caveat, and simply for convenience, in the discussion that follows the terms 'left idealism/realism' will be used.

The main features of the left realist critique of left idealism are as follows:

- Left idealists did not take seriously the harms caused by conventional crime (especially its impact on socially and economically deprived communities) preferring instead to focus their attention on the crimes of the powerful.
- For left idealists, crime rises were illusory, and public fears resulted from media-fuelled moral panics.
- Left idealists romanticized the crimes of the powerless, seeing them as forms of political resistance.
- Along with administrative criminology (see Chapter 2) left idealism had little interest in the causes of crime, emphasizing instead processes of criminalization.
- Left idealists refused to contribute to practical policies aimed at reducing, or redistributing, criminal victimization. Thus they remained aloof from any processes that involved them interacting with the institutions of the capitalist state, such involvement being seen as mere liberal reformism, and counterproductive in terms of the ultimate goal of the socialist transformation of society.

Needless to say, these accusations led to a spirited response from those labelled left idealists:

- Left idealists underlined their refusal to work within the constraints imposed by state definitions of crime and the 'crime problem', and rejected attempts to essentialize crime, as if it possessed some inherent common features, such as harmfulness or immorality. Left idealists stressed the importance of recognizing the significant harms caused by white collar, corporate and state crime.

- As far as engaging with the 'real' world is concerned, left idealists defended themselves by arguing that left idealism had always been interventionist in a practical sense. The chief difference between it and left realism was that, while the latter focused on 'the community' and institutions such as the police and local authorities within the context of an assumed (or at least hoped for) consensus, left idealists operated within a context of conflict. In other words, left idealist interventions have tended to be concerned with issues of corruption, discrimination, miscarriages of justice and human rights violations when they have manifested themselves in institutions of the state, rather than with crime reduction as traditionally understood. This has often involved making links with and supporting groups within the community; for example, women, gays and lesbians, and minority ethnic groups.

Since these emerging disputes and the broad split into two types of radical criminology in the 1980s, the nature of 'critical criminology' has become much more complex. Both left realism and so-called left idealism have continued to develop in terms of theory and practice, but the lines of demarcation are much more blurred nowadays. Having said that, two important proponents of critical criminology/left idealism, Chadwick and Scraton (2006), are keen to emphasize continuing differences between left idealism and left realism. On the other hand, although Young (1998), in his retrospective review of *The New Criminology*, makes reference to what he sees as left idealism's continuing preoccupation with criminalization processes, he also stresses the common ground shared by all critical criminologists, including left realists.

At the same time, other scholars, who describe their work as 'critical', have come onto the scene, bringing new ideas, or reworking old ones, and new challenges (e.g. within the context of feminist perspectives, studies based on the concept of masculinities, abolitionism and cultural criminology – all are discussed in detail under the named chapters). Thus, and reflecting developments across the world of academia, critical criminology has become increasingly diverse and fragmented. One important dimension to this relates to critical criminology's theoretical foundations. During its early developmental period in the 1970s, it was explicitly based upon neo-Marxist social theory, and its proponents had a political commitment to the transformation of a capitalist society into a socialist one. Although there are strong and important continuities in terms of theoretical ideas and political sensitivities, today critical criminology draws upon a range of theory and, significantly, socialism is only referred to infrequently. And when it is, the reference is often symbolic, for example, seeing socialism as a 'beacon' prodding us to challenge inequality and injustice, rather than as a type of society that may eventually come into being (see, for instance, Bauman and

Tester 2001). The shift from an explicitly Marxist critical criminology towards one that embraces a variety of theoretical discourses could be seen as reflecting, wittingly or unwittingly, a post-modernist rejection of 'grand narratives', that is, placing all your eggs in one theoretical basket, as it were. However, there is a danger of overstating the degree of unanimity during the 1970s with regard to interpretations of both Marxism and socialism. Most obviously, there were Marxist scholars who repudiated the idea that a Marxist criminology or sociology of deviance was possible.

Yet there were also disputes among those who concurred that such a project was viable and desirable. Hence the arguments at the time over the 'young' and 'old' Marx; over the 'humanistic' Marx; and over the sometimes deterministic ideas found in Marx's (and Engel's) writings. As far as socialism (or communism) was concerned, this was, of course, a corollary of being a Marxist, though in practice, it tended to function as a flag to rally around. There was certainly no consensus regarding precisely what a socialist society would look like and, indeed, Marxist theory itself cautioned against attempting such a task. Clearly, the lack of references to socialism within contemporary critical criminology is in part due to the collapse of socialist/state socialist societies around the world since the late 1980s, and their move towards economies based upon neo-liberal, 'unfettered' markets. Seen as an epic failure, the 'socialism' associated with these societies is nowadays hardly likely to inspire popular support for political movements whose aim is to replace capitalism with socialism. At the same time, within critical criminological discourses, the 'natural' enemies of Marxism, in the shape of the bourgeoisie or capitalist class, has been replaced by 'the powerful', the authoritarian state, or some functional equivalent, and capitalism by neo-liberal markets.

All criminological theories are political, either in terms of explicit or implicit political intent, and/or consequences. Throughout its history, this had been most obviously the case with critical criminology; it has always been transparently about more than crime and deviance *per se*. Critical criminology continues this tradition today; crime and deviance remain core concepts but, as always, are utilized as the basis for critique. Hence the continuing engagement, at the levels of theory and practice, with issues of injustice, human rights, racism and sexism, inequality, and so on. In the past such issues were linked explicitly to the nature of capitalism, and analysed within the context of Marxist social theory, while today there are references to neo-liberal markets, and Marxism is more of a silent partner. However, from the perspective of critical criminologists, these issues remain and still require urgent attention and resolution. That is what critique is all about.

In spite of the diversity and fragmentation referred to earlier, we can, albeit in broad brushstrokes, outline the main features of critical criminology at the present time.

- There is a rejection of the deterministic, individualized explanations of criminality associated with positivism. Criminality, and indeed all social action, is seen as the product of a dialectical relationship between both structure and agency. Thus, although criminality does not result from social, psychological or biological factors over which the individual has no control, it does arise within structural contexts involving, for instance, social inequalities, discriminatory practices, and cultural understandings of masculinity and femininity. A particular emphasis is placed upon neo-liberal markets, globalization, individualism and increasingly intense forms of consumerism.

- While there are continuing debates between left idealists and left realists (and others) over definitions of 'crime' and the 'crime problem', there is agreement that from the point of view of harmfulness and financial costs, the most serious crimes, or transgressions, are carried out by states, corporations and the more wealthy members of society. At the same time, rule-breaking of this sort tends to be relatively invisible, and therefore avoids public scrutiny and prosecution. However, left idealists are more interested in those events and situations that cause harm, rather than those that happen to be defined as criminal (see, for example, Hulsman 1986) – though left realists argue that much conventional crime is harmful.

- Market societies are characterized by inherent inequalities and social divisions. In such societies, the criminal law, its enforcement and its prosecution are seen as protecting the interests of the powerful, rather than the powerless. In tandem with this, the state will seek to neutralize the anxieties associated with late modernity and arising from, for example, job insecurity and significant levels of unemployment and social exclusion, by shifting attention to issues of law and order. Thus the state will foster and exploit public worries regarding crime, antisocial behaviour, immigration, and so on, and this in turn acts to legitimize the introduction of new legislation and more intrusive forms of social control surveillance (for an early version of this approach see Hall et al. 1978). Furthermore, it is argued that discriminatory practices relating to class, gender, 'race' and sexual orientation operate not only at the level of the individual, but become institutionalized within criminal justice processes as a whole. When discussing issues of blame and punishment, critical writers often employ the concept of penality. This concept is intended to capture the totality of a specific penal system and the historical, social, political, and so on contexts within which that system develops and functions.

- Along with other criminologists, critical criminologists argue that social order is largely a product of informal, rather than formal, in the shape of the criminal justice system, modes of control. However, they also argue that the criminal justice system – and prisons in particular – does not lead to reductions in criminality; on the contrary, the system is more likely to increase criminality. Abolition-ism is one type of critical criminology that focuses on the counter-productive nature of the criminal justice and penal systems (see Chapter 1).

● The post-structuralist work of Foucault on the theme of knowledge, ideologies and power has been especially influential among critical criminologists (Foucault 1977). This directs attention to the ways in which power is linked to the production and dissemination of socially accredited, 'correct' knowledge regarding the 'crime prob-lem', those responsible for it, and how the state and its criminal justice agencies should respond.

● Unlike left realists, left idealists continue to place more emphasis on social censures and processes of criminalization, rather than the causes of criminality. Again, these processes are analysed within structural contexts of, for example, social and economic deprivation, social exclusion, racism and sexism.

● All critical criminologists are committed to some notion of 'progres-sive' politics. This can, of course, mean many things and incorporate varying degrees of radicalism, though, broadly speaking, critical political agendas cluster around notions of equality and justice. Over the years there has been much critical work on corruption and cover-ups, for example, in Northern Ireland and in relation to accidents at work. More recently, particular prominence has been given to the issue of human rights violations (see, for instance, Cohen 2001).

● Finally, critical criminologists are (by definition, one might say) antagonistic towards right-wing criminology, such as right realism. They are also highly critical of administrative criminology for ignoring the structural contexts within which criminal motivations develop, and for attempting to reduce the complexities of social action to graphs, charts and computer models; crime science too is castigated for what are seen as its scientific pretensions (see Chap-ters 2 and 15).

As the left realist Young (2002) argues, critical criminology continues to have an influential presence within the field of criminology. Likewise, and speaking as a 'left idealist', Scraton (2002) stresses the importance of critical criminology in terms of analysing and challenging the authoritarianism of the state and its criminal justice and penal institutions in contemporary society – this view is explored further in Chapter 1.

Further reading

As a catalyst and inspiration for the development of critical criminology the polemical *The New Criminology*, by Taylor, I., Walton, P. and Young, J. (1973) London: Routledge & Kegan Paul, is essential reading. It is also worth reading the follow-up, 'companion' text: Taylor, I., Walton, P. and Young, J. (eds) (1975) *Critical Criminology*. London: Routledge & Kegan Paul. Here we see important debates stimulated by the earlier text beginning to develop (especially in Paul Hirst's chapter). Useful texts on left realism are: Lea, J. and Young, J. (1984) *What is to be Done about Law and Order?* London: Penguin; Matthews, R. and Young, J. (eds) *Confronting Crime*. London: Sage Publications. The case for a critical alternative to left realism will be found in: Scraton, P. (ed.) *Law, Order and the Authoritarian State: Readings in Critical Criminology*. Buckingham: Open University Press; and Scraton, P. and Chadwick, K. (1991) Challenging the new orthodoxies: the theoretical imperatives and political priorities of critical criminology, in K. Stenson and D. Cowell (eds) *The Politics of Crime Control*. London: Sage Publications. Also worth reading is a collection of essays built around the notion of social censure: Sumner, C.S. (ed.) (1990) *Censure, Politics and Criminal Justice*. Buckingham: Open University Press.

Some critical writers have, in more recent years, begun to develop a pan-European critical criminology; see, for example, van Swaaningen, R. (1997) *Critical Criminology: Visions from Europe*. London: Sage Publications; Bergalli, R. and Sumner, C.S. (eds) (1997) *Social Control and Political Order: European Perspectives at the End of the Century*. London: Sage Publications; Ruggiero, V., South, N. and Taylor, I. (eds) (1998) *The New European Criminology: Crime and Social Order in Europe*. London: Routledge; and Taylor, I. (1999) *Crime in Context*. Cambridge: Polity Press.

On the issue of human rights see Cohen, S. (2001) *States of Denial: Knowing about Atrocities and Suffering*. Cambridge: Polity Press. On crimes of the state see Green, P. and Ward, T. (2004) *State Crime: Governments, Violence and Corruption*. London: Pluto Press. On corporate crime see Pearce, F. and Tombs, S. (1998) *Toxic Capitalism: Corporate Crime and the Chemical Industry*. Aldershot: Dartmouth. On corporate and state crime see Tombs, S. and Whyte, D. (eds) (2003) *Unmasking the Crimes of the Powerful: Scrutinising States and Corporations*. New York: Peter Lang.

Walton, P. and Young, J. (eds) (1998) *The New Criminology Revisited*. Basingstoke: Macmillan, is a collection of readings that reassess the contribution made by *The New Criminology*, and review the current state of critical criminology.

Good, more up-to-date discussions of critical criminology will be found in: Pavlich, G. (2000) *Critique and Radical Discourses on Crime*. London: Ashgate; Carrington, K. and Hogg, R. (eds) (2002) *Critical Criminology: Issues,*

Debates and Challenges. Cullompton: Willan Publishing; Hillyard, P., Tombs, S., Pantazis, C. and Gordon, D. (eds) (2004) *Beyond Criminology: Taking Harm Seriously.* London: Pluto; Sumner, C.S. (2004) The social nature of crime and deviance, in C.S. Sumner (ed.) *The Blackwell Companion to Criminology.* Oxford: Blackwell Publishing; Coleman, R. (2004) *Reclaiming the Streets: Surveillance, Social Control and the City.* Cullompton: Willan Publishing; Barton, A., Corteen, K., Scott, D. and Whyte, D. (eds) (2007) *Expanding the Criminological Imagination: Critical Readings in Criminology.* Cullompton: Willan Publishing.

8 Cultural Criminology

This chapter should be read in conjunction with Chapter 16. Cultural criminology is a fairly recent, and still evolving, theoretical perspective. It seeks to apply the methodologies, ideas and theories associated with cultural studies to illicit behaviour and responses to it, including, importantly, media representations. Cultural criminology has, though, drawn on a wide range of sociological and criminological sources, complicating the task of outlining its defining features. The major influences have come from work in the 1960s and 1970s on the sociology of youth subcultures, especially that carried out by the Birmingham Centre for Contemporary Cultural Studies, symbolic interactionism, elements of new deviancy theory, phenomenology and the 'appreciative' and 'naturalistic' sociology of David Matza. In addition, cultural criminology is explicitly interdisciplinary, drawing on, for example, the work of anthropologists and geographers, and has incorporated certain ideas associated with post-modernist social thought, not the least of which, as the discussion so far indicates, is a rejection of a grand narrative (i.e. an overarching, universally applicable organizing principle, or theoretical paradigm, such as Marxism). Cultural criminology can also be seen as constituting a form of critical criminology, in that it has strong affinities with the work of critical theorists in criminology and an explicit commitment to critique (see Chapter 7).

This perhaps bewildering array of intellectual sources is in many ways reminiscent of the 'misfit' sociology of the 1960s (as Geoff Pearson described the new deviancy theory of that period). There are also echoes of this earlier sociology in the nature of the subject matter – 'edgework', 'thrill', 'pushing the boundaries' – and, seeking to capture the visceral excitement of illicit behaviour, a style of writing less prosaic than that usually associated with academia. Accordingly, in the titles of major texts there are references to 'seduction' (Katz 1988); 'carnival' (Presdee 2000); 'energy' (Young 2003); and to cultural criminology being 'unleashed' (Ferrell et al. 2004). In short, cultural criminology is passionate and sometimes messianic.

Within the context of academic criminology, its main critique is directed towards administrative criminology and 'crime science' perspectives on crime and criminality (see Chapter 2). Administrative criminology is centrally concerned with the prediction and prevention of crime. Its research is strongly oriented towards the policy requirements of central and local government, and the police and other agencies with an interest in crime prevention, or at least reduction. Within this framework, and drawing on various bodies of knowledge, for example, sociology, geography, forensic science and psychology, crime science attempts to amass and analyse 'hard', 'objective' data, and to use these data in order to build up predictive profiles of types of offender, patterns of offending, successful anti-crime strategies, and so on. From the perspective of cultural criminology, this is a seriously flawed project because a) it is a spurious attempt at being 'scientific', and b) it fails to engage with and understand the lived experiences, meanings and motivations of offenders. This critical stance in relation to administrative criminology is one of the reasons why cultural criminology has recently found favour among left realists, notably Jock Young (see Chapter 11). Unsurprisingly, *culture* lies at the heart of cultural criminology. Analyses of culture though are situated within the context of contemporary late-modern societies. These societies are seen as characterized by such things as uncertainty, intense consumerism, enhanced levels of social control, anxiety and, perhaps paradoxically, a high degree of boredom. They are also societies where the media, in their various forms, have penetrated into all aspects of social life (the term 'media-saturated' is often used). A more detailed examination of the concept of culture can be found in Chapter 16, though we can note that it is defined and used in a variety of ways within the social sciences.

Cultural criminologists are strongly committed to qualitative research methodologies, and have carried out a wide range of ethnographic and 'appreciative' studies of transgressive subcultures; that is, subcultures whose rule-breaking and risk-taking activities violate the norms of conventional society. This work has spanned a broad spectrum and includes, for instance, 'edgework' manifested in scaling city skyscrapers and BASE jumping (Lyng 1990, 1998; Ferrell 2001); urban graffiti artists (Ferrell 1996); and terrorists (Hamm 2004). Analyses incorporate a number of interconnected dimensions, in the sense that they involve particular transgressive subcultures, the interrrelationship between these subcultures and those who seek to place controls on their behaviour, and the mediated representations of these subcultures in factual and fictional accounts in the mass media. On this basis, there is an emphasis on the interactional processes through which understandings, lifestyles, identities and meaning are constructed. From this perspective, illicit behaviour and responses to it are both products and producers of culture. On a generalized level, the main features of cultural criminology can be outlined as follows:

- In line with phenomenology, studies of subcultures are guided by naturalistic and appreciative principles. The aim is to provide accounts of subcultures from the perspectives of the participants – to see the social world as they see it and produce an account that they would recognize. All this in a spirit of 'appreciation' rather than condemnation, though on occasion there is a fine line between appreciation and approval. Some writers, Presdee (2000) for instance, also draw on their own experiences as a member of a transgressive subculture.

- The nature and internal dynamics of a subculture are explored, or 'read', as cultural phenomena. Thus a subculture possesses a collective identity deriving from the shared symbolic meanings attached to such things as style, language and demeanour as well as the illicit activities with which it is associated; they share the symbolic meanings, or understandings, of these things. The illicit activities of a subculture are conceptualized by cultural criminologists as cultural artefacts.

- Albert Cohen argued in the 1950s that typical juvenile delinquent behaviour was not instrumentally motivated, that is, was not engaged in for material rewards (see Chapter 16). In a similar vein, cultural criminologists argue that much crime is not instrumental in nature: 'an awful lot of crime, from joyriding to murder, from telephone kiosk vandalism to rape, involves more than instrumental motivation' (Young 2007: 19). However, whereas Cohen linked delinquency to 'status frustration', cultural criminologists link crime to emotional factors. More specifically, they see much crime as motivated by excitement, thrill and the rush of adrenaline that comes from risk-taking behaviour. This approach is captured well in the title of Katz's (1988) influential book on cultural criminology: *The Seductions of Crime*. However, we can note that more recently, and writing from a left realist perspective, Young, has also linked these motivations to relative deprivation (see Chapter 11).

- This understanding of crime has, say cultural criminologists, two important implications from the point of view of administrative criminological approaches to crime control. First, crime control measures based upon a view of the offender as an instrumental, rational choice-maker will be much less effective in cases where criminal motivations are rooted in human emotions. And, second, that the extra risk attendant on such measures may act to stimulate further an individual's motivation to offend (it is not uncommon, for example, for so-called joy-riders to taunt the police and 'challenge' them to a highly dangerous car chase).

- Representations of illicit activities, including specifically criminal ones, in a globalized, all-pervasive, mass media are also analysed. Therefore close attention is paid to the mediation of images and texts, through which understandings of crime, and so on are culturally constructed (e.g. Ferrell et al. 2004). As I have written elsewhere:

These meanings are produced, reproduced, circulated, reshaped, absorbed or rejected, in a multiplicity of complex and continuous processes of interaction and interpretation. Individuals enjoy their fifteen minutes of fame, or infamy; a small boy becomes a feral, uncontrollable 'rat-boy'; violent criminals are transformed into romanticised lovable celebrities; whole communities are stigmatised as the barbarians at the gate; exploited migrant labour is recast as a threat to the 'British way of life'. In this frenzy of images and signs, where the media act as mediators of reality, the distinction between fact and fiction dissolves.

(Tierney 2006: 335)

Importantly for cultural criminologists, these processes involving the media, transgressive subcultures and agents of social control are interactional. The images and understandings of subcultures that are constructed and reproduced by the media, feed into social control processes and public perceptions. They also influence the ways in which members of transgressive subcultures and agents of social control understand and see themselves. At the same time, the media, for example, film and music, and other aspects of culture, such as fashion, are themselves influenced by illicit subcultures. It is an endless, fluid process, in effect a power struggle, where the meaning of crime, criminals, law and order, and so on are contested, not fixed or consensually agreed upon.

• Some ethnographic studies by cultural criminologists move beyond 'appreciation' to approval and celebration of the attributes and activities of the subcultures concerned. A study of 'urban anarchy' by the American cultural criminologist Jeff Ferrell (2001) provides a good example. Drawing on ethnographic studies, he examines the subcultures within the context of what he sees as a distinctly dystopian late-modern urban landscape. Contemporary cities, he argues, are characterized by a plethora of rules and modes of social control. These have created a rigid regimentation of social life coupled with a culture of exclusion constructed around notions of 'outsiders' and 'undesirables' (see also Davis 1990; Vaneigem 2001). The end result, says Ferrell, is that cities have become bland, Disneyland-style entities. In fact, he has also argued that a key feature of late-modern societies is 'institutional boredom' (Ferrell 2004). All sorts of illicit urban subculture, for instance, graffiti artists, BASE jumpers and skateboarders are seen as challenging the blandness and boredom of urban life. For Ferrell, these activities represent a form of political resistance. Conceptualizing some, or all, deviant behaviour as 'political' has a long history in critical criminological thought – it was, for example, a strong feature of the work of BCCS. The idea is returned to briefly below, and discussed further in

Chapter 7. Presdee (2000) argues that human beings have a wilder side to them, a 'second life' that is repressed by the stultifying conformity and rationality of contemporary society. In the past, this second life exploded periodically in the form of carnivals, which provided a temporary licence for large numbers of people to gather together in public spaces and let their hair down. Afterwards, life returned to 'normal' – until the next time. In late-modern society, says Presdee, transgressive behaviour, in the form of 'edgework', drug-taking, heavy consumption of alcohol, and so on, erupts periodically in an attempt to recapture a sense of carnival and reanimate one's second life.

We can see why cultural criminology has become increasingly influential in recent years. By rejecting research agendas based on crime control and quantitative methodologies, it offers a radical alternative to administrative criminology and crime science. It thus refuses to join the ranks of the crime control industry as part of the 'fight against crime'. In addition, its naturalistic approach takes us under the skin and into the emotional excitement surrounding various criminal and non-criminal subcultures. Many other types of criminology, just like Ferrell's late-modern city, are for cultural criminologists boring.

Cultural criminology is not without its critics though. Some have criticized it for glorifying and romanticizing the actions of criminals. Howe (2004), for example, argues that in celebrating the 'seductive' nature of crime, including violent crime, Katz loses sight of the victims. On the other hand, it could be argued that this was not what Katz set out to do, that he was only concerned with providing an understanding of crime from the perspective of the criminal or, more accurately, a certain sort of criminal. As Young (2003: 391) says: 'I have no doubt that much crime is mundane, instrumental and opportunistic in motivation and that there are people whose response to crime is cool, calculated and rationalistic'. This is an interesting comment from Young when read within the context of his desire to incorporate the insights of cultural criminology into a left realist perspective. Left realist analyses developed around an understanding of crime as instrumental and rational (and drew on Merton's notion of relative deprivation), that is, crime as described by Young in the above quote. This type of crime though is clearly different to the types of crime, and other transgressive behaviours, discussed by Young from the vantage point of cultural criminology. This is not to suggest a contradiction in terms of theoretical analysis; it does, however, raise questions regarding where the line between instrumental and non-instrumental rule-breaking is to be drawn, on what basis, and to what extent they co-exist in the same behaviour.

There is also the issue of politicizing the criminal and non-criminal actions of the subcultures under scrutiny; in other words, seeing their 'resistance' as a form of political action. It is certainly the case that efforts to 'reclaim the streets' are looked on approvingly by Ferrell and, along with others, he sees cultural criminology itself as a form of resistance, though with a mission to reclaim criminology, rather than the streets. However, it should be recognized that Ferrell is focusing on very specific types of subculture, and is not suggesting that crime, or any other type of transgressive behaviour, is political *per se* – a view that distances his work from that of a number of earlier critical criminologists.

The emergence of cultural criminology has over the past few years rekindled debates about the concepts of culture and subculture (see also Chapter 16). Garland, for instance, has pointed to a lack of consistency in how the word 'culture' is used:

- Sometimes culture is identified as one, among many, factors shaping aspects of social life. Used like this, we might say, for example, that art, music, eating and drinking are part of the culture of a society.
- At other times, though, it is used to distinguish between one society, or section of society, and another. An example of it being used in this sense is when someone refers to 'British drinking culture' (seen as different to French or Spanish drinking culture): 'Understood in this way, a culture is a more-or-less bounded, more-or-less unified, set of customs, habits, values and beliefs' (Garland 2006: 423).

Taking the first of these, Garland acknowledges the analytical value in abstracting culture and using it as an explanatory concept. However, as he sees it, problems arise when other aspects of social life, for instance, political power, economic and social structure, are displaced and ignored: 'separating out aspects of human action and social practice that are, in fact, inseparably intermeshed and integrated' (p. 428). Put simply, there is a danger of seeing culture as *the* single explanatory or causal factor. One criminologist who has sought to integrate 'culture' and 'structure', and thus locate transgressive behaviour within a social structural context is Young (2003). Drawing on Merton's theory of anomie and his concept of relative deprivation (see Chapter 3), and Katz's cultural reading of transgression, the title of his article sums up what he sets out to achieve: 'Merton with energy, Katz with structure'.

When used in the second of the above senses, Garland's chief concern is that it leads to a tendency to exaggerate the extent to which norms, values and beliefs are encompassed and shared by a particular group or whole society. It is, he says, as if all members are totally at one in this respect and collectively can be distinguished from other groups or other societies (as if, for example, 'British drinking culture', not only unites all British citizens, but sharply differentiates them from citizens of other countries). Garland recog-

nizes that the concept of subculture within the context of cultural criminology in effect subsumes both of the above understandings of culture,
though in his view this has created a yet to be resolved tension between the
two as: 'scholars ... frequently slide over into a broader conception of what
"culture" entails, going beyond the study of subcultures, styles and artistic
works to study the production of social meaning more generally' (Garland
2006: 426).

As well as taking cultural criminologists to task for, as he sees it, failing
to give sufficient attention to factors other than culture (economic, political,
psychological, etc.), O'Brien (2005) is also critical of the way in which they
conceptualize both culture and subculture. He argues that when the concept
of 'culture' is used, it tends to refer to 'mainstream' society (which includes
the media and social control agencies), and carry with it negative connotations. However, when the concept of 'subculture' is used, as in Ferrell's (1996)
study of the subculture of urban graffiti artists, it is infused with highly
positive connotations. According to O'Brien, the result is that in terms of
norms, values, beliefs and lifestyles, members of mainstream society are
characterized as bland, conformist and boring, and in the process sharply,
and unflatteringly, differentiated from members of the transgressive subculture, who are apparently the opposite.

This raises a number of interesting issues regarding so-called 'mainstream' society. While cultural criminologists may discount corporate crime
and white-collar crime because it is instrumental, rather than expressive,
there are many examples of transgressive behaviour among 'respectable'
members of straight society that is motivated by risk, thrill or emotion (in
addition to the carnival of 'binge drinking' sessions), or where instrumental-
ism and expressiveness are combined. The behaviour may involve embracing
aspects of the dominant culture, yet still be transgressive in nature. Each day
millions of 'respectable' people engage in 'edgework' by logging on to an
online poker site and gambling away their hard-earned money. 'Respectable'
people also engage in serial adultery, search the Internet for hard core
pornography, smoke cigarettes, use illicit drugs and drink themselves into a
stupor each evening after work. More seriously, some 'respectable' people
sexually abuse their children and rape their wives. It might be argued that
some or all of these have forfeited their right to being described as respectable, but where would that place them in relation to the transgressive
subcultures of cultural criminology? Thus, and importantly, there is a danger
of only associating transgressive behaviour with marginalized, exotic subcultures. Clearly, there are echoes here of Liazos' (1972) argument (see Chapter 10) that concentrating on such groups functions to reaffirm stereotypical
understandings of the typical 'deviant' – the usual suspects.

The concepts of culture and subculture are discussed further in Chapter 16.

Further reading

A special issue of the journal *Theoretical Criminology* (Volume 8, No. 3, August 2004) is devoted to cultural criminology. See also the recently published journal *Crime, Media, Culture: An International Journal*, London: Sage Publications.

A good introduction to work that focuses on the thrill and risk attached to crime is Katz, J. (1988) *Seductions of Crime*. New York: Basic Books. On the same theme, though situating his study within a structural context, is Mullins, C.W. (2006) *Holding Your Square: Masculinities, Streetlife and Violence*. Cullompton: Willan Publishing. Mullins provides an insight into the minds and social worlds of seriously violent men. They are not, for instance, binge drinkers up for a bit of 'bovver' before they enjoy a late night kebab. They are men like 'Red', who felt so humiliated when a stranger in a bar slapped him across the face, that he waited until the man concerned emerged at closing time, and then put seven bullets in his head. In addition to the sources already referred to above, Ferrell, J. and Sanders, C.R. (eds) (1995) *Cultural Criminology*. Boston, MA: Northeastern University Press, contains a collection of chapters outlining for the first time the main arguments of 'cultural criminology'. Hayward, K. (2004), *City Limits: Crime, Consumer Culture and the Urban Experience*. London: Glasshouse Press, analyses the relationship between crime and the city in late modernity, paying particular attention to consumerism. One of the most influential studies illustrating the interrelationship between transgression and the media is Cohen, S. (1972) *Folk Devils and Moral Panics*. London: MacGibbon and Kee.

For an up to date, accessible overview of cultural criminology see: Ferrell, J., Hayward, K. and Young, J (2008), Cultural Criminology, London: Sage.

9 Feminism

There is no consensus among feminists regarding the desirability, or possibility of a specifically feminist criminology. Not only are there many different sorts of criminology, involving a variety of agendas and theoretical orientations, there are also many different sorts of feminism, thus juxtaposing 'feminist' with 'criminology' is somewhat problematic. Broadly speaking, there are five major strands within feminism: liberal, radical, socialist, black and post-modernist.

- For liberal feminists, inequalities between men and women result from sexist attitudes and stereotypes, and the discriminatory processes that prevent women from achieving parity with men. The central task has been one of creating an equal society where in effect gender becomes irrelevant, a task predicated on the idea that men and women are basically the same. Liberal feminists have, therefore, placed great stress on the notion of equal opportunities and rights in the public sphere through the introduction of such things as legislation aimed at preventing sex discrimination. Walklate (2003) sees a close relationship between liberal feminism and traditional criminology, in the sense that each believes that social scientific methodologies can be used to produce objective knowledge relating to the criminality of men and women, and the operation of the criminal justice system. Thus criminological work by liberal feminists has, to a significant extent, concerned itself with redressing the balance from the point of view of knowledge about male and female offenders, and their respective treatment by the criminal justice system. Naffine (1997) has described this approach as 'feminist empiricism', an approach criticized by her and other feminists for simply assuming that traditional methods of enquiry, providing they are cleansed of their sexist biases, can be used to establish a 'truthful' account of women, crime and social control. In addition, this approach has been criticized for assuming that it is possible to insert this 'new' knowledge into the theoretical models of (non-feminist) traditional criminology.
- The key concept in radical feminism is patriarchy – the domination of women by men. For radical feminists, patriarchy is deeply engrained in the structures of society and is universal in scope. From their perspective, the liberal feminist programme represents mere reformist tinkering with the system, and would not produce the

desired effects for women. Rather, the system itself and its patriarchal institutions should be dismantled and fundamentally reorganized; only in this way will male power be eradicated. Within the context of criminology, as well as resisting dominant patriarchal assumptions and theories, radical feminism is especially associated with research into the violence done to women by men. As Brown-miller (1975: 15) famously said in her study of rape: 'It is nothing more or less than a conscious process of intimidation by which *all* men keep *all* women in a state of fear' (emphases in original). It is also associated with 'standpointism', that is, empathetic research carried out on women by women. Rather than attempting to be 'scientific' and detached, such research seeks to understand the feelings and emotions of women, thereby bypassing the (sexist) interpretations provided by men. Only in this way, say radical feminists, can truthful and authentic accounts be brought to light (see, for example, Hartsock 1983; Harding 1991). Given the importance placed on patriarchy, the relevance of this sort of feminism to criminology is, as Walklate (2003: 80) says: 'largely dependent upon whether or not "men" as men are considered the central concern of the criminological project'. Radical feminists have attracted a range of criticisms. They have been accused of essential-izing and polarizing the differences between women and men. This, it is said, has led them to conjure up a totally negative picture of all men, and a totally positive picture of all women, together with a tendency to see all women as the same.

- Socialist feminist criminology shares many of the concerns of critical criminology, especially where each is Marxist, or neo-Marxist in orientation (see Chapter 7). Each analyses crime and responses to it within the context of capitalist or market society, seen as grounded in exploitative class relations and inherent inequalities and, in consequence, being fundamentally criminogenic. The femi-nist version though gives greater prominence to women and the place of gender in its analyses. The subordination of women is, therefore, linked not just to class, but also to ideological understand-ings of women's 'correct' role in society, for example, as carers in domestic settings. None the less, the intersection of gender and class is a crucial dimension, thus much research has focused on the specific experiences of lower-class women, for instance, within the context of police work and imprisonment.

- Black feminism arose on the basis of a critique of liberal and radical feminisms, which, in Europe and North America, were accused of ignoring the differences between white women and black women (and indeed other minority ethnic groups), in terms of their respec-tive structural location in, and experiences of, society. Post-colonial theory has had a significant influence on this type of feminism, and black women are seen as, in a sense, doubly oppressed – because of gender and 'race'. In fact, some writers, such as hooks [*sic*] (1988), see them as triply oppressed, being caught up in a matrix of gender, 'race' and class.

• Post-modernist feminism is in varying degrees critical of all the above versions of feminism. The critique arises from profound differences in epistemology between post-modernist thought and the rest. Post-modernists reject the whole idea of a 'modernist project', and in so doing reject the belief that 'scientific' methods can be used to uncover some 'true' reality. There is a stress on the individual and the notion of difference, and a rejection of research aimed at generalizations within the framework of a grand narrative (see Chapter 14 for a discussion of post-modernist thought in general). Many criminologists, including feminists, have seriously questioned the relevance of post-modernist contributions.

It should be pointed out that while the above provides a general overview of the main varieties of feminism, in terms of research agendas, methodologies and theory, there are overlaps between one and another. Some feminists argue that the major division is between 'liberal' and 'critical' (in the widest sense) feminisms. Daly (2006), for example, provides a dichotomic representation based upon what she sees as two major axes: one drawing on liberal theory; the other on critical social theory. Some of these overlaps, as well as differences, will become apparent in the discussion below.

It is clear that a unified 'feminist criminology' does not exist, and whether it *could* exist is a moot point. None the less, since the last part of the twentieth century, feminist writers have made a significant contribution to criminological theory and practice. What though makes it specifically 'feminist'? Certainly, gender, both feminine and masculine, is a core issue, though this alone does not necessarily distinguish a feminist contribution from a non-feminist one. The key dimension to feminism is that research agendas and theoretical formulations are always ultimately oriented towards women, and to a desire to, in some sense, impact positively on the place and experiences of women in society. It is then not simply a question of studying women; after all it is possible for a non-, or even anti-feminist to carry out research that focuses on women. The major difference is that feminist work is carried out within the context of certain sorts of agendas, for example, relating to liberation, equality or human rights. In fact, a feminist perspective could be in evidence in a research project focused entirely on men and masculinities, in that its relevance will be judged according to its implications for women. This reminds us that the origins of feminist criminologies lie in the women's movement of the 1960s and will, in contemporary times, to some extent reflect the actual and potential concerns of that movement. Indeed, many feminists have challenged the idea that they should only study women, arguing that to do so would encourage further the marginalization of feminism within criminology. Some, however, have argued that only women can/should study women because, for instance, women are better placed to empathize with other women and are able to draw on their own experiences and feelings (see the above reference to 'standpointism' – p. 81).

Hidden from view

Although there had been some earlier examples in the United States, in Britain, the first significant feminist contribution to the criminological field was Carol Smart's (1976) *Women, Crime and Criminology*. Here Smart addressed women's criminality and victimization, as well as criminology itself as a (male) gendered discipline. Early examples of feminist contributions to the field, such as Smart in the 1970s and 1980s, made the point that the discipline of criminology was dominated by men, and that what they studied was basically other men. In other words, women were invisible in terms of criminality, criminology and criminologists. The discipline, and especially what was called mainstream criminology, was still imbued with positivist sensibilities and outmoded assumptions regarding women. Additionally, male criminologists were accused of failing to acknowledge their own maleness. The aim then (and now) was not simply to redress the balance by studying more women; rather, it was to position gender as a core concept in criminology – studying men and women, and drawing on concepts of femininity and masculinity, it was argued, could contribute to a better understanding of crime in general and criminal justice responses to it. While it is clear that since the 1970s a significantly higher proportion of academic criminologists are women, and that feminism has had a major impact on criminology, many feminist voices continue to counsel that there is no room for complacency. Naffine (1997), for instance, argues that criminology still tends to be male-dominated, and that these males still tend to ignore their own maleness. More recently, in a review of the field, Gelsthorpe (2002: 112) made the point that while many might believe that criminology 'has been well and truly (if paradoxically) "penetrated" by feminism (this) is not the case. Doubts are still expressed'.

Various explanations for criminology's lack of interest in female offenders have been put forward. The most obvious is that men are more likely than women to engage in crime and, as a consequence, criminologists have traditionally concentrated on male offenders, especially younger offenders from lower-class backgrounds. In Britain and the United States official statistics have for many years consistently shown an offending rate for males four or five times greater than that for females. Currently, in England and Wales, around 80 per cent of known offenders are male and, overwhelmingly, it is men who are responsible for the most serious crimes, especially crimes that involve the use of violence. Silvestri and Crowther-Dowey (2008: 56) have summarized Home Office figures (for 2003) in order to show (in brackets) the percentage of offenders in the following crime categories who are male:

- Violence against the person (85%)
- Sexual offences (96%)
- Robbery (88%)
- Burglary (91%)
- Theft and handling stolen goods (78%)
- Fraud and forgery (73%)
- Criminal damage (88%)
- Drug offences (86%)

Although self-report studies have indicated less of an imbalance (Box 1983), this tends to result from the inclusion of offences at the less serious end of the spectrum. When explaining the lack of interest in female offenders, Heidensohn (1985) has also noted that male criminologists have always been drawn to the tough, macho world of the male criminal, while at the same time finding it extremely difficult to gain access to groups of female offenders. During the 1980s, a significant amount of feminist work, and oriented at least in part towards a liberal agenda, turned its attention to illuminating women's experiences as offenders and as victims (though many feminists prefer the term 'survivors'). In the post-war period, both in Britain and in the United States, there were some small increases in the proportion of offenders who were female. By the mid-1970s some criminologists were suggesting that these increases were linked to the greater equality and opportunities enjoyed by women as a result of the Women's Liberation Movement (Adler 1975; Simon 1975). However, Smart (1979) argued that these increases appeared before the movement had made any impact. Later on, Carlen (1990) argued that the explanation for increases in female offending in the 1970s and 1980s lay in worsening economic conditions and the resultant increases in poverty. These sorts of anxiety regarding women and their transgressions surface regularly in the mass media, and are usually constructed around a theme of women becoming more like men. One of the more recent examples is that of young women, alcohol consumption and the emergence of a so-called 'ladette' culture (for a brief, but useful discussion of this, see Silvestri and Crowther-Dowey 2008).

Distortions and stereotypes

The critique of traditional criminology that accompanied the development of feminist perspectives pointed to the distortion and crude sexist stereotyping found in those, albeit relatively rare, examples where criminologists have studied female offenders: 'the majority of these studies refer to women in terms of their biological impulses and hormonal balance or in terms of their domesticity, maternal instinct and passivity' (Smart 1976: xiv). The end result is that criminal men are seen as 'normal' human beings, and criminal women as 'abnormal'. Feminists argue that that view of offending women has not disappeared from contemporary criminology.

An early example is provided by the biological positivism of Lombroso and Ferrero (1885) (see Chapter 13). They argued that the criminal behaviour of 'born criminals' resulted from a condition of atavism; that is, such individuals were throwbacks to an earlier stage of human evolution, and therefore 'degenerate'. In their view, relatively few female criminals were in this category. However, unlike their male counterparts, such females were difficult to identify from their external appearance. This, they reasoned, was because women as a whole were less developed, in an evolutionary sense, than men, meaning that atavistic characteristics would not be so obviously in evidence. While most female criminals were not atavistic, they were, however, seen as unnatural aberrations from normal woman, who were naturally endowed with various non-criminal characteristics, such as passivity, reserve and domesticity.

In the middle of the twentieth century, the American Pollak (1950) put forward the view that women committed just as much crime as men, but because of their biology and nature, they were able to hide their offences. He argued that they had a natural caring role in society, and that this protected them from external scrutiny. However, Pollak is particularly identified with the view that women possess two key natural attributes: deceitfulness and secretiveness, and these led them to commit certain sorts of crime. For Pollak, faking orgasm was evidence of deceitfulness, and concealing menstruation evidence of secretiveness. Although less crude than these examples, similar sorts of criminology continued in the twentieth century. Cowie et al. (1968), for instance, said that because of fundamental biological differences between the sexes, boys find it more difficult to deal with stressful situations, and this lack of self-control explains why they are more likely to engage in crime than girls are.

Doing criminology

Since the emergence of feminist scholarship, there have been intense debates among feminist criminologists – or, given that some wish to detach themselves from 'criminology', feminists interested in studying crime, and so on – regarding what it means to 'do' criminology. Of particular importance in this context are debates centred on theory: what is it that makes feminist criminological theory 'feminist'? Clearly, as indicated at the beginning of this chapter, much depends on which type of feminism one subscribes to, as well as one's views on the merits of already existing criminological theory. A number of early feminists questioned the relevance of the major strands of criminological theorizing to the issues and agendas of feminism; for example, strain theory and labelling theory, on the grounds that these theories were designed to explain male rather than female crime. Some, such as Shacklady Smith (1978), were more optimistic and discussed the extent to which gender could be incorporated into some of these different theories. In general, though, feminists were dubious that this kind of project could succeed. In particular, the point was made that women, just as much as men, experience the various social factors that in the literature of criminology are associated with crime (e.g. anomie, poverty, exposure to media representations and unemployment), and yet are much less likely to engage in crime. Thus a key question is: what is it that differentiates men and women in terms of the impact of these sorts of social factors?

Heidensohn (1994) points out that the notion of control was one of three major themes in feminist research during the 1980s and 1990s (the others being: patriarchy, and economic and social marginalization). This prompted an upsurge of interest in control theory among some feminists, not because the theory is in itself 'feminist', but rather that it has the potential to help explain women's lack of involvement in crime. Thus control theory found favour because it posed the question: why do people *not* break the law? (See Chapter 6.) Meanwhile, the issue of the viability of a specifically feminist criminology continued to generate much debate. Some argued that such a criminology did exist (e.g. Greenwood 1981; Brown 1986), while others (e.g. Smart 1981) highlighted the divisions among feminist writers, divisions based upon research agendas, methodologies, politics and theoretical formulations.

Post-modern feminism

By the late 1980s and early 1990s, a number of feminist scholars interested in the field of crime and deviance began to draw on ideas associated with post-modernist thought (Cousins 1980; Cain 1989, 1990; Smart 1990). Sometimes described as 'post-feminism', post-modern feminism has been strongly influence by post-structuralism. It has notably drawn on Derrida's (1976) notion of 'deconstruction' and the view that the language used to give meaning to the social world is never neutral, and does not provide a 'true' understanding of that world. Some accounts become dominant, not because they are 'truthful', but because they reflect hierarchies of power. According to Derrida, the words constituting language are based upon dualities, for example, good/bad, beautiful/ugly, deviant/non-deviant and, especially significant in the context of this discussion, woman/man. Although these binary opposites create what seems to be an ordered social reality, they are simply *versions* of reality, giving the illusion of an essential difference between one and the other. Post-modern feminists, therefore, reject the dichotomy between woman and man:

> The assumption that each person has one fixed sex, one sexuality, and one gender is replaced by crosscutting sex, sexuality, and gender constructs that capture the complexity of gendered experience.

> (Lanier and Henry 1998: 282)

One major implication of rejecting the notion of 'woman' is that it distances post-modern feminism from standpoint feminism, given that the latter is concerned to give a voice to the experiences of women as women.

Post-modern feminists have also cautioned against a feminist engagement with criminology as an academic discipline, arguing instead for a feminist approach that detaches itself from criminology and its misleading assumptions and essentializing tendencies. From their perspective, criminology's central referent – 'crime' – suggests that criminal behaviour is different in kind from non-criminal behaviour, as if it possessed certain essential features; by definition, these features are negative ones such as harmfulness and badness. Smart put forward the radical view that feminists should abandon criminology (but not 'crime', though it should not be tied to traditional definitions):

> The thing that criminology cannot do is deconstruct 'crime'. It cannot locate rape or child sexual abuse in the domain of sexuality, nor theft in the domain of economic activity, nor drug use in the domain of health. To do so would be to abandon criminology to sociology; but more importantly, it would involve abandoning the idea of a unified problem which requires a unified response – at least at the theoretical level.

> (Smart 1990: 7)

As Carlen (1992: 62) says, a struggle over the 'meaning of things' has always been a feature of social science discourses, feminist or otherwise, and the purpose of theory is to 'produce new meanings that will empower'. Thus she is arguing that feminists should 'stay in', rather than vacate, the academic field of criminology. For Carlen, the key task facing feminists is to develop strategies that allow them to, as it were, stay in without selling out. There have also been ongoing debates regarding whether or not feminists should orient their research to issues of policy. Some, such as Smart (1990), are not enthusiastic about this type of research, basing their concerns on the view that research carried out within a 'traditional' criminological framework will have only a minimal impact from the point of view of the avowed aims of this research – for example, the creation of a fairer system of criminal justice for women.

This returns us to the question: what makes feminist criminological theory 'feminist'? Carlen (1992) provides a thoughtful overview of the debates surrounding this question, and concludes that *a* feminist criminology does not exist, that it is not desirable and that it is not possible. It is undesirable on the grounds that any totalizing, universal theory would detach supposedly distinct genders, together with patriarchal processes, from all other social, political, cultural and economic structures and processes that contribute to crime and social control. The main reason that it is not possible, she argues, is that apart from patriarchy, feminist perspectives have failed to develop explanatory concepts that are distinctively 'feminist'.

Summarizing developments in feminist criminology since the 1970s, Heidensohn and Gelsthorpe (2007) identify three phases: feminist empiricism, feminist standpointism (each discussed above) and, currently, deconstructionism. This third phase, which has emerged over the last ten years or so, reflects the increasing influence of critical social theory, post-structuralism and post-modernism on feminist theory. In this context though the stress has to be on 'critical'. Deconstructionism, a theoretical strategy associated with post-modernist thought, concerns itself with how people and things are represented and made 'real' through discourse and texts. This 'reality' then has implications for subjective understandings of identity, for example, what it means to be female or male, and for 'difference' between one human being and another. From the perspective of feminist criminologists, texts and messages embedded in social, criminological and legal discourses carry deep, and problematic representations of women and men. However, feminists such as Smart (1995), although influenced by post-modernist theory, have questioned that idea that 'discourse' is the only reality, arguing that innovative sociological methods can illuminate the 'reality' of discourse and social relations, and the interactions between the two realms. Daly (1997) too argues along these lines, in the process pointing to the development of 'three modes of analysing sex/gender': class-race-gender; doing gender; and sexed bodies. In summary:

> Class-race-gender focuses on the intersections of different social relations on women's (and men's) lives; doing gender (and subsequently doing masculinity) centres on the situations and social practices that produce gender; and sexed bodies focuses on sexual differences and on the relationship of sex and gender as corporeal and cultural categories.

(Daly 2006: 167)

Clearly, in recent years analyses of gender, crime and control by feminist criminologists have become increasingly complex and multifaceted. What has emerged though are anti-deterministic theoretical formulations that recognize the multiplicity of gender identity and its fluid and contingent nature.

Further reading

For accessible introductions to feminist criminology (along with other criminologies), see Chapter 5 in Walklate, S. (2003) *Understanding Criminology: Current Theoretical Debates*, 2nd edn. Buckingham: Open University Press; and Chapter 18 in Williams, K. (2004) *Textbook on Criminology*, 5th edn. Oxford: Oxford University Press.

More advanced texts are Gelsthorpe, L. and Morris, A. (eds) (1990) *Feminist Perspectives in Criminology*. Buckingham: Open University Press; Rafter, N.H. and Heidensohn, F. (eds) (1995) *International Perspectives in Criminology*. Buckingham: Open University Press; Smart, C. (1995) *Law, Crime and Sexuality: Essays in Feminism*. London: Sage Publications; and Daly, L. (1997) Different ways of conceptualising sex/gender in feminist theory and their implications, *Theoretical Criminology*, 1(1): 25–51.

10　Labelling Theory

Labelling theory emerged in the 1960s and was a core element of what came to be known as new deviancy theory. New deviancy theory incorporated an eclectic mix of theoretical influences; for example, interactionism, phenomenology and Marxism (Pearson 1975 described this 'odd theoretical cocktail' as 'misfit sociology'). Emerging initially in the United States, by the last part of the 1960s it had begun to have a profound influence on a younger generation of more radical British sociologists whose interests lay in areas of crime and deviance. However, as the name of this theoretical development indicates, the spotlight was on deviance, and those involved described what they were doing as 'the sociology of deviance' rather than 'criminology'. The popularity of new deviancy theory can be linked to certain key features:

- It offered a radical alternative to the traditional approaches to the study of rule-breaking that had dominated the field for so long. In Britain, these approaches were to a significant extent non-sociological, preoccupied with juvenile delinquency, oriented towards a positivistic (see Chapter 13) search for the causes of crime, and locked into the policy requirements of, for instance, the Home Office. New deviancy theory, on the other hand, gave its attention to a very wide range of so-called deviant behaviours, rejected the determinism associated with positivism in favour of a stress on voluntarism, and shifted the emphasis away from policy-oriented research.
- On a cultural level, new deviancy theory seemed to be congruent with the 'do your own thing', anarchy-style sensibilities of the 1960s' counterculture. Both new deviancy theory and the counterculture rejected the notion of a consensus in favour of a plurality of cultures, or subcultures. Furthermore, and allied to this, they both questioned the assumption (an assumption implicit in orthodox criminology) that deviant or criminal behaviour equated with 'bad' behaviour; in other words, they took a morally relativistic stance.
- On a political level, new deviancy theory's critical, even iconoclastic, stance in relation to social control agencies and processes, and with it a rejection of the view that sociological studies of crime and deviance should necessarily contribute to the 'war on crime', was attractive to those radical academics who aligned themselves with the Marxist/socialist New Left.

The origins and subsequent popularity of labelling theory are particularly associated with the American sociologist Howard Becker. The following famous quote from Becker provides the basis for understanding labelling theory (though by the early 1970s he preferred to use the term 'perspective', rather than theory):

> Social groups create deviance by making the rules whose infraction constitutes deviance, and by applying those rules to particular people and labeling them outsiders. From this point of view, deviance is *not* a quality of the act the person commits, but rather a consequence of the application by others of rules and sanctions to an 'offender'. The deviant is one to whom that label has been successfully applied; deviant behaviour is behaviour that people so label.

(Becker 1963: 9)

Here Becker is making two points (see also Erikson 1962 and Kitsuse 1962, two other labelling theorists). First, he is stressing that no behaviour is inherently deviant; deviance only exists because social rules exist (the same can be said of crime, which only exists because criminal laws exist). Those activities considered deviant in a particular society are not fixed, but alter over time and, similarly, there are differences between one society and another regarding what is considered to be deviant. For this reason, deviant behaviour is not synonymous with, for example, perverted, or unnatural, or bad, or immoral behaviour. Thus while in the media and, indeed, general conversation, deviance is often used in this way, that is, as a term of disapprobation, within the context of criminology or the sociology of deviance, it is not (for further discussion of this, see Chapter 7). From a sociological perspective deviant behaviour only has meaning in relation to specific social rules.

The second point made by Becker takes us into the heart of labelling theory: that deviance is not the result of breaking rules *per se*, but rather the result of a social audience defining and labelling specific cases of perceived rule-breaking as deviant (it was sometimes referred to as social reaction theory). The word 'perceived' is important in this context, for it may happen that the social audience gets it wrong, and an individual or group is labelled deviant when they have not broken any rules. Labelling, it is argued, is likely to have a social and psychological impact on those defined as 'offenders'. Ascribed the status of 'deviant', they will be treated as such by other members of society (they may be shunned, or experience intense surveillance or hostility), which in turn may affect how they see themselves and their subsequent behaviour (e.g. coping strategies, or acts of resistance in the shape of further deviance – described by Becker as a 'deviant career'). Drawing on the work of earlier American symbolic interactionists (especially

Cooley 1902 and Mead 1934), labelling theorists were interested in the ways in which understandings of self, others and situations were the product of interactional processes, processes based upon negotiation and interpretation, through which understandings of 'what things mean' are constructed.

Although in theory, and whether justified or not, any behaviour could be labelled deviant, in practice, of course, behaviour so labelled generally involves rule-breaking. However, while rule-breaking is widespread throughout society, labelling theorists argue that many of those involved escape being labelled deviant. This means that they avoid experiencing a negative societal reaction and concomitantly are able to maintain an image of themselves as non-deviant. Lemert (1951, 1967) introduced the term 'primary deviation' to describe rule-breaking behaviour that avoided being labelled as deviance. Given the ubiquitous nature of such behaviour, he argued that it was pointless to attempt to establish the causes of primary deviation. Labelling theory's lack of interest in the causes of deviance subsequently attracted quite a lot of criticism, though it should be noted that establishing causes was not what it was designed to do. Lemert used the concept of 'secondary deviation' to describe rule-breaking behaviour that does get labelled deviant by a social audience. Again, this emphasizes the central argument from labelling theory that deviance is created by societal reactions, and in that sense is the cause of deviance. A key factor here is the relative power possessed by those seeking to apply the label. Clearly, authority figures such as police officers, judges or members of the medical profession are, potentially at least, in a stronger position than others to make the label stick. Other factors have to be taken into consideration though. The rule-breaker may be able to keep their behaviour secret, or the circumstances surrounding the behaviour (e.g. being drunk) may allow it to be normalized, or defined as a temporary aberration, or they may possess enough social and economic resources to nullify efforts to label them deviant.

Labelling theory, then, broke with traditional approaches to deviance that had focused on the deviant actor and tried to explain why they did it. Attention shifted from the deviant themselves to those in a position to apply the deviant label. From this perspective, deviance is *constituted*, or created, by the labellers rather than the labelled. As Lemert put it:

> This is a large turn away from older sociology which tended to rest on the idea that deviance leads to social control. I have come to believe that the reverse idea, i.e., social control leads to deviance, is equally tenable and the potentially richer premise for studying deviance in modern society.

(Lemert 1967: v)

For a case study seeking to show how this process works in practice, see Lemert's (1967) study of stuttering among native North Americans in British Columbia, Canada.

This break with a traditional, common-sense conceptualization of deviance in favour of a constitutive approach was also associated with the sociological phenomenology and ethnomethodology developing in the 1960s and early 1970s. For phenomenologists, the nature of social reality does not exist 'out there' waiting to be discovered, but rather resides in the subjective meanings shared by society's members (see, for example, Phillipson 1971; Schutz 1972). Ethnomethodology (literally 'people's methods') concentrates on the spoken word and the tacitly understood ways in which language is used to create and sustain an ordered social world. Looking specifically at rule-breaking behaviour, an example provided by the ethnomethodologists, Hester and Eglin (1992) illustrate well a constitutive approach to deviance and, therefore, a rejection of a common-sense approach based upon what Pollner (1974) calls 'mundane reasoning'. From the perspective of Hester and Eglin, and regardless of what 'really' happened, a crime cannot exist until it is officially defined as such. In this example, they focus on the response of a police chief to the trial judge's acquittal of a group of strikers. The police chief was convinced that they had, in fact, committed a crime:

> From the police chief's point of view, for something to be 'unlawful' it is not crucial that a judge finds it so; rather its unlawfulness exists independently of judicial response ... Judges, in this view, do not constitute crime in their judicial work, rather they merely respond to its already existing criminal character. This is mundane reasoning *par excellence*: it presumes some independent factual domain of criminality against which human perceptions can either correctly or incorrectly correspond.
>
> (Hester and Eglin 1992: 129)

We can begin to see some complex issues and debates opening up here; fundamentally, at what point can a deviant act and a deviant person be said to exist? (See Ditton 1979 for a sophisticated analysis of the role of social control in the creation of deviance and crime.) Returning to labelling theory, it should be noted that while its adherents were nominally committed to a constitutive approach, their work was not always consistent in this respect. Becker's (1963: 20) typology of deviance and conformity, for instance, has over the years generated much debate. His typology is based on two variables: actual behaviour and perceptions of that behaviour by a social audience (see Table 11.1).

Table 11.1

	Obedient behaviour	Rule-breaking behaviour
Perceived as deviant	1. Falsely accused	2. Pure deviant
Not perceived as deviant	3. Conforming	4. Secret deviant

'1' refers to a non-rule-breaker who, in spite of this, is 'unjustly' labelled deviant; '2' is a rule-breaker who is 'justly' labelled deviant; '3' is a non-rule-breaker who 'justly' is not labelled deviant; and '4' is a rule-breaker who manages to hide the fact and is 'unjustly' not labelled deviant. At first glance, all this seems quite logical, even obvious.

However, looked at within the context of a supposedly constitutive model of deviance, some discrepancies emerge, specifically with regard to the categories 'falsely accused' and 'secret deviant'. As Pollner (1974) argued, although someone who is 'falsely accused' may be innocent, the fact that they are perceived to be deviant, and hence labelled as such, in effect places them in the same category as the 'pure deviant'. In other words, from the point of view of a constitutive model, whether or not they really did it is irrelevant; what matters is the construction of a deviant status as a result of interactions with a social audience. The concept of a 'secret deviant' has been similarly criticized (see, for example, Gibbs 1966; Taylor et al. 1973; Pollner 1974) on the grounds that someone who is able to cover their tracks, thereby avoiding being labelled deviant, is, according to a constitutive model, *not* a deviant, secret or otherwise. Gibbs (1966) also criticized Lemert's concept of primary deviation on the grounds that such behaviour cannot logically be described as deviant if it has not been so labelled. Later on Becker (1974) acknowledged that the notion of a 'secret deviant' is misleading, and stated that 'potential deviant' would have been a more appropriate term. However, someone in the 'conforming' category could also be categorized as a 'potential deviant', given there are no guarantees that someone engaging in obedient behaviour will not be labelled deviant.

Innocents abroad?

Labelling theorists never suggested that prior to being labelled deviant, rule-breakers were 'innocent' members of society, unaware that their rule-breaking would be disapproved of. However, this did not stop some critics from arguing otherwise. Akers (1967: 46), for example, stated: 'One sometimes gets the impression from reading this literature that people go about minding their own business, and then – "wham" – bad society comes along and slaps them with a stigmatised label'. It is true that one sometimes gets this impression, but only – by definition – in the case of Becker's 'falsely accused'; *sometimes* that is precisely what happens. In general, the deviant groups studied by labelling theorists had chosen (within the context of their particular circumstances) to engage in that behaviour in the knowledge that it was disapproved of, and even illegal. However, labelling theory was infused with a degree of ambivalence regarding the wrongfulness or harmfulness of the behaviours studied, coupled with a critical view of reactions on the part of social control agents. This was facilitated by a tendency to concentrate on relatively harmless deviant lifestyles and 'crimes without victims'. Becker (1967) argued for an 'appreciative' approach to the study of deviance, rather than the condemnatory approach found in traditional criminology, and asked: 'Whose side are we on?' In fact, given that labelling theory was influenced by the libertine-leaning ideals of the 1960s counterculture, it is not surprising that sometimes studies of deviant cultures shifted from appreciation to celebration.

This raises an important question (and one relevant to present-day studies of deviance): on what basis did labelling theorists decide that a particular form of behaviour was deviant? It certainly did not reflect their personal disapproval, but who 'out there' in society was thought to be expressing disapproval and labelling the behaviour deviant? For labelling theorists, society was composed of a plurality of subcultures (and therefore a plurality of norms and values), thus the notion of a consensus and with it a majority view was highly problematic. Are some forms of behaviour, then, seen as deviant because of the views of a powerful minority, or denunciation in the mass media, or what? There was in labelling theory a tension between a focus on micro interactional processes of deviantization, and an identification of examples of deviance based upon a societal, or macro, level of analysis. Taking labelling theory's argument that rule-breaking, potentially deviant behaviour is everywhere to its logical conclusion, it would be more productive to allow for the possibility of deviance in all social relationships, including very small groups.

Wilkins' concept of deviancy amplification introduced a strongly ironic ingredient to the labelling process. He argued that under certain conditions social control responses intended to reduce, or even eradicate, a particular example of deviance can, as a latent function, have the opposite effect, and increase the amount and frequency of the deviance. This links up with Becker's concept of a deviant career and Lemert's concept of secondary deviation, by focusing on the impact of labelling on self-image and subsequent behaviour. According to Wilkins, an intolerant, heavy-handed response (e.g. on the part of the police, the courts or the media) to rule-breaking is likely to be counterproductive. Intolerance of even minor infractions of a particular rule increases the number of individuals stigmatized as deviant. This, in turn, creates an amplification spiral – a vicious circle – whereby those involved become increasingly isolated from the wider, conformist society, develop a deviant identity, engage in more rule-breaking, and stimulate an even stronger social control reaction, which then affirms the original concerns of the wider society.

The deviancy amplification process is well illustrated by Young's (1971) study of marijuana users in Notting Hill, London. Influenced by lurid stories in the mass media concerning the supposedly 'perverted' lifestyles of drug users, a scandalized general public, in tandem with the mass media, demanded that 'something be done'. A heavy-handed response on the part of the police, and 'tough' sentencing by the courts, transformed a relatively minor problem into a more serious one. Seeing themselves as under siege from 'straight society', drug use became a form of symbolic resistance to authority and a source of collective identity. Furthermore, while the notion of amplification cannot be reduced to mere 'copy cat' behaviour, there will be situations where publicity in the mass media will lead to other newcomers being attracted to the behaviour in question.

As a final point on this, looked at within the general context of labelling theory, the amplification of deviance can occur in two senses:

1   There is an actual increase in the amounts and frequency of the deviance (involving a range of original participants, with perhaps new ones joining in).
2   There is no increase in the amounts and frequency of that behaviour, however, because of more intense enforcement, or those concerned becoming more brazen, more participants are labelled deviant.

S. Cohen (1972) drew on Wilkins' concept of deviancy amplification in his study *Folk Devils and Moral Panics*, the title of which brought to prominence two other key concepts associated with labelling theory. In this study Cohen focused on two youth groups that emerged in the mid-1960s in England – mods and rockers – and analysed the ways in which mass media representations and the response of the police and courts created a deviancy amplification spiral. It began with exaggerated and sensationalized mass media accounts of inter-group fighting and acts of criminal damage one Easter bank holiday weekend in 1964. Misleading images of mods in conflict with rockers were conjured up. Soon the mass media were explaining the behaviour by situating it within the context of a generalized understanding of the 'problem with today's youth': too much money, boredom, indiscipline, and so on. However, at the beginning only extremely loose affiliations existed, and these tended to be based upon neighbourhood territoriality, rather than being a so-called mod or rocker. However, Cohen paints a graphic picture showing how, within a short period of time, an amplification of deviance occurred, and with it an escalation in actual amounts of violence and other forms of disorder. It was, in other words, a self-fulfilling prophesy. Two years on, and large numbers of young people across the country were calling themselves 'mods' (relatively few opted to become 'rockers').

The study shows how societal reactions were instrumental in creating folk devils – a demonized and stigmatized section of society – in the shape of mods and rockers. Cohen's concept of moral panic refers to exaggerated alarm among members of a society in response to a group or condition perceived to be posing a threat to that society's moral well being. Hall et al. (1978) used the term in a Marxist analysis of the British state's response to a crisis of legitimacy during a period of social and economic decline in the 1970s. According to this analysis, in an effort to reassert its legitimacy, the state deflected attention away from the deeper sources of Britain's social and economic problems by exploiting public anxieties surrounding issues of 'race' and immigration. Hall et al. argue that the state was instrumental in creating a moral panic around 'muggings' (i.e. street robbery), and in the process linking muggings to black youth specifically, thus in turn creating a folk devil in the shape of the 'black mugger'.

In a more recent review, Thompson (1998) discusses the key defining characteristics of a moral panic, and these are in accord with the work of S. Cohen (1972) and Hall et al. (1978) above. First, there is relatively intense media interest and coverage over a specific time period. Second, this coverage involves a significant exaggeration of the scale and harmfulness of the events concerned. Third, those involved are represented as folk devils. Fourth, there is an emphasis on the connections between the behaviour or condition under scrutiny and deeper moral issues afflicting that society.

The concepts of moral panic and (though perhaps to a lesser extent) folk devil have over the years entered into wider usage, especially within journalism, if sometimes in a sloppy fashion. They have also continued to generate debate within criminology and the sociology of deviance. One issue arises from conjoining moral with *panic*. The notion of panic suggests alarm, anxiety, even fear, when in particular cases anger may be the primary emotional reaction in relation to concerns regarding threats to the moral order. Clarke (2003) has questioned the assumption that members of the public will inevitably panic when faced with highly threatening situations.

Waddington (1986) has focused on the idea that a moral panic represents an exaggerated or disproportionate response to such threats, questioning the implication that an alternative, 'rational' and proportionate response is something that can be assessed (see also Sacco 2005). In terms of objective, measurable criteria, this is, of course, correct. However, there is an important issue raised by this argument. A number of writers have pointed to terrorism as an example of a contemporary moral panic (e.g. Chapman and Harris

2002). They have then gone on to highlight various repercussions, ranging from attacks on civil liberties to increased security measures at airports. Obviously, informed judgements regarding whether or not these repercussions are disproportionate or not would, by definition, require privileged access to the intelligence gathered by security services. However, even then, the notion of 'proportionate' would be open to interpretation. Thus although there is no objective, scientific method for calibrating the balance between 'freedom' and 'security', it does not follow that analyses of responses to terrorism based on the concept of moral panic necessarily lack credibility or legitimacy. Other writers have reviewed the idea of moral panics within the context of media-saturated contemporary societies (see, for example, McRobbie and Thornton 1995).

One argument is that nowadays moral panics are sometimes used as a marketing strategy, so that a band, type of music, style of dress, and so on, is associated with, for instance, danger, or rebellion, or edginess. This though is not an entirely new feature of popular culture. The music and fashion industries were not slow to exploit mod culture in the mid-1960s, to the extent that, as mentioned earlier, by 1966 large numbers of young people were calling themselves 'mods', enjoying 'mod bands', wearing 'mod' clothes and watching 'mod' music programmes, such as *Ready Steady Go*, on television. Likewise, by the time Young's study of drug users was published in 1971, drug-referenced 'psychedelia' had become a powerful motif within popular culture, taking in music, fashion, graphic design, cinematography and literature. As Nuttall put it:

> Nine months after the first gatherings in Haight-Ashbury (in San Francisco) girls and office workers were wondering down the Brighton and Blackpool seafronts, jangling their souvenir prayer-belts, trailing their Paisley bedspreads, brandishing daffodils and trying to look tripped out. The Beatles had gone 'flower power' and it was up to the kids to do their best to follow.
>
> (Nuttall 1970: 200)

As always, of course, this commercialization went hand in hand with a sanitization of the original cultural movements – what we might call the antibiotic effect of commercial interests. With so many young people across the country identifying with mod culture, they were not encouraged to engage in violence and acts of criminal damage. Neither were those flirting with psychedelic culture encouraged to take too seriously the hippie invitation to 'turn on and drop out' of school or work.

The radical turn

Within a relatively short space of time, there emerged a number of what were destined to become highly significant criticisms of labelling theory. They were significant in that they laid some of the foundations for the subsequent development of a much more radical perspective on crime, deviance and social control – the 'new criminology' (see Chapter 7). These criticisms can be summarized as follows:

- In their analyses of labelling processes, labelling theorists were criticized for concentrating on low-level agents of social control, such as police officers, teachers and social workers. This, it was argued, ignored the role played by those with significant economic and political power (in the orchestration of moral panics, for instance) and, more importantly, ignored their role in defining particular types of behaviour as deviant or criminal in the first place (see Liazos 1972; Thio 1973). This critique, therefore, focused on the powerful as rule-makers.
- Labelling theorists were also criticized for perpetuating stereotypical images of deviant groups – marginalized, powerless and exotic. In his critique, Gouldner (1968) said the deviant was represented as an 'underdog', while Liazos (1972) referred to 'nuts, sluts and perverts' ('preverts' in the original spelling). See also Thio (1973). According to these critics, the outcome was that labelling theory failed to expose the 'real' deviants in American society, for example, corporate fraudsters and the politicians responsible for the violence of the Vietnam war. This critique focused on the powerful as rule-breakers.
- The third criticism is particularly associated with Gouldner (1968). For him, labelling theory was at fault for characterizing the deviant as 'man-on-his-back': a helpless victim of the labelling process. Gouldner proposed an alternative view, one that characterized the deviant as 'man-fighting-back'; that is, as someone who actively chooses to engage in deviant behaviour in order to challenge dominant norms and values. This critique suggested that deviance represents a form of political action.

Looking back, it is clear that new deviancy theory – and in particular labelling theory – had a major impact on the study of crime, deviance and social control. The ideas generated by labelling theory led to an upsurge in interest in this field among sociologists. Of particular importance was a concern to interrogate the conceptual language of criminology and the sociology of deviance, thereby challenging taken-for-granted understandings. The employment of the theories and methods of interactionism was to have a lasting effect on the sociology of deviance and this continues today. At the same time, and as discussed above, key criticisms of labelling theory influenced subsequent developments in radical criminology.

Further reading

The key original early texts are Lemert, E. (1951) *Social Pathology*. New York: McGraw-Hill; Kitsuse, J. (1962) Societal reaction to deviant behaviour, *Social Problems*, 9: 247–56; Becker, H.S. (1963) *Outsiders: Studies in the Sociology of Deviance*. London: Macmillan; Wilkins, L. (1964) *Social Deviance: Social Policy, Action and Research*. London: Tavistock; Lemert, E.M. (1967) *Human Deviance, Social Problems and Social Control*. Englewood Cliffs, NJ: Prentice-Hall; Goffman, E. (1968) *Stigma: Notes on the Management of a Spoiled Identity*. London: Penguin. Two important readers from this early period are Becker, H.S. (ed.) (1964) *The Other Side: Perspectives on Deviance*. New York: Free Press; and Rubington, E. and Weinberg, M.S. (eds) (1968) *Deviance: The Interactionist Perspective*. Basingstoke: Macmillan. And a more recent reader is Downes, D. and Rock, P. (eds) (1979) *Deviant Interpretations*. Oxford: Oxford University Press.

The classic British study of 'folk devils' and 'moral panics' is Cohen, S. (1972) *Folk Devils and Moral Panics*. London: MacGibbon and Kee. For an early British study drawing on the concept of deviancy amplification, see Young, J. (1971) *The Drugtakers: The Social Meaning of Drug Use*. London: MacGibbon and Kee.

Goode, E. and Ben-Yehuda, N. (1994) *Moral Panics: The Social Construction of Deviance*. Oxford: Blackwell; Thompson, K. (1998) *Moral Panic*. London: Routledge; and Hunt, A. (1997) Moral panic and moral language, *British Journal of Sociology*, 48(4): 629–48, provide good overviews of the concept of moral panic.

Focusing on 'mugging' specifically, Waddington, P.A.J. (1986) Mugging as a moral panic: a question of proportion, *British Journal of* Sociology, 32(2): 245–59 critically questions the notion of an 'exaggerated' response to deviance. McRobbie, A. and Thornton, S.L. (1995) Re-thinking 'moral panic' for multi-mediated social worlds, *British Journal of Sociology*, 46(4): 559–74 provides a critical review of the concept of moral panic within the context of media-saturated, information-rich, contemporary societies, and in a similar vein: Critcher, C. (2003) *Moral Panics and the Media*. Buckingham: Open University Press, and Jewkes, Y. (2004) *Media and Crime*. London: Sage Publications.

11 Left Realism

During the early 1980s a division began to open up within the neo-Marxist, critical criminology that had emerged at the beginning of the 1970s; by the middle of the 1980s an alternative critical criminology, described as left realism, had come into being. Interestingly, Ian Taylor and Jock Young, two of the authors of one of the key texts associated with the earlier critical criminology (*The New Criminology*, Taylor et al. and published in 1973) played major roles in laying the groundwork for, and then developing, left realism (Young 1975; Taylor 1981). In fact, these and other proponents of left realism – notably, Richard Kinsey, John Lea and Roger Matthews – to a significant extent developed their ideas as part of a concerted critique of the earlier critical criminology, which they labelled disparagingly as 'left idealism' (see Chapter 7), a label rejected by the criminologists concerned. While left realists described the new paradigm as critical/radical, and themselves as 'socialists', left realism was more social democratic and reformist in orientation than the critical criminology that had preceded it.

At the core of left realism is an entreaty to 'take crime seriously', meaning that critical criminologists should appreciate the harmfulness of conventional crime, such as burglary and robbery and, as a corollary, strive to develop causal explanations, together with devising practical policies aimed at reducing victimization from this type of crime. As Gross (1982: 51) complained: 'on crime, more than on most matters, the left seems bereft of ideas'. It can be noted that administrative criminology too was criticized for failing to address the causes of crime, and concentrating instead on situational crime prevention strategies (see Chapter 2).

While 'left idealists' gave serious attention to the crimes of the powerful, they were accused by left realists of showing little interest in conventional crime (much of which is carried out by the least powerful), apart from discussing it in terms of processes of criminalization, moral panics and exaggerated public fears, or some romantic notion of political resistance. At the same time, said left realists, crime rises as measured by official statistics were seen by left idealists as a mere illusion. This, they argued, ignored the real problems faced by those living in lower working-class neighbourhoods, whose fear of crime is rational, rather than the result of media-fuelled, misplaced 'moral panics'. Furthermore, such residents are doubly victimized – by crime *and* a lack of money. Left idealists were also admonished for adopting a sympathetic, or even supportive stance in relation to so-called 'crimes without victims', for example, those involving drugs, and sometimes in relation to 'crimes with victims', especially if the perpetrators are in some sense 'oppressed'. The refusal to 'take (conventional) crime seriously', argued left realists, had over many years allowed those on the political right, who did appear to take it seriously, to seize the issue of 'law and order' and make it their own.

From the start, one of the priorities for left realism was to build up an accurate picture of the crime problem, especially in working-class neighbourhoods. The major tool for doing this was localized victim surveys, such as the two carried out in Islington, London (Jones et al. 1986; Crawford et al. 1990). By concentrating on relatively small geographical areas, and using sensitive interviewing techniques, these surveys were felt to provide much more accurate information on victimization than was provided by recorded crime figures, or the large sweeps of the British Crime Survey, which is also based upon victims' accounts. Left realists argued that since the 1960s, Britain had experienced real increases in amounts of crime, coupled with a greater sensitivity towards, and fear of, crime among the general public. Thus although they cautioned against taking official crime statistics at face value, left realists did agree with the general trends indicated by these statistics. A second priority was to develop a causal explanation of these crime rises, which puzzlingly occurred during periods of low unemployment and increasing affluence, as well as during periods of high unemployment and less affluence.

A left realist explanation of the causes of crime has been refined over the years, and is well represented in the work of Jock Young (see, for example, Young 1986, 1987, 1994, 1998), who has sought to develop a 'holistic' model. As a basis, he argues that different groups in society define crime, and the 'crime problem', in different ways, and that these definitions are not fixed, but are constantly changing. Different perspectives will be found among offenders, victims, systems of informal control, and systems of formal control – these four elements are referred to as the 'square of crime'. Specific definitions of crime are seen as resulting from the interrelationships among the four. As the discussion above indicates, special attention is paid to victims' definitions of crime, however, and criticizing both positivist criminology and 'idealist' critical criminology, Young further argues:

> ... that crime is inevitably the product of action and reaction and that the failure of previous criminologies is that they have problematized one component and ignored the other. Thus positivism focuses on crime and tends to take the definition of crime for granted whereas constructionism (that is, labelling theory, abolition-

ism and much of critical criminology) problematizes the way in which crime is defined and constructed yet tends to ignore crime itself.

(Young 2006: 235)

For Young and other left realists, one crucial outcome of the interplay between action and reaction is that increases in crime have been accompanied by increases in public concerns, or fears, about crime – the 'worst of all worlds' as Young puts it.

As far as offenders are concerned, from Young's perspective, the major source of crime and indeed rising crime rates since the 1960s is lower-class, male subcultures. These subcultures are seen as collectivities that reproduce, affirm and express key values relating to toughness, machismo and patriarchy, values highly conducive to criminal behaviour. In addition, he argues that since the 1960s we have witnessed in Britain and elsewhere an increasing emphasis on consumerism and an ethos of individualism, and that these too has been incorporated into the value systems of these subcultures.

Drawing on Merton's anomie theory (see Chapter 3), Young argues that the intense consumerism and individualism characterizing late modern societies have led to an increase in relative deprivation. In this formulation, relative deprivation is not an objective condition based upon a lack of money and material possessions *per se*, but a subjective condition, whereby an individual feels that they have not achieved the material rewards commensurate with what they consider to be reasonable expectations and, as a consequence, experience a sense of injustice. Relative deprivation is, therefore, a key causal factor when explaining rising crime rates, in that it is believed to have led to an increasing propensity to acquire material possessions by illegitimate means. For left realists, it is this subjective element that explains why during the 1930s, for instance, when there was much more unemployment and poverty than in the post-war period, crime rates were relatively low. In Britain at that time, it is argued, people may have been economically deprived, but they had significantly lower expectations in terms of the material possessions they could reasonably expect to acquire. Thus, and in common with critical criminologists in general, Young rejects a simplistic, positivist causal relationship between rising crime rates and such things as poverty and unemployment.

More recently, however, Young (2007; Hayward and Young 2007) has augmented this explanation of criminality by drawing on the work of cultural criminologists (see Chapter 8), and in the process shifted away from an emphasis on acquisitive property crime. His argument now is that much crime, or transgressive behaviour, is motivated by emotion and a desire for thrill and excitement, rather than monetary or material gain (even in cases where the latter rewards are present). Crime of this sort is though still linked to relative deprivation (together with a 'crises of identity'), in that while the individuals involved feel resentment, frustration, humiliation, and so on because of their failure to achieve in a material sense, their reactions are oriented towards expressive rather than material goals (there are echoes here of Cohen's 1955 work on 'status frustration' among delinquent boys – see Chapter 16).

Left realists are highly critical of left idealist versions of critical criminology. They are accused of remaining aloof from an engagement with practical policies aimed at reducing criminal victimization, and improving the criminal justice system, so that it becomes fairer and more just. This, they said, was because left idealists viewed the police, the courts, prisons, and so on as working in the interests of the powerful, and that any 'improvements' would only represent a liberal tinkering with the capitalist system. Left realists argued that an all or nothing commitment to a socialist transformation of society, seen by left idealists as a necessary precondition for the achievement of fairness and justice, was misplaced Utopianism. In a similar vein, left idealists were also criticized for their refusal to develop anti-crime policies based upon the mobilization of local communities so that they worked in unison with local authorities, police and other relevant organizations. Again, said left realists, this resistance to taking crime seriously had historically opened the door to the political right and their non-progressive policies.

Therefore, in response to what they saw as a policy deficit on the part of the political left, various criminologists writing from a left realist perspective put forward a range of practical policy suggestions (see, for example, Gross 1982; Einstadter 1984; McMullan 1986; Matthews 1992a); these included such things as 'citizen defence squads', 'supportive neighbourhood (crime prevention) networks' and victim–offender mediation schemes. They also forged links with Labour Party-controlled local authorities in an effort to develop anti-crime strategies. Left realists underlined the point that policies based upon mobilizing local communities were 'progressive' and directed at improving the lot of, in particular, poorer working-class people. The aim was reduce the victimization of vulnerable groups with some left realists arguing explicitly for a redistribution of victimization – from more to less impoverished neighbourhoods.

The work of left realists has stimulated a great deal of critical debate over the past two decades with strong reactions coming from, in particular, those critical criminologists characterized as left idealists. One issue relates to how 'crime', as in the phrase 'taking crime seriously', is conceptualized by left realists. While there are many different types of crime, it is argued that left realists in practice essentialize the concept because of their primary focus on conventional crime (in spite of acknowledging the problems caused by corporate and white-collar crime). It is also argued that using the term 'crime' places the criminologist in the position of having to address only those activities that happen to be defined as criminal in a particular society, thereby ignoring other harmful, though non-criminal, activities. Although left realists such as Young point to the different definitions of crime arising from the dynamics of 'the square of crime' (as discussed above), all parties – and notably respondents in victim surveys – are nominally locked into official legal categories. Furthermore, critics have argued that there is an implicit assumption in left realism that all crime is by definition necessarily harmful to those living in poorer working-class neighbourhoods. In some situations, the argument runs, crime will be judged to be beneficial by many residents, for example, when smuggling rings make cheap alcohol and cigarettes available, or when cheap, albeit stolen, spare parts for broken household appliances are on sale in the local pub.

At the core of the left realist characterization of the 'crime problem' is the information derived from localized victim surveys, which, as mentioned above, invite respondents to think about their victimization in terms of general understandings of 'crime'; rather than, for instance, 'harmful events'. Additionally, because of their nature such surveys will not bring to light certain sorts of crime; for example, corporate crime. A further dimension to this takes us back to Young's argument that there have been real increases in crime since the 1960s, due to a corresponding emphasis on individualism and an increase in relative deprivation. He incorporates into this argument the view that the public has also become gradually more sensitive towards crime, making them more anxious or fearful, and thereby increasing the likelihood of criminal victimization being disclosed to the interviewer. In other words, the suggestion is that in the past people had a higher tolerance level in relation to certain types of victimization. In fact, he argues that public sentiments can be situated on a tolerance-criminalization continuum, and that since the 1960s public sentiments have shifted more and more towards the 'criminalization' end, meaning that people have become increasingly likely to report their experiences of victimization in victim surveys. One problem with this formulation is that it is difficult to assess the relative importance of a lack of public tolerance compared with other factors, such as relative deprivation and individualism, which are also linked to crime rises. It is theoretically possible that a lack of tolerance, emanating from greater sensitivity, could explain *all* increases in amounts of victimization as re-flected in victim surveys. Another problem when making historical compari-sons is that in the past equivalent victim surveys did not exist.

As far as engaging with policy is concerned, left idealists have always argued that, contrary to what left realists say, they do engage with practical issues of policy. However, these interventions have tended not to be con-cerned with crime prevention as traditionally understood, but rather with issues of corruption, discrimination, miscarriages of justice and human rights violations when they have manifested themselves within the institutions and practices of the state. Left idealist criticisms of the practical policies devised by left realists have focused on the nature of the local community and its relationship with the police and local authorities. One argument is that drafting residents into the criminal justice process when responding to offenders may, as a consequence, lead to interventions becoming even more Draconian than they are at present. Another is that left realists have failed to appreciate the lack of homogeneity within many local communities, which, because of divisions based upon class, gender, 'ethnicity' or age, could generate tension and conflict, rather than a resolution of problems. Tension and conflict could also be generated within the context of 'partnerships' between the community and the police and local authorities, for example, because of an imbalance in terms of power and resources. Finally, some have been highly critical of the way in which left realists conceptualize 'the community', in that there seems to be an assumption that those living in a particular neighbourhood constitute two quite separate and identifiable types: non-offenders (i.e. 'the community') and offenders (i.e. 'the rest'). Those critical of this view argue that in reality individuals often move in and out of these categories.

Finally, given that both left realism and left idealism are part of the critical tradition in criminology and the continuing disputes between them, it is difficult to avoid discussing one without referencing it against the other. However, there are overlaps between the two. Each agrees that both the conventional crimes of the relatively powerless and the (corporate and state) crimes of the relatively powerful are harmful and should be subjected to criminological analysis. They also share some common ground at the level of theory, for example, that 'crime' has no ontological reality – it depends on how it is defined in specific jurisdictions. On the other hand, there are major disputes between the two, disputes that have important implications in terms of different understandings of what it means to 'do criminology'. As the above discussion indicates, the key differences between left realism and left idealism can be seen in relation to the emphasis placed on one type of crime rather than another; how these substantive concerns are translated into 'progressive' policies; and the theories and concepts associated with the respective approaches, in particular, the divergent definitions of 'crime' itself.

Further reading

For an early precursor of left realism, see Taylor, I. (1981) *Law and Order: Arguments for Socialism*. London: Macmillan. Two early texts making the case for, and outlining the contours of, left realism are Lea, J. and Young, J. (1984)

What is to be Done about Law and Order? London: Penguin; and Matthews, R. and Young, J. (eds) (1986) *Confronting Crime.* London: Sage Publications. Examples of left realist localized victim surveys are Kinsey, R. (1984) *The Merseyside Crime Survey: First Report.* Liverpool: Merseyside County Council; Jones, T., Maclean, B. and Young, J. (1986) *The Islington Crime Survey.* Aldershot: Gower; Crawford, A., Jones, T., Woodhouse, T. and Young, J. (1990) *Second Islington Crime Survey.* London: Middlesex Polytechnic; and Anderson, S., Kinsey, R., Loader, I. and Smith, C. (1991) *The Edinburgh Crime Survey.* Edinburgh: Scottish Office.

For a collection of readings with various contributors assessing the arguments of left realism, see Young, J. and Matthews, R. (1992) *Rethinking Criminology: The Realist Debate.* London: Sage Publications. Subsequent developments in left realism are discussed in Young, J. (1994) Incessant chatter: recent paradigms in criminology, in M. Maguire, R. Morgan and R. Reiner (eds) *The Oxford Handbook of Criminology,* 1st edn. Oxford: Clarendon Press; and Young, J. (1999) *The Exclusive Society.* London: Sage Publications.

The influence of left realism is in evidence outside of Britain, in North America, for instance, Lowman, J. and Maclean, B. (eds) (1992) *Realist Criminology.* Toronto: University of Toronto Press; Currie, E. (1995) *Confronting Crime.* New York: Pantheon; and Currie, E. (1998) *Crime and Punishment in America.* New York: Metropolitan Books.

Analyses that have incorporated ideas from cultural criminology into left realism are Young, J. (2003) Merton with energy, Katz with structure, *Theoretical Criminology,* 7(3): 389–414; and Young, J. (2007) *The Vertigo of Late Modernity.* London: Sage Publications.

12 Masculinities

Gender refers to socially constructed understandings of maleness and femaleness, that is, masculinity and femininity. These understandings are produced, affirmed and reproduced in culture, social structure and social relations. Thus masculinity and femininity are associated with certain traits or attributes, and often these are essentialized, in the sense that they are thought to reflect fundamental differences between men and women, not just in terms of biology/sex, but also as social beings. Sociologists and anthropologists though have highlighted the fact that understandings of masculinity and femininity are not fixed and universally agreed upon. Even in a given society at any given time, these understandings will vary significantly. Furthermore, the way in which an individual translates these understandings into actual behaviour can vary enormously, depending on particular circumstances. It is because of this that the plural terms masculinities and femininities are used.

Criminological research into masculinities and crime emerged out of the feminist criminology developing in the 1970s, where gender was the core concept. A specific interest in masculinity arose because men are much more likely to engage in criminal behaviour than women are, especially with respect to the more serious and violent offences. Thus although the relevance of, for instance, class, ethnicity and age, were acknowledged, masculinity was seen by many as the key explanatory concept. Early work by radical feminists concerned itself with male violence towards women, in particular domestic and sexual violence (see Chapter 10), and focused on male power, or patriarchy, rather than male traits and attributes *per se* (see, for example, Brownmiller 1975). The problem with this kind of approach though is that it tends to polarize men and women and make generalizations about *all* men (and women), in the process ignoring how masculinities and femininities are socially constructed and variable. Increasingly, however, work was produced that did address the complex processes and structures within which masculine and feminine identities and relationships are socially constructed, though because of its links with criminal behaviour, special attention has been given to masculinities.

One of the difficulties with foregrounding masculinity in this way though is that while it is recognized that masculinity and femininity cannot be polarized in terms of different and universal attributes, some distinctions between the two need to be identified, otherwise what would explain the differences in offending? As a result, analyses attempted to theorize the social construction of masculinity in terms of culturally approved attributes.

However, while these theories acknowledge that the meaning of masculinity (and femininity) is fluid, and contingent upon particular circumstances, there is, as Jefferson (1997) points out, a tendency for analyses to make men synonymous with masculinity, and women synonymous with femininity. In addition, and also noted by Jefferson (1997), if the intention is to identify masculine attributes that are linked to criminal behaviour, then it is likely that these attributes will be negative in character. Although there is some variation in the detail, masculinity is typically associated with such things as toughness, daring, hardness, aggressiveness and stoicism. By contrast, femininity is usually associated with 'non-criminal'-inducing attributes such as, caring, passive, maternal, affectionate and tender. However, there is a danger of, in effect, conflating three separate things into one:

1 being male in terms of biology;
2 being male in terms of ways of thinking and behaving;
3 the attributes supposedly defining masculinity.

And what of women? In some accounts, there is an implication that, because criminality is a product of masculine attributes, women who commit crime must be 'masculine'; in other words, 'abnormal'. On the other hand, both criminal *and* non-criminal men are viewed as 'normal'. A further dimension to this is that some analyses of men and crime have concentrated solely on masculinity (culture) and ignored the relevance of the male body (biology). These have been strongly criticized by Allen:

> The body is denied any place in the formation of subjectivity, consciousness, or personhood ... Behaviours and practices such as criminalities are thus investigated as solely matters of mind, attitude, influences, identities, cultural patterns. In an area of behaviour as sexed as criminalities, the fact that mainly persons with the sexed bodies of men predominate is accorded no significance.
>
> (Allen 1989: 31)

Developing theory

The last 20 years or so have seen a large growth in research and theory on the theme of masculinities and crime. For some (notably, Cain 1989, 1990; Smart 1990), taking their work in this direction offered a feminist alternative to what they saw as the 'masculinist' and modernist discipline of criminology (see Chapter 9). One of the most influential contributors to debates about masculinities is Connell (1987). He addresses issues of patriarchy and the male domination of women, but initially his work was developed around a critique of radical feminist analyses of male violence towards women, which he saw as essentializing the differences between men and women, and misleadingly characterizing all men as oppressors of women. In Connell's view, there exist multiple masculinities, and these are contingent upon 'race', class, sexual orientation and social circumstances. As a result, there are different male identities and 'masculine' forms of behaviour. He does though point out that some models of masculinity are highly admired because of their association with power, physical strength and wealth, attributes employed in the dominance of women, and other men. He describes these models as 'accredited' – John Wayne and Mohammed Ali were two examples of one type of accredited 'tough masculinity'. Later on he introduced the terms 'hegemonic' (i.e. dominant) and 'subordinated' (i.e. gay, 'weak') forms of masculinity (Connell 1995), seeing these as produced and reproduced in the social structure and culture of society, though over time subject to change. Focusing on the delinquent behaviour of young males, Messerschmidt (1993, 1997) developed Connell's work on 'hegemonic masculinity' within the context of what he called 'structured action theory'.

Hegemonic masculinity involves various accredited attributes, such as aggressiveness and competitive individualism, and these are part of the dominant culture into which males are socialized. Opportunities to accomplish masculinity and appropriate self-identity are provided by paid employment, authority over women, and (hetero) sexual prowess. However, legitimate opportunities are not equally distributed, therefore, some men turn to crime as an alternative means for achieving masculinity. This explanation of crime, based upon an individual's response to block opportunities, has strong echoes of R.K. Merton's 'strain theory (see Chapter 3). According to Messerschmidt, for some men crime is a way of 'doing masculinity'. He develops this further by arguing that the meaning of masculinity varies according to the individual's structural position in society, which is based on hierarchies of class and 'race', and this in turn influences the types of criminal, or other transgressive behaviour the individual engages in in order to 'do masculinity'. Thus, for example, among boys from lower-class minority ethnic groups, a lack of achievement in school, routine humiliation and a perceived lack of power means that they are more likely to 'do masculinity' through violent crime, such as street robbery. White, middle-class 'college boys', on the other hand, are more likely to engage in non-violent transgressive behaviour, such as heavy drinking or criminal damage.

The concept of 'hegemonic masculinity' has stimulated a good deal of critical debate over the years, as well as some revisions by Connell and Messerschmidt (2005) to their earlier formulations. One major criticism is that the concept is burdened with having to explain too much. As Collier (1998) points out, it refers to a list of 'masculine' attributes as well as the causes of male criminality, though much criminal behaviour does not in any obvious way require hegemonic masculine attributes. Many have criticized the concept for being tautological:

> Masculinity is depicted as both primary and underlying *cause* (or source) of a social effect (crime); and, simultaneously, as something which itself *results from* (after all, it is accomplished through) recourse *to* crime.
>
> (Collier 2004: 293, emphases in original)

Hood-Williams (2001) and Jefferson (1996) have argued that Messerschmidt's structured action theory is unable to explain the precise dynamics that lead particular men to commit particular types of crime – only some men, whatever their class or 'racial' background, decide to use crime to do masculinity. Criticizing structured action theory for being deterministic, Jefferson (1997, 2002) has developed a psycho-social theory that emphasizes male subjectivities. On this basis, he has explored how, depending on the situation, men embrace different understandings of masculinity in order to assuage their psychological anxieties. Many of these criticisms can be summed up as follows:

> ... we are left with many questions as to how 'masculine' qualities relate to what men do in concrete and material ways. These analyses also leave unanswered questions of the relationship of masculinity to the individual and the 'embodied social selves' of men. Further, they fail to help us understand the dimensions of the unities and differences among men.
>
> (Heidensohn and Gelsthorpe 2007: 388)

More recently, Connell and Messerschmidt (2005) have revised their work on masculinities in response to the various criticisms that emerged. Notably, they have placed much greater emphasis on cultural understandings of femininity *and* masculinity, acknowledging that one only has meaning in relation to the other. In addition, they have given more attention to masculinity in a globalized world and, given the different demands and anxieties that unfold as men go through life, the ways in which understandings of masculinity can over time change significantly.

Further reading

Some of the key texts are Connell, R.W. (1987) *Gender and Power*. Cambridge: Polity Press; Connell, R.W. (1995) *Masculinities*. Cambridge: Polity Press; Messerschmidt, J.W. (1993) *Masculinities and Crime*. Lanham, MD: Rowman and Littlefield; and Connell, R.W. and Messerschmidt, J.W. (2005) Hegemonic masculinity: rethinking the concept, *Gender and Society*, 19(6): 829–59.

A good overview of the field is provided by Jefferson, T. (1997) Masculinities and crime, in M. Maguire, R. Morgan and R. Reiner (eds) *The Oxford Handbook of Criminology*, 2nd edn. Oxford: Oxford University Press; and Part iv (Gender and the masculinity of crime) in Sumner, C. (ed.) (2004) *The Blackwell Companion to Criminology*. Oxford: Blackwell Publishing.

13   Positivism

Positivism is a theoretical perspective that takes the view that social life can be studied objectively and scientifically by employing research methods comparable to those used in the natural sciences. It first emerged in the early part of the nineteenth century, in the shape of sociological positivism, and the work of the Frenchmen Comte de Saint-Simon and Auguste Comte, the former credited with coining the word 'positivism', and the latter the word *sociologie*. Comte described sociology as the scientific study of society, and the ultimate task was to discover the social laws that governed the nature of society. The modernist project that began with the Enlightenment was now grounded in the fervent belief that social life could be understood and controlled through the application of rigorous scientific methods. It was this belief that was to underpin the development of positivist criminology.

In this chapter we examine the origins, early stages, and key features of a specifically criminological positivism that appeared in the late nineteenth century. By then three varieties of positivism were in evidence: sociological, biological and psychological. The basic premise of positivism is that criminal behaviour is caused by more or less deterministic factors over which the individual has little or no control. Whereas sociological positivism locates these factors in the social environment, biological positivism locates them in the body, and psychological positivism in the mind. Positivists were highly critical of the earlier classical criminology that had emerged out of the Enlightenment during the eighteenth century. For them, classical criminology was merely pre-scientific, philosophical speculation.

By the end of the nineteenth century and in the early twentieth century, positivism was the dominant criminological perspective in Europe, though it was the biological and psychological versions, rather than the sociological (in spite of its earlier appearance) that took centre stage. In the United States, though, sociological positivism was by the 1920s making significant contributions to criminology (see Chapter 4). Having said that, these three types of positivism did not exist in separate worlds and, as we shall see, biological positivism, for instance, incorporated ideas from both sociology and psychology. Positivism in all of its guises was to retain its dominant position within criminology for a considerable length of time. In fact, it was not until the 1960s that positivist criminology came to be seriously challenged (see Chapter 10). In the discussion that follows the focus is primarily on biological positivism. See discussions of sociological positivism and criminology in Chapters 3, 4 and 15.

One of the most famous figures in biological positivism is the Italian physician and physical anthropologist, Cesare Lombroso, whose writings were published in the late nineteenth century and early twentieth century. His most influential book was *Criminal Man* (*L'Uomo Delinquente*), originally published in 1876. Lombroso helped popularize what is in effect the most obvious, clear-cut example of positivist criminology. For him, the cause of an individual's criminal behaviour lies in their genetic make-up, and thus they are born criminals. He is particularly associated with the notion of *atavism*, together with the view that criminals can be identified on the basis of their physiological outward appearance and discernible irregularities in the brain. Influenced by Darwin's evolutionary theory, he believed that some individuals could be categorized as atavistic, meaning that because of their genetic make-up, they represent a throw-back to an earlier stage of human evolution. Such individuals, therefore, are seen as endowed with 'instincts' and desires suited to earlier, more primitive and harsher times, but out of sync, as it were, with modern societies. At the time there was a racist dimension to this view, in that many writers also argued that whole groups of indigenous peoples living in those parts of the world colonized by the European powers, and described as 'savages', represented examples of atavism. Lombroso's perspective on the atavistic criminal is well illustrated in his report of an autopsy that he carried out on a famous bandit called Vilella:

> At the sight of that skull, I seemed to see all of a sudden ... the problem of the nature of the criminal – an atavistic being who reproduces in his person the ferocious instincts of primitive humanity and the inferior animals. Thus were explained anatomically the enormous jaws, high cheek bones, prominent supercillary arches, solitary lines in the palms, extreme size of the orbits, handle-shaped or sensile ears found in criminals, savages and apes, insensibility to pain, extremely acute sight, tattooing, excessive idleness, love of orgies, and the irresistible craving for evil for its own sake, the desire not only to extinguish life in the victim, but to mutilate the corpse, tear its flesh and drink its blood.
>
> (Lombroso 1911: xiv–xv)

The inclusion of tattooing in this list of genetically determined physiological and psychological attributes appears odd, given that it is obviously a product of social learning. For Lombroso though tattoos were of special significance and he spent some time studying those individuals who had them. In his view, such individuals are much more likely to engage in anti-social behaviour, including crime, than those who have no tattoos.

It is important to add that following numerous revisions and additions, five editions of his book were eventually published, and the number of pages grew from a mere 200 in the first edition to over 3000 in the final one. It is clear that in this and other publications he was grappling with a variety of complex issues such as:

- the proportion of criminals who can be defined as 'atavistic';
- whether or not *all* criminal behaviour is caused by a person's (pathological) genetic make-up;
- whether *all* those genetically predisposed to criminality, that is, so-called 'born criminals' actually offend, and if not why not?

These intellectual ruminations led Lombroso to put forward four categories of criminal. First, there are the atavistic, born criminals discussed above; second, those who are mentally insane, or have what we describe nowadays as learning difficulties, together with alcoholics and epileptics; third, those given the intriguing title of 'criminaloids', which refers to individuals who commit crimes when suitable opportunities arise; and fourth, criminals seized by overwhelming passions arising from jealousy, anger, and so on. However, Lombroso did gradually temper his biological/genetic model some-what by recognizing the relevance of various social and environmental factors. None the less, the notion of the born criminal remained a significant dimension to his work, and he argued that around a third of criminals could be characterized as 'atavistic'. Of the four categories above, the first three are linked to genetic factors and are, in that sense, being characterized as 'born criminals'.

A number of Italian biological positivists – Ferrero, Ferri and Garofalo – worked with Lombroso during the late nineteenth century and early twenti-eth century, and were known collectively as the Italian School. Their influence spread throughout Europe, though much less so in Britain, where psychological positivism (or psychological medicine) took precedence over biological positivism. Thus by the late nineteenth century, classical criminol-ogy, which saw criminals as hedonistic, pleasure-seekers who, on the basis of free will, rationally weigh up the costs and benefits of offending, had been largely replaced by positivist criminology. Now, free will disappeared from the equation and criminals had become determined beings, forced into offending by biological or psychological factors outside of their control. Furthermore, by arguing that all offenders should be treated equally in a court of law; that is, they should be judged according to the seriousness of the offence, the classical school effectively disallowed any consideration of mitigating factors.

Positivism, on the other hand, opened the door to mitigation, given that offending arose from force of circumstance. Put simply, an offender is not really to blame for their offending. This, therefore, shifted the emphasis away from the punishment fitting the crime, towards the punishment (in the sense of 'treatment') fitting the criminal. In reality, though, courtroom processes and penal policy have been based on a mixture of the two approaches. The growth of positivism at that time was facilitated by a number of developments. Across Europe, all branches of science had gained in status, thus the voices of those criminologists promising to 'scientifically' determine the causes of crime became increasingly seductive. Concomitantly, the growing status of science, together with its technological accomplishments, encouraged the development of educational and training opportunities and a wider dissemination of knowledge, through learned societies and publications. Furthermore, a growth in the number of prisons created ready-made laboratories for the study of criminals.

Further developments

While positivist criminology embraces biology, psychology and sociology (and is certainly more sophisticated today than it was in the late nineteenth century), it does possess certain general defining features distinguishing it from other types of criminology. These can be summarized as follows:

- *Scientific methodology*: the use of scientific research methods in order to amass objective, factual knowledge regarding the social world, which is seen as existing 'out there' waiting to be discovered. The emphasis is on dispassionate observation and measurement, and the suspension of all personal opinions and values.
- *Causal-corrective orientation*: the use of scientific data to establish the causes of criminality and to develop appropriate interventions to correct the problem.
- *Determinism*: criminal behaviour does not result from voluntarism or free will; rather, the individual is compelled to commit crime due to biological, psychological or social forces outside of their control.
- *Difference*: criminals are viewed as being qualitatively different to non-criminals.
- *Pathology*: differences between criminals and non-criminals are a consequence of some 'sickness' or dysfunction of a biological, psychological or social nature.
- *Treatment/rehabilitation*: given that those individuals who commit crime are not at fault, as their behaviour was not freely chosen, then punishment is illogical. Responses should be directed at correcting the pathological sources of criminality, or treating those affected. Note that sociological positivism may identify problems in the social environments of offenders, such as poverty or lack of educational qualification, thus directing attention to aspects of social life.

It should be stressed that the concept of the atavistic criminal has been totally discredited by contemporary geneticists. Furthermore, no evidence has been found for the existence of a 'criminal gene'. However, the quest for some biological source of criminality – in other words, attempts to locate criminal dispositions within an individual's constitution – continued throughout the twentieth century and into the twenty-first century. Some biological positivists, notably in the late nineteenth century and early twentieth century, took a particular interest in tracing the genealogy of 'criminal families' and, on that basis, argued that criminal genes are passed on from one generation to the next. The two most famous studies were carried out in the United States: on the Juke family (Dugdale 1877) and the Kallikak family (Goddard 1914). Studies of this sort, which aimed to show that deviant behaviour had a genetic basis, are replete with references to 'feeblemindedness' (the title of Goddard's book), 'low intelligence' and 'degeneracy' and, along with other biological studies during that period in history, stimulated the growth of the eugenics movement in the United States and other parts of the world. Members of the movement took these studies to what they saw as their logical conclusion: interventions by the authorities to prevent those labelled 'degenerate', and so on from producing children. As a result:

> Viewed by the authorities as having 'bad blood lines', showing signs of 'feeblemindedness', belonging to the wrong 'race', being 'deviant' etc., hundreds of thousands of Americans were prevented from having children. At least 60,000 were coercively sterilised; thousands more were erroneously placed in mental institutions, not permitted to marry, and in some cases 'un-married' by state officials. It was not until the evidence of the Nazi extermination camps emerged that the eugenics movement began to lose influence, and when the war ended, what were formerly known as eugenics institutions became genetics institutions.
>
> (Tierney 2006: 60)

There is also a long history of research into the links between body shape and criminality, research based upon measuring large samples of criminals and comparing them with non-criminal control groups. One of the most famous (and much criticized) earlier studies was carried out by Hooton (1939). His basic argument was that in terms of strength and performance, the bodies of criminals are inferior to the bodies of non-criminals, the suggestion being that the physiology of the body somehow reflects a genetic predisposition to criminality. Sheldon (1949) focused on delinquent youth, arguing that their delinquency was passed on from their parents genetically, who also tended to have been delinquent. He also believed that, when compared with their non-delinquent counterparts, delinquent youths were much more likely to possess athletic, muscular bodies (which contradicted Hooton's findings). Glueck and Glueck (1950) put forward a similar argument. On a critical note, while some children will inherit a genetic propensity to develop athletic and muscular bodies from their parents, it is difficult to see how this is connected to an *inherited* predisposition towards criminal or delinquent behaviour. From an interactionist perspective, there are social processes that can explain what some see as genetically determined outcomes. First, an individual's body shape will contribute to the ways in which they are responded to in interactions with others as they grow up, and this will help shape an individual's identity, including in some cases a delinquent one. Second, rather than body shape providing evidence of inherited criminal motivations, those endowed with stronger bodies may be more likely to be recruited into and thrive in delinquent subcultures.

Over the years, many studies have sought to establish causal links between criminality and an individual's biology. Some have focused on the XYY sex chromosome syndrome (Price and Whatmore 1967); some have concentrated on psychoses and brain malfunction (Shah and Roth 1974); and some have explored the biochemical bases of criminal behaviour, analysing such things as sexual hormones (Ellis and Coontz 1990) and blood sugar levels (Virkkunen 1987). An influential recent development is socio-biology, an approach that examines the interaction between individuals' biological characteristics and their social and/or physical environment. One of the major figures in socio-biology is Mednick, whose work is mainly relevant to situations where, in spite of 'appropriate' socialization, an individual still engages in antisocial behaviour. In these cases, the antisocial behaviour is said to result from the individual having a 'sluggish' automatic nervous system (Mednick et al. 1987).

Other socio-biologists, such as Jeffery (1977), have concentrated on how individuals' genetically determined biological characteristics can interact detrimentally with their physical environment (e.g. in neighbourhoods that are highly polluted), leading to criminal behaviour.

Some critical points

The main criticisms directed at biological positivism can be summarized as follows:

- Concepts of 'crime' and 'criminal' are taken for granted and treated as if they possessed some inherent, essential qualities. Crime though is a relative concept, in that definitions of crime vary between one society and another, and between one time in history and another within the same society. Thus it is misleading to suggest that 'criminal' events reflect absolute or objective morality regarding right and wrong, or agreed understandings of harmfulness. Criminality is, therefore, being linked to forms of behaviour that over time are not fixed, but can be extremely fluid in terms of how they are judged.

- The variety of acts defined as criminal within a particular jurisdiction is enormous, thus generalized statements about the causes of 'crime' cannot be made. In practice, a fairly narrow range of crimes is involved – state crime, and corporate and white-collar crime are usually ignored.
- Research is carried out on apprehended and already processed 'criminals'. These though may not be representative of criminals (or types of criminal) in general. Furthermore, it is assumed that those selected for 'non-criminal' control groups actually are non-criminal.
- The meanings that individuals give to their behaviour and complex interactional processes are not taken into account, leading to highly deterministic accounts of social action.
- Social structure, including structures of power and conflict, as well as cultural and subcultural dimensions to social life, are ignored.
- It is extremely difficult to separate out, and measure, the relative importance of the various factors involved, including myriad social and psychological ones.
- Sometimes politicians and policy-makers have been tempted to embrace biological and psychological explanations of criminality, as they deflect attention away from causal factors located in social structure, or resulting from government policy itself. Sociological positivism though does direct attention to social structural issues.

Further reading

Two original texts by Lombroso are Lombroso, C. (1911) *Criminal Man*. New York: G.P. Putnam; and Lombroso, C. (1913) *Crime: Its Causes and Remedies*. Boston, MA: Little Brown. Also from this early period by a member of the Italian School is Ferri, E. (1901) *Criminal Sociology*. Boston, MA: Little Brown. Work from this period is examined by Shah, S.A. and Roth, L.H. (1974) Biological and psychophysiological factors in criminality, in D. Glaser (ed.) *Handbook of Criminology*. London: Rand McNally.

A more recent discussion from the perspective of genetic theory is Jones, S. (1993) *The Language of Genes*. London: Harper Collins. For an illuminating study of the eugenics movement, see Black, E. (2003) *War Against the Weak: Eugenics and America's Campaign to Create a Master Race*. New York: Four Walls Eight Windows. For a good, accessible discussion of biological and psychological positivism, see Hopkins Burke (2001) *An Introduction to Criminological*

Theory. Cullompton: Willan Publishing. The views of socio-biologists will be found in: Mednick, S.A. and Christiansen, K.O. (eds) (1977) *Biosocial Bases of Criminal Behavior.* New York: Gardner. Herrnstein, R.J. and Murray, C. (1994) *The Bell Curve: Intelligence and Class Structure in American Life.* New York: Free Press argue that a major cause of criminal behaviour is low IQ.

For a discussion of the place of positivism in the historical development of criminology, see Tierney, J. (2006) *Criminology: Theory and Context,* 2nd edn. Harlow: Pearson Longman.

14   Post-modernism

This chapter begins with a general discussion of post-modernism and an overview of some of the implications of post-modernist thought from the point of view of 'doing criminology'. Following this, there is a discussion of constitutive criminology, an approach to the study of crime that has been particularly influenced by post-modernist ideas (post-modern feminism is discussed in Chapter 9).

Broadly, the term post-modernism is used to describe:

- the nature of society, now described as 'post-modern', and seen as qualitatively different to an earlier 'modern' society;
- a variety of ideas, concepts and modes of analysis oriented towards an understanding of post-modern society, and thus described as post-modern thought. It should be noted though that post-modernism is 'best described as an area, a loose collection of themes, rather than as in itself a coherent philosophy' (Lea 1998: 165).

The foundations of post-modernism as an intellectual project lie in the second half of the twentieth century, in the work of an eclectic mix of writers and thinkers. These intellectual sources encompassed literary criticism, linguistic philosophy, art and architecture, psychoanalysis and social science. The work of various French, post-structuralist theorists that emerged in the 1970s was particularly influential; for example, Derrida (1976), Foucault (1977), Lyotard (1984) and Baudrillard (1988) – among these, Foucalt having the most influence in terms of subsequent developments in criminology. Post-structuralism represented a critique of structuralism. Structuralism is founded on the view that society is made up of observable 'structural' components, such as the institutions relating to economic, political and family life, which through their interconnections and functions constitute the overall social system. The belief is that modes of analysis based upon the logic, conceptual language, and methodologies of the social *sciences* can illuminate the nature of these deep structures and how they shape, or in some cases determine, social relations and behaviour. Thus from the perspective of structural Marxists, such as Althusser (1971), the capitalist economy, state and legal system have reality as structural entities, and are therefore analysed not in terms of individuals and their subjectivities, but in terms of rules, stable patterns, coherence and functional interdependence, which as a whole constitute a capitalist mode of production. Post-structuralists, on the other hand, prioritize individuals and their subjective understandings (i.e. agency), arguing that this is what gives meaning to the social world, not the structures that individuals happen to be caught up in. In so doing, they reject the idea that the social 'scientist', armed with their concepts, insights and privileged knowledge, can somehow gaze down on human society and discern what is 'really' going on.

The social world is not seen as an already existing, knowable entity 'out there'. For post-structuralists, what we refer to as society exists only in and through discourse – the language and texts that create it and give it 'reality'. For Foucault (1977), knowledge is created through language and, rather than being grounded in fixed, 'truthful' meanings, it is subjective and fluid. From this perspective, 'expert', intellectual discourses associated with particular disciplines, such as sociology and criminology, cannot lay claim to special status because of their knowledge about the 'real' world. This notion of the relativity of knowledge lies at the core of post-modernism, and hence the view, for example, that no one theoretical school can ever corner the market in 'correct' knowledge.

During the 1980s, post-modernist ideas were beginning to surface in design, fashion and architecture, and with them notions of irony, playfulness and pastiche. Architects, for instance, began to design buildings that broke free from received wisdom and rules regarding 'style' and 'taste', especially in relation to the brutally stark modernist structures that we now associate with the 1960s. 'Pastiche' was reflected in new kinds of building based upon a mixture of architectural styles, from the past and the present; these buildings that were no longer 'Victorian', or 'Georgian', and so on.

Although the American C. W. Mills (1959) seems to have been the first sociologist to use the term 'post-modern', it was the work of another American sociologist, Daniel Bell (1960, 1973), which was to have the most influence on subsequent sociological post-modernist thought. Forty years before the British Labour Party were to incorporate it into the 'third way' philosophy of New Labour, Bell introduced the phrase 'the end of ideology'. He used it to capture what he predicted would be a major, global transforma-tion in the nature of political belief systems: an end to 'extreme' political ideologies; specifically, Communism and National Socialism. As he saw it, this would result in a blurring of the traditional boundaries between the political Right and the political Left. Later on, he predicted the emergence of what he called 'post-industrial society', a society based upon a service industry and consumption, rather than manufacturing industry and 'fordist' production methods (hence the term 'post-fordist'). Both of these ideas were embraced by post-modernist thinkers, and used as part of a critique of modernist politics and economics which, as they saw it, were no longer relevant in the 'post-modern' world.

The critique of modernism

Modernism emerged during the seventeenth-century and eighteenth-century Enlightenment period (see Chapter 5), and continued to develop through the nineteenth and twentieth centuries. It was, as Morrison (1995: 453) says: 'underpinned by a faith in certain grand narratives ... particularly those of progress, self-advancement and emancipation'. A modernist view of the world is based on a belief in linear progress, that the material world and the social world can be controlled and gradually improved by applying rational scientific knowledge. During the nineteenth century, the modernist project had been further enhanced by the promises held out by positivist social science (see Chapter 13). From the perspective of positivism, scientific methods, comparable to those used in the natural sciences, can be used to study and make sense of the social world, with the ultimate aim of improving the sum of human happiness. By the end of the nineteenth century, positivism had turned its attention to the study of crime, and remained the dominant perspective in criminology up until the 1960s and the advent of new deviancy theory (see Chapter 10). Under the influence of positivism, traditional criminology focused on establishing the causes of crime, and then devising strategies aimed at controlling it. However, it was not positivism (and its so-called scientific methods) in itself that was criticized by post-modernism; after all, by the 1970s, criticisms of positivism were commonplace within criminology (e.g. on the part of phenomenologists, labelling theorists and neo-Marxists).

What attracted criticism (or, as post-modernists put it 'critique') was the entire modernist project, a project grounded in a belief in progress through the accumulation of rational, scientific knowledge and, at the same time, a growth in 'experts' who were privy to this knowledge and motivated by a commitment to improve people's lives. For post-modernists, the modernist belief in progress is entirely misplaced, and the modernist project has been a profound failure. While they acknowledge that science, technology and social planning have in some ways improved the quality of life for many people, this does not equate with 'progress'. The social and scientific developments associated with modernity have had, say post-modernists, many negative and extremely harmful consequences; for instance: innumerable wars and human destruction; the death camps of the Stalinist USSR and Hitler's Germany; degradation of the environment and global warming; and a massive growth in intrusive forms of surveillance and modes of social control.

However, for post-modernists, not only did the modernist project fail, during the latter part of the twentieth century, the societies that grew out of modernism underwent a qualitative transformation and in the process became (or are becoming) 'post-modern'. The main features of a post-modern society or 'condition' are:

- *Diversity, difference and the loss of the social*: the 'loss of the social' refers to a condition where previously stable institutions, such as traditional family and community life, patterns of work and class, have dissolved and no longer have salience in terms of providing a solid context within which people are socialized. Now, say post-modernists, all is change, fluidity and flexibility. Relatively fixed roles and ways of thinking based on, say, class position, have given way to plurality and an emphasis on identity rather than class. In a post-modern society, individuals are freed from traditional constraints on identities, lifestyles and modes of thought – these things can be explored and experimented with in ever changing situations, and no longer exist as a unified whole. The loss of definitive moral foundations to guide behaviour is one important dimension to this, given its implications for deviance (Gardiner 1996). This loss does not mean an end to morality, but it does mean that previously authoritative sources have disappeared. Post-modernists argue that the 'scientific' methodologies of modernism are incapable of making sense of a social world characterized by such diversity, fragmentation and a multiplicity of models of order. Foucault's work has relevance here in that he argues that power and control have become dispersed throughout society and are no longer monopolized by the state and its agencies. Thus while norms and values may have been detached from some absolute source, they still have a presence (as obligations and expectations, etc.) within, for example, the workplace, the community and among peer groups on the street.
- *Post-industrialism and post-fordism*: a post-industrial society describes a society where manufacturing industry and an emphasis on production have given way to one based on a service industry and consumption. This is sometimes referred to as 'post-fordism'; in other words, there has been a significant shift away from the forms of mass production associated with Henry Ford in the early part of the twentieth century; now flexibility is the key. Post-modernists argue that these developments have led to a transformation of the older class structure, making analyses of society rooted in class relations (such as a Marxist analysis) obsolete.
- *Hyper-consumerism*: for post-modernists, contemporary society is characterized not just by consumerism, but hyper-consumerism. The incessant pressure to consume not only provides the economic life-blood for a post-industrial society, it is a key ingredient in the production and reproduction of identities and lifestyles on the part

of consumers (see Chapter 8 for a discussion of the relationship between this and transgressive behaviour).

- *The end of ideology*: this returns us to Bell's notion of the 'end of ideology' and the dissolution or blurring of traditional understandings of 'left' and 'right'. It is as if the 'pick and mix' ethos of aesthetics, taste, identity and lifestyle has entered and captured the political arena.

- *Globalization*: this refers to a process whereby previously local or national phenomena relating to economic, political and cultural life, have been transformed into interconnected, global phenomena. Technological developments have facilitated the growth in mass and instantaneous communications and the rapid movement of people from one part of the world to another. Usually, particular emphasis is placed on economics; specifically, the growth in transnational, unregulated neo-liberal markets. Globalization is said to have led to increasing homogeneity among nations from the point of view of economics, politics and culture.

Repudiating modernist assumptions, ideas and modes of analysis, post-modernists argue that alternative – that is, 'post-modernist' – concepts, theories and methods are required to make sense of the social world. Broadly speaking, these can be summarized as follows:

- There is a rejection of grand narratives: some overarching, universalized, organizing principle or explanatory model. Within the context of modernism, grand narratives include notions of progress and self-advancement, as well as theoretical formulations such as Marxism.

- The idea that the social world exists 'out there' waiting to be understood, providing that appropriate concepts and methodologies are used, is also rejected. Particular disapprobation is reserved for positivism and its faith in rational and objective scientific analysis. Post-modernists, therefore, question the view, found in traditional criminology, that social life is orchestrated by stable institutions and processes constituting a patterned and ordered society, based upon equilibrium. For them, society is characterized by change, instability and contingency. There may be order, and yet it is always shadowed by, and subject to, disorder. From this perspective, it is futile to search for the causes of crime (or any other social behaviour), as normally understood.

- Rather than the rational actor found at the centre of modernist thought, post-modernists refer to the 'decentered' subject, a concept intended to illustrate that individuals are caught up in, and constrained by, language.

• Language or discourse is of particular importance for post-modernists. Unlike modernists, post-modernists take the view that the words used to give meaning to the world are not neutral artefacts that bring to light a 'real' understanding of the world. Rather, language forms of the basis of discourse, which represents bodies of knowledge, but these are only representations of versions of knowledge. Some of this knowledge may become privileged and widely accepted as 'correct', but that is a product of power, rather than inherent truthfulness. Discourses are communicated through various types of 'text' and, for post-modernists, a text never possesses one, absolute, 'real' meaning – it is always open to an infinite range of interpretations. The device of 'deconstruction' (Derrida 1976) is employed by post-modernists to, as it were, decode a text in order to bring to light the author's previously unspoken and unacknowledged values and prejudices. The modernist view that language is simply a neutral mechanism for engaging in social relations and making sense of the world is strongly rejected by post-modernists. Drawing on the psychoanalytical theories of Lacan (1981), they argue that the discourses that people use reflect and express their desires and understandings of who they are as human beings. They are, therefore, never neutral.

There are varieties of post-modernism, and continual internal developments and debates, making an attempt at a general overview extremely difficult. For instance, there are what have been called 'sceptical' and 'affirmative' versions of post-modernism. Sceptical post-modernism takes the view that all knowledge is relative and there is no way to determine the 'truth'. Affirmative post-modernism, however, takes a more positive view, and argues in favour of engaging with political programmes.

Post-modernism has attracted its fair share of criticism. Some have described it as an intellectual fad, filling a gap in the market left by Marxism falling out of favour. One such critic is Callinicos (1989), who goes on to argue that the apparently new ideas associated with post-modernism were already in evidence in the classical sociological theories of Marx, Durkheim and Weber. Along with others, he also argues that although post-modernists reject the idea of grand narratives, ironically, post-modernism is itself a grand narrative. There are those, such as Eagleton (1996), who are extremely critical of the post-modernist argument (especially in the case of the 'sceptical' version) that all accounts of the social world and all tastes in music, art and literature and so on, are equally valid. There is also a criticism summed up in the question: what is it for? In other words, outside of the realms of intellectual academia, what is its relevance in terms of political action and social policy? Finally, Cohen (1998: 101), looking back to the 1960s, makes the point that many of the key conceptual ideas in post-modernism (e.g.

deconstructionism) were present in the sociology of deviance 'well before Foucault made these subjects intellectually respectable'. Downes and Rock also take up this theme:

> There is a sense in which the sociology of deviance is born post-modernist, that is, in the emphasis it gives to the importance of accounts, hierarchies of credibility and vocabularies of motive. In the highly unequal division of labour that goes into the social construction of reality, sociologists of deviance have long aimed to redress the balance between those in and those outside power. The attempt, however, is to mediate between different accounts, rather than to grant them equal validity.
>
> (Downes and Rock 2007: 312)

Constitutive criminology

Constitutive criminology is particularly associated with Stuart Henry and Dragon Milovanovic (1994, 1996, 1999), and represents an 'affirmative' version of post-modernism, focusing specifically on issues of crime and criminality. Along with post-modernism in general, constitutive criminology has drawn on a wide range of intellectual sources and theories; for example, deconstructionism, discourse analysis, post-structuralism, topology theory, chaos theory and catastrophe theory. Even this cursory glance at some of its intellectual influences indicates that we are dealing with a highly complex theoretical formulation, one requiring, for instance, some competency in mathematics before it can be fully comprehended. Indeed, many commentators, including some academic criminologists, have said that it is too difficult to understand. There is no suggestion here that problems of comprehension should be blamed on an author's lack of ability to present material in clearly written English. The problem lies in the inherent complexity of the ideas, concepts and theories informing this type of criminology. Snider (2004: 245), for instance, writes: 'Henry and Milovanovic's (1999) almost incomprehensible (to me, at least) constitutive criminology ...'. While Colvin, in a review of one of their books, says: 'The reader who is not already familiar with post-modernist work and its often obscure language, however, will find it exceedingly difficult to extract the author's ideas'. Schwartz and Friedrichs (1994: 228) though are less generous: 'It is the difficulty of imagining how a body of work will ever attain a broad influence when the "style" of writing ... is so dense and so obscure that it is largely inaccessible to all'.

In spite of these observations, the following discussion endeavours to provide at least a broad overview of what constitutive criminologists are saying (hopefully, this will assuage any sense of foreboding on the part of readers).

To begin with, constitutive criminology works with its own definition of 'crime', one that is not dependent on the criminal law in a particular jurisdiction. Thus crime is not simply defined as, for example, behaviour that breaks the law. Other critical theorists have developed alternative definitions of crime, detached from criminal law definitions (see Chapter 7). For Henry and Milovanovic (1996: 116), 'crime' is 'the power to deny others their ability to make a difference'. Or, in other words: 'the harm resulting from humans investing energy in harm-producing relations of power. Humans suffering such "crimes" are in relations of inequality' (Lanier and Henry 1998: 283). Crime is therefore defined in terms of harm, and harm is manifested in the disrespect accorded to a 'victim' through the social actions of an 'offender': 'People are disrespected in numerous ways but all have to do with denying or preventing us becoming fully social beings' (Henry and Milovanovic 2006: 66). A 'fully social being' describes a condition where an individual has the freedom to engage with others and the world around them in the context of an absence of harm. Crime, therefore, comprises these key elements: inequalities in power, disrespect, harm and diminishing an individual's worth as a social being. Constitutive criminologists take this formulation further by distinguishing between 'crimes of reduction' and 'crimes of repression'. The former refers to crimes where the victim is left in deficit, due to being deprived of property or dignity (e.g. as in the case of a street robbery). The latter refers to crimes that block the opportunity for an individual to advance socially (e.g. racial discrimination).

Labelling theorists also take a constitutive approach to crime (and deviance), though here 'constitutive' has a different meaning to that found in constitutive criminology (see Chapter 10). For labelling theorists, crime is constituted by labelling processes, culminating in someone being legally defined as 'a criminal', and their behaviour as 'crime'. For constitutive criminologists, on the other hand, crime seems to be a quality of the act, and is therefore independent of labelling processes. One practical problem with this definition of crime is actually identifying specific examples. Given that 'harms', as defined by constitutive criminology, can range from the extremely trivial to the extremely serious (and victim perceptions are of crucial importance here), how is one to judge where the line between crime and non-crime is to drawn?

Rather than the *causes* of crime (a concept that runs counter to its theoretical position), constitutive criminology seeks to explore how crime is *co-produced*. Instead of attempting to specify particular social factors that cause (or at least influence) someone to become an offender, as traditional criminology does, constitutive criminologists take what they call a 'holistic' approach to show how crime is co-produced by society as a whole. In other words, crime is conceptualized as the product of a totality comprising social structure, culture and individuals. However, emphasis is placed on human agency, so that individuals are seen as active participants in the production and reproduction of social structure and culture, and in the fluid, contingent processes out of which are constructed particular forms of social behaviour, including criminal behaviour. Importantly, constitutive criminologists do not focus on one type of participant – say, the offenders, to find out 'why they did it' – rather, their analyses bring all participants who, from their perspective, are implicated in the constitution of crime, into the frame: offenders, victims, criminal justice personnel; in fact, anyone who contributes to, and consumes, discourses oriented towards the phenomenon of crime. Thus in the latter category, for instance, documentary and feature film-makers, writers, academic criminologists and cinema audiences can be found. Although constitutive criminologists have redefined crime, so that it is not necessarily equated with criminal law violation, this list suggests that they none the less perceive a significant overlap between their definition and a more formal, conventional definition.

All these are included because of the enormous importance placed on discourse and the discursive processes, right across society as a whole, that in combination constitute crime – hence 'constitutive criminology':

> This reconception of crime, offender, and victim locates criminality not in the person or in the structure or culture but in the ongoing creation of social identities through discourse and it leads to a different notion of crime causation. To the constitutive theorist, crime is not so much *caused* as *discursively constructed* through human processes, of which it is one.
>
> (Lanier and Henry 1998: 284, emphases in original)

Thus crime is located in particular social identities, themselves a product of crime-related discourses. According to constitutive criminologists, offenders are people who have constructed a particular sort of social identity, whereby they become 'an "excessive investor" in the power to dominate others ... and magnifying differences between themselves and others' (Lanier and Henry 1998: 284). Crime-related discourses found in the media are given special attention in terms of the co-production of crime.

Looked at from the point of view of its implications for justice policy, constitutive criminologists argue for 'replacement discourses': the deconstruction of existing discourses and their reconstruction or replacement by alternative discourses on crime that possess less harmful meaning. One example of this is Barak's (1999) 'newsmaking criminology'. Here the argument is that the discourses of academic criminology, while not representing some higher 'truth' (an idea of course rejected by post-modernists), should be incorporated into the discourses of the news media in order to provide alternative conceptualizations and accounts of crime, offenders and victims. The ultimate aim is construct discourses that are less harmful *vis-à-vis* offenders and victims. Another example relates to the way in which a courtroom operates. As Vold et al. (2002) illustrate, both the offender's and the victim's narrative accounts are translated by professionals, such as barristers and judges, into an established legalistic narrative – 'legalese' – that conforms with the discursive expectations of the court. For constitutive criminologists, this process renders the accounts of victims and offenders 'invisible'; that is, it is exclusionary in character.

Further reading

Useful texts on post-modernism are Baudrillard, J. (1988) *Selected Writings*. Stanford, CA: Stanford University Press; Harvey, D. (1989) *The Condition of Post-modernity: An Enquiry into the Origins of Cultural Change*. Oxford: Blackwell Publishing; Rosenau, P.M. (1992) *Post modernism and the Social Sciences: Insights, Inroads, and Intrusions*. Princeton, NJ: Princeton University Press. For an exploration of Foucault's post-structuralism, see Foucault, M. (1980) *Power/Knowledge: Selected Interviews and Other Writings 1972–77* (ed. C. Gordon). Brighton: Harvester Press.

Notwithstanding their complexity, two major texts on constitutive criminology are Henry, S. and Milovanovic, D. (1996) *Constitutive Criminology: Beyond Postmodernism*. London: Sage Publications; and Henry, S. and Milovanovic, D. (eds) (1999) *Constitutive Criminology at Work: Applications to Crime and Punishment*. New York: State University of New York Press. There is a more accessible, though much shorter, discussion in Chapter 12, Lanier, M.M. and Henry, S. (1998) *Essential Criminology*. Boulder, CO: Westview Press. For a critical analysis of the relevance of constitutive criminology to policy, see Cowling, M. (2006) Post modern policies? The erratic interventions of constitutive criminology, *The Internet Journal of Criminology* (www.internetjournalofcriminology.com/Cowling).

15   Right Realism

Right realism is a neo-conservative type of criminology and is particularly associated with the American, James Q. Wilson. As a policy adviser to President Reagan during the 1980s, he was strongly positioned to have his ideas on crime taken seriously and acted upon by powerful individuals, which is precisely what happened. While many theorists in criminology can be situated within either a positivist or classical tradition, that is, their work is oriented towards either a positivist concern with the causes of criminality, or a classical concern with crime prevention, Wilson's work has reflected each of these traditions. Taken together, these two dimensions provided the basis for right realism (see Chapters 5 and 13 for further discussion).

Working in partnership with Herrnstein (Wilson and Herrnstein 1985), he developed a neo-positivist, bio-social explanation of the causes of criminality. In other words, criminality was seen as resulting from the interrelationship between biology and social environment. The argument was that because of their genetic make-up, some individuals are more likely than others to engage in criminal behaviour. However, in tandem with this, they also argued that this genetic predisposition could be controlled through appropriate social conditioning in the family, school, and so on. According to Wilson and Herrnstein though the problem was that some families and communities were inadequate to the task, and pointed their fingers at the underclass in general – seen as the major source of crime – and single-parent families in particular. We can see here an indication of how Wilson and Herrnstein tapped into, and perhaps helped ferment, commonsense, populist understandings and agendas among sections of the American public and importantly neo-conservative politicians. It is also worth noting that a decade later, Herrnstein and Murray (1994) argued in their book *The Bell Curve* that black people and Latinos were, when compared with white people, handicapped by having lower, genetically determined IQs; hence, according to the authors, their over-representation within the so-called underclass and their greater propensity to engage in criminal behaviour. Clearly, these arguments proved, to put it mildly, to be controversial. Needless to say, the authors are neither black nor Latino.

However, it was Wilson's work on the prevention of crime, rather than the causes of criminality, which was destined to have the most influence on both academic criminology and criminal justice policy. Specifically, his work played a major role in the subsequent development of what Young (1988) dubbed 'administrative criminology' in Britain and the United States, a site where the concerns of some academic criminologists and criminal justice policy-makers became intimately intertwined. This dimension to Wilson's work reflected a desire to develop a 'realistic' approach to dealing with the crime problem, which meant focusing on crime prevention, rather than on attempting to address what he saw as the bio-social causes of criminality. Clearly, outside of a eugenics programme, nothing could be done to alter an individual's genetic make-up. As far as an individual's social environment is concerned, Wilson had a jaundiced view of social welfare programmes aimed at improving the life experiences and chances of the poor, and argued that the social, economic and cultural transformations required to ensure that appropriate social conditioning took place would not only be impractically epic in scale, but also politically and morally unpalatable. Thus in line with administrative criminology in general, while there is an acknowledgement that crime is linked to various causal factors, these causal factors are in effect made irrelevant (thereby echoing the ideas associated with the early classical school). The existence of criminally motivated individuals is taken as given, and the focus is on the practical ways in which such individuals can be prevented from translating their motivations into criminal behaviour.

Right realism focuses very specifically on street crime, such as mugging and burglary, seen as the type of crime that citizens are especially concerned about. It is grounded in a critique of previous liberal positivist policies in the United States (and by implication many other societies) for failing to deal with it. Wilson and others (see Wilson and Kelling 1982, 1989; Kelling and Coles 1996) pointed out that in spite of a large investment in both social and criminal justice policies, a significant amount of which was directed at deprived urban neighbourhoods, from the 1960s onwards crime continued to rise inexorably. They also pointed out that this rise in crime happened to coincide with a sustained increase in standards of living. From this perspective, improved social welfare programmes and a more affluent society had failed to deliver any dividend in terms of reductions in predatory crime. What was required, they said, was a more realistic and tougher approach to the crime problem, again indicating the populist appeal of right realism.

Wilson and Kelling (1982, 1989) were particularly interested in those neighbourhoods where community ties had weakened significantly and informal modes of social control were ceasing to be effective. According to Wilson and Kelling, in such neighbourhoods people's lives are blighted by the gradual encroachment of disorder and minor criminality, with an increase in 'problem' families, unruly youth, incivilities and the inward migration of marginalized groups such as the homeless, street beggars and people with drink problems; what is left of the 'community' is seen as being under siege from disreputable 'others'. Hand in hand with this are signs of physical deterioration manifested in, for instance, abandoned vehicles, litter and graffiti – a neglected and decaying physical environment sending out the wrong signals, and symbolically encapsulated in the title of the article in which they first floated these ideas: 'Broken Windows' (Wilson and Kelling 1982). Under these circumstances, members of the community increasingly withdraw into their homes or, if they have the resources, move to another neighbourhood. Thus a vicious and downward spiral of social and physical decline is set in motion, leading eventually to a situation where more and more predatory criminals move in, creating a neighbourhood that now has serious problems of crime and disorder.

This evocative model of neighbourhood decay and descent into lawlessness is rather different from that put forward by the Chicago School at an earlier period in the twentieth century (see Chapter 4). For Wilson and Kelling, high crime areas result from an invasion of disreputable individuals, whose criminality is rooted in bio-social factors. The Chicago School, on the other hand, pointed to the social structural features of the criminal area as the source of the problem, rather than the individuals living there. Indeed, a central argument from the Chicago School was that when people left such areas they did not take their criminality with them, while from a bio-social perspective, criminals carry their criminality around with them like an albatross nesting on their shoulder.

For Wilson and Kelling, a descent into high levels of crime could be prevented, providing that action was taken before a neighbourhood reached the tipping point in terms of social and physical decline, and the police were earmarked to play a central role. What they called for was a return to a more traditional order maintenance police role, one based upon high visibility community patrols. Rather than focus their resources on crime-fighting, they argued that the police should concentrate on dealing with the sources of disorder – incivilities, unruly youth, the homeless, and so on, referred to above – in a firm manner. In short, 'zero tolerance' policing. With this kind of support, they said, community ties would be strengthened and informal social controls reactivated, with a corresponding improvement in the quality of life. An integral part of this process would be that people would begin to take responsibility for reversing the physical deterioration of the neighbourhood: they would, as the slogan puts it, revert back to 'mending broken windows'.

Although many found Wilson and Kelling's reasoning seductively convincing, it did also stimulate a great deal of critical debate. The policing of 'order' rather than 'crime' raises issues relating to the police officer's legal mandate:

> ... if the police are allowed on such a loose mandate to control all manner of activities, it is very difficult to make them accountable

and ensure that they act with integrity. It also opens the possibility of discriminatory decisions by police officers, or at least of claims of such by members of the public.

(Williams 2004: 426)

Wilson and Kelling have also been criticized for concentrating on a reduction in conventional predatory crime as the ultimate goal and, in the process, ignoring the crimes of the powerful, for example, corporate crime. Others have questioned whether disorder leads to high crime levels, rather than vice versa, or is there a symbiotic relationship between the two? Some commentators criticized their analysis for detaching what is happening in these neighbourhoods; for example, high unemployment from a wider, and indeed global, context of structural social and economic change (Matthews 1992a). This raises important issues relating to the marginalized or disreputable individuals selected for disapprobation and the targets of zero tolerance policing. As Lilly et al. put it:

> The theory's potential downside, however, is its implicit disinterest in why communities have people who are homeless, panhandling for money, alcoholic, mentally ill, loitering on street corners, and willing to commit predatory crimes. There is little consideration that these personal conditions were not created by social disorder but rather developed while growing up in families and communities affected by structural inequality and concentrated disadvantage.

(Lilly et al. 2007: 259)

It also raises the question of where such people are supposed to move to. The likelihood is that they will end up in those neighbourhoods that for Wilson and Kelling have gone beyond the tipping point, neighbourhoods where crime and disorder have reached such proportions that it is too late to start repairing broken windows. As they see it, the only option in these neighbourhoods is tough law enforcement, backed up by the certainty of punishment, which translates into punitive prison sentences.

Wilson, along with other right realists, reject what is seen as the 'excuse-making' industry – liberal positivist explanations that linked criminality to social circumstances. For right realists, the source of the crime problem lay with disreputable individuals who made a rational choice to exploit criminal opportunities and commit predatory crime (this is the core argument of administrative criminology). Such individuals are, therefore, seen as being fully responsible for their actions, and such things as poverty or unemployment cannot be used to excuse their behaviour. However, Wilson's argument that some individuals are predisposed towards criminality, because of a combination of genetic endowment and social conditioning, *is* congruent with the view that the causes lie outside of individuals' control. If this is the case, then it suggests that they are not to blame. It also poses questions regarding the concept of *rational* choice in this formulation, and this is discussed in Chapter 2. Another problem arises from the central argument that individuals who commit crime are blameworthy and deserve the punishment commensurate with making a bad decision. From this perspective, the social, economic and cultural contexts in which crime occurs simply melt away. And yet Wilson and Kelling believe that crime is more likely to occur in poorer, deprived neighbourhoods, which suggests that living in such neighbourhoods, rather than others, is hardly irrelevant from the point of view of criminal motivations.

Analyses of crime and disorder by right realists were clearly in accord with commonsense, populist and authoritarian sentiments among many American citizens, including neo-conservative politicians. Individuals, rather than 'society', were blameworthy and deserved strong punishment; social and economic deprivation provided no excuses; liberal, welfare-oriented policies had failed, so cut-backs in welfare spending appeared to be justified; and local communities, with a little help from the police, should take responsibility for social control in their neighbourhoods. Although the arguments from right realism have generated a great deal of criticism, especially from liberal and critical criminologists, these criticisms are not based upon a callous indifference to the myriad problems, including problems of crime and disorder, faced by people living in economically and socially deprived neighbourhoods; in fact, quite the opposite. There are many neighbourhoods that, as a result of global, national and local processes, enter into a period of decline. One symptom may be a rise in predatory crime and other forms of problematic behaviour, such as drug-dealing and prostitution, which severely disrupt the civilities and orderliness of everyday life. Such developments, which obviously create significant problems and anxieties for residents, are not taken lightly by critics of right realism. However, taking these things 'seriously' as, for instance, left realism does (though with a more progressive agenda than right realism – see Chapter 11) is only a starting point. The key issues concern how these developments are understood and explained, and what the implications are in terms of policy interventions.

Further reading

The major right realist text emphasizing the biological basis of criminality, and the over-representation of criminality among the 'underclass' is Wilson, J.Q. and Herrnstein, R.J. (1985) *Crime and Human Nature: The Definitive Study of the Causes of Crime*. New York: Simon and Schuster. For a strident critique, see Gibbs, J.P. (1985) Review essay: crime and human nature, *Criminology*, 23:

381–8. In Wilson, J.Q. (1985) *Thinking About Crime*. New York: Vintage Books, the author sets out his right realist agenda.

The 'broken windows' thesis is outlined in Wilson, J.Q. and Kelling, G.L. (1982) Broken windows: the police and neighborhood safety, *Atlantic Monthly*, 249(3): 29–38. More up-to-date discussions are: Kelling, G.L. and Coles, C.M. (1996) *Fixing Broken Windows: Restoring Order and Reducing Crime in Our Communities*. New York: Simon & Schuster; Kelling, G.L. (1999) Broken windows, zero tolerance and crime control, in P. Francis and F. Penny (eds) *Building Safer Communities*. London: Centre for Crime and Justice Studies. Useful critiques are: Lilly, J.R., Cullen, F.T. and Ball, R.A. (2007) *Criminological Theory: Context and Consequences*, 4th edn. Thousand Oaks, CA: Sage, and Matthews, R. (1992) Replacing 'broken windows': crime, incivilities and urban change, in R. Matthews and J. Young (eds) *Issues in Realist Criminology*. London: Sage Publications. Critical reviews of zero tolerance policing are provided by: Eck, J. and Maguire, E. (2000). Have changes in policing reduced violent crime? An assessment of the evidence, in A. Blumstein and J. Wallman (eds) *The Crime Drop in America*. Cambridge: Cambridge University Press, and Harcourt, B.E. (2001) *Illusions of Order: The False Promise of Broken Windows Policing*. Cambridge, MA: Harvard University Press.

16　Subcultural Theory

Clarke et al. provide a useful definition of culture (all were members of the Birmingham Centre for Contemporary Cultural Studies, and their work is returned to below, along with a more detailed examination of the concept of culture):

> The 'culture' of a group or class is the peculiar and distinctive 'way of life' of the group or class, the meanings, values and ideas embodied in institutions, in social relations, in systems of beliefs, in mores and customs, in the uses of objects and material life … A culture includes the 'maps meaning' which make things intelligible to its members … Culture is the way the social relations of a group are structured and shaped: but it is also the way those shapes are experienced, understood and interpreted.

> (Clarke et al. 1976: 9)

Studies of subcultures focus on the cultural attributes, as indicated above, associated with particular, identifiable groups in society. They constitute *sub*cultures because these cultural attributes are seen as different to those of the wider society. The notion of *deviant* or *delinquent* subcultures is used to designate specific social groups whose members share a culture that encourages, is conducive to, or requires deviant or delinquent behaviour. The wider society, against which such groups are referenced, is often described as 'mainstream', or 'conventional', or 'conformist', or even 'middle-class'. The notion of youth subculture can be differentiated from that of youth culture in that while the latter refers to cultural attributes widely dispersed among a younger generation (involving, for instance, music, styles of dress and hairstyles), the former focuses on specific youth subcultural formations such as skinheads, punks or Goths.

Subcultural strain theory

The early versions of subcultural theory, which emerged in the 1950s and early 1960s in the United States, took the form of subcultural strain theory. Here, delinquent subcultures are seen as resulting from 'strains' in the lives of those involved. At a key moment, usually early adolescence, these strains become particularly pertinent, and the formation of delinquent subcultures represents a way of dealing or coping with the problems associated with them. The classic study from this period is Cohen's (1955) *Delinquent Boys*. There are some similarities with Merton's version of strain theory (discussed in Chapter 3), in that both Cohen and Merton link the source of strains to the nature of American society itself. However, Cohen's work can be distinguished from Merton's in three important ways. First, unlike Merton, who explored the deviant reactions of the individual to strain, Cohen explored group reactions in the shape of subcultures. Second, whereas Merton emphasized the instrumental motivations behind deviant reactions (i.e. they were directed at achieving material rewards), Cohen argued that typical adolescent delinquency is malicious and non-instrumental (involving, for instance, fighting and criminal damage). And third, unlike Merton, Cohen introduced a psychological dimension to his theory – what he calls 'psychogenic factors' – seeing these and subcultural factors working in combination 'in most cases'. Therefore, some boys, due to psychogenic factors, are seen as being more likely to turn to delinquency than others. Cohen was also influenced by the concept of differential association developed by Edwin Sutherland during the 1940s as a key element of his social learning theory (Sutherland and Cressey, 1970). It explains delinquency in terms of the influences arising from interactions with significant others, whose norms and values encourage delinquent behaviour (see Chapter 4).

Although Cohen was quick to point out that not all lower-class boys engaged in delinquency, and that middle-class boys were not immune to its attractions, he did none the less see delinquency as 'typically' concentrated among lower-working-class boys (he describes such boys as 'corner boys' – a term he borrowed from Whyte ([1943] 1955). In Cohen's account, this results from the way in which status is ascribed to individuals in American society. It is, he says, a society dominated by mainstream, middle-class standards relating to such things as educational prowess, demeanour and speech, against which all individuals are judged. Compared with other sections of society, the home and family background of lower-class boys and indeed, the entire milieu in which they grow up is seen as culturally deficient, thus their socialization fails to provide sufficient resources to compete on equal terms in the status stakes. As a consequence, and usually coinciding with early adolescence, such boys experience 'status frustration'. This, of course, would not occur if the boys were unconcerned about achieving status according to middle-class standards. However, a key dimension to Cohen's theory is that in general lower-class boys do value middle-class status, and *are* concerned about 'the contempt or indifference of others' (Cohen 1955: 123) they are faced with when they fail to achieve it. When this happens, they experience, in Cohen's words, a 'problem of adjustment':

> To the degree to which he values middle-class status, either because he values the good opinion of middle-class persons or because he

has to some degree internalised middle-class standards himself, he faces a problem of adjustment and is in the market for a 'solution'.

(Cohen 1955: 119)

Cohen argues that there are three ideal type 'solutions' available to the lower-class corner boy:

1   *Stable corner boy*: here the response is based upon hedging one's bets and in effect making the best of a bad job. It may involve minor delinquent acts, but the boy is careful not to stray too far from conventional norms.
2   *College boy*: this is a boy with aspirations of middle-class status and, therefore, seeks to achieve such status through educational success.
3   *Delinquent boy*: it is boys in this category that Cohen's study focuses on. For them, the solution to a lack of middle-class status lies in the formation of a delinquent subculture.

In his analysis of the third of these, the delinquent boy, Cohen uses the concept of 'reaction formation', a psychological concept that originated in the work of Freud. It refers to a situation where the failure to achieve something that is desired – in this case middle-class status – leads to an individual vehemently rejecting what had previously been an object of desire. The delinquent boy does not reject the idea of achieving status *per se;* rather, he joins others in the same position and forms a delinquent subculture, and the subculture is now the source of status, though now it is no longer based upon middle-class standards. According to Cohen, the strength of feeling is so strong that the subculture is in fact a contraculture, in that its norms and values are inversions of middle-class norms and values, and towards which there is now extreme hostility. The delinquent activities associated with the subculture – fighting, criminal damage, and so on – express this hostility and importantly provide a source of status for the boys. Status is now ascribed according to the standards of the subculture.

A further example of American subcultural strain theory from that period is Cloward and Ohlin (1960). As with Cohen, they too draw on the work of Merton and Sutherland, though they also introduce ideas from Durkheim (see Chapter 3). A common thread running through the work of Merton, Cohen, and Cloward and Ohlin is the strain arising from thwarted ambition, within the context of a society that promises, though fails to deliver, equality of opportunity. Following Durkheim, the assumption is that in the absence of strain; that is, in a meritocracy where reward matches ability, the likelihood of deviant or delinquent behaviour would be reduced accordingly. Cloward and Ohlin though differ from Cohen by arguing that strain is more likely to be felt by those lower-class boys who aspire to achieve middle-class status and, therefore, seek to compete with their middle-class counterparts in the spheres of education and employment. Consequently, for Cloward and Ohlin it is those described as 'college boys' by Cohen who are most at risk of engaging in delinquency. These lower-class boys, they say, tend to be more intelligent than others from the same social class and, as a result, will have been encouraged to 'better themselves'. Unfortunately, as they pursue this pathway, they experience strain arising from the fact that achieving success is not based simply on one's 'ability'. Other factors, such as having the right contacts, or accent, or social background enter into the equation, factors that place the boys in a significantly disadvantaged position. This, say Cloward and Ohlin (and reflecting ideas from Durkheim and Merton), creates for some a strong sense of moral injustice and anger, to the extent that they react by ceasing to be committed to the norms and values of middle-class society. In this formulation, it is these angry failures who are the most likely candidates to join delinquent subcultures.

Interestingly, Cloward and Ohlin pursue their analysis by arguing that the world of deviant subcultures mirrors that of conventional society, in that it exhibits its own structural inequalities. *Criminal* subcultures are associated with more tightly organized lower-class neighbourhoods, where adult criminals keep the younger delinquents in check (e.g. by controlling conflict between gangs) in order to prevent their largely property crime activities coming to the attention of a wider audience. *Violent* subcultures are found in more disorganized neighbourhoods where these controls are significantly less effective. At the bottom of the pecking order are *retreatist* subcultures, which are mainly associated with illicit drug use.

Taking stock of the above studies raises a number of critical points:

- The *raison d'état* of subcultural strain theory is that lower-class delinquents early on in their lives internalize a middle-class value system, typically desire middle-class status, then as a result of being thwarted in this quest (i.e. experience 'strain') turn to delinquency. There are two fundamental questions in relation to this. First, does delinquency require 'strain'; in other words, does it necessarily result from something going 'wrong'? And, second, do lower-class boys *typically* desire middle-class status at some earlier stage in their lives? This is looked at in more detail in the discussion of cultural diversity theory below.
- The identification of most delinquency with lower-class males does reflect the story told by official crime statistics, though these may overstate their rates of delinquency when compared to middle-class males (see Hirschi 1969).
- Cohen has been criticized for equating non-delinquent, mainstream values with middle-class culture, which suggests conversely that the values of lower-class culture are inherently delinquent in nature. From this perspective, lower-class members of American society can

only be 'saved' from delinquency by internalizing (and holding on to) middle-class values. Thus we have to question this negative assessment of lower-class culture and the perhaps idealized assessment of so-called middle-class culture. Furthermore, if lower-class culture is associated with delinquent values, why does the onset of delinquent behaviour require the previous internalization of middle-class values?

• Cohen has also been criticized for overstating the degree of hostility towards middle-class culture (arising from 'reaction formation') felt by delinquent boys (Short and Strodtbeck 1965; Downes 1966).

Cultural diversity theory

Cultural diversity theory has its roots in the work of the Chicago School carried out in the 1920s and 1930s (see Chapter 4). Unlike subcultural strain theory, cultural diversity theory does not see lower-class delinquency as resulting from thwarted ambitions following the internalization of middle-class values. Rather, delinquent behaviour and subcultures are seen as developing 'naturally' within specific 'criminal areas', or neighbourhoods in towns and cities. Within these socially and economically deprived areas, it is argued, children are socialized into a set of norms, values and beliefs at variance with those of mainstream society, norms, values and beliefs that allow and encourage delinquency. Thus delinquent values are 'culturally transmitted' from one generation to the next.

Broadly speaking, it was this approach, rather than subcultural strain theory, which influenced early sociological studies of delinquency in Britain. The first of these studies to refer to the concept of subculture was carried out in a deprived area of Liverpool by Mays (1954). In fact, Mays argued that the area itself constituted a subculture characterized by norms and values strongly at variance with those of the rest of the city. Almost without exception, the youngsters brought up in the area to a greater or lesser extent engaged in delinquency, which was seen as a normal outcome of their socialization into the delinquent norms and values of the area. In this study, Mays makes explicit reference to the absence of 'strains', as understood by Cohen, in the boys' lives. They experienced strains or tensions in the sense that they faced a range of problems resulting from social and economic deprivation; however, these were not related to status frustration resulting from a failure to succeed according to middle-class standards. Morris (1957) came to a similar conclusion in his study of a deprived 'criminal area' in the London borough of Croydon. He did though give particular attention to the confluence of social class and the local municipal housing market. Delinquency, he said, was not distributed evenly among lower-working-class families; rather, it was concentrated in particular 'criminal' neighbourhoods, and these were the result of the local authority's policy of lumping so-called 'problem families' together on the same estates.

In an earlier study set in the English Midlands, Carter and Jephcott (1954) also pointed to differences within the lower working class measured in terms of 'respectability', and hence amounts of delinquency among young males. They found that residential patterns were based upon a central division between the 'roughs' and the 'respectables', and this was the outcome of decisions made by the respective groups regarding where they wanted to live. Further British studies also rejected the notion of status frustration as an explanation of delinquency, at least in a British context. Again, the general conclusion was that delinquency was a 'normal' outcome of growing up in certain areas (see Miller 1958 who spoke of the 'focal concerns' of such areas; that is, the key values linked to understandings of maleness and toughness, and Willmott 1966).

The most sophisticated early British study to develop an explanation of delinquency based upon cultural diversity theory was that of Downes (1966). In this study, set in the working-class areas of Stepney and Poplar, in the East End of London, the structural bases and cultural nuances surrounding what he saw as 'typical' English delinquent subcultures are brought to life. Downes' delinquent boys had not internalized middle-class values (e.g. as a result of schooling), nor did they desire middle-class status. Thus there was no 'problem of adjustment' or 'status frustration' as described by Cohen. Delinquent behaviour was rooted in the norms and values that pervaded the unskilled manual working-class families and neighbourhoods in which they lived. Young boys growing up in these neighbourhoods, says Downes, are from an early age socialized into a culture infused with notions of toughness, daring, adventure and excitement; they are also neighbourhoods where criminal activities are commonplace among all age groups. There was no desire on the part of the boys to 'escape' from this into a middle-class, or even skilled working class, occupation and lifestyle. In this sense, there was no resentment or frustration with their working-class status, though they were dissatisfied with various aspects of their lives. In common with most people, they would unsurprisingly have welcomed more money in their pockets, but within the context of their subcultural value system, a college education, followed by a middle-class occupation were not seen as desirable aspirations. However, this disinterest in a middle-class lifestyle did not reflect overt hostility towards the wider society. As Downes says, there was no evidence of the 'reaction formation' documented by Cohen. The boys were essentially conformists in that they conformed to the cultural values in which they were immersed, rather than rebels (with or without a cause) against society.

Parker (1974) paints a similar picture in his study of young people in a working-class area of Liverpool. The boys in Downes' study were also profoundly dissatisfied with their experiences of the education system and, later on (after leaving school at the earliest opportunity) the unskilled work into which they went. As Downes explains, in this situation where they 'dissociate' themselves from schooling and the world of work, the core problem faced by the boys was finding some space and activities in their lives through which they could live out the values into which they had been socialized; it is here that we see the emergence of a 'delinquent solution'. With much of the day taken up with either school or work, only their leisure time provides an opportunity to live out these values, and thereby find some meaning and satisfaction. This enormous emphasis placed on leisure and what it should deliver creates what Downes describes as an 'edge of desperation'. For the boys, many legitimate leisure activities that could deliver these values were effectively out of bounds, either because they lacked the money required, or the activities themselves were not seen as attractive. There is, however, one 'area of excitement to which he has absolutely untrammelled access' (Downes 1966: 249), and that area is delinquency.

Criticisms of subcultural theory

Subcultural theories of delinquency, such as those discussed above, have attracted a number of criticisms, summed up by Heidensohn (1989) as follows:

- They tend towards *deterministic* explanations in the sense that young working-class males are seen as in effect passively internalizing delinquent values.
- Proponents of subcultural theory ignore the more-or-less conventional majority and turn the spotlight on the more spectacular minority involved in relatively serious delinquent behaviour. There is, therefore, a problem of *selectivity*.
- They fail to address the implications of *gender*, thus issues of masculinity and femininity remain unexplored.
- The tendency towards deterministic explanations is connected to a lack of attention being paid to *conformity*: why do others, living in the same social environment, avoid internalizing delinquent values?
- While Cohen's version of strain theory avoids this, other subcultural theorists generally conceptualize delinquent youth lacking in moral regulation, as if they lived in *anomic* enclaves, untouched by the wider society and conventional values (see Chapter 3 and, discussed below, Sykes and Matza 1957).

The Birmingham Centre for Contemporary Cultural Studies

A large amount of work on youth subcultures came out of the Birmingham Centre for Contemporary Cultural Studies (BCCCS) during the 1970s. However, while 'culture' and 'subculture' were key explanatory concepts, the work was situated within a neo-Marxist theoretical framework and, although looked at in this chapter, can be seen as part of the critical tradition in criminology (see Chapter 7). Analyses of youth subcultures, such as teddy boys, mods, rockers and skinheads, placed the subcultures within the context of class inequality and conflict, and a dominant (or hegemonic) culture. An early and sophisticated example was Cohen's (1972) study of the mod and skinhead subcultures that emerged in working-class neighbourhoods in the East End of London during the 1960s. This was a time of profound social and economic change in these neighbourhoods, and Cohen argued that the subcultures represented an attempt, on a symbolic level, to recapture a rapidly disappearing sense of community.

Although some studies concerned themselves with specifically delinquent subcultures, the majority focused on 'deviant' working-class subcultures, which were counter-posed against a hegemonic, ruling-class culture/ ideology. Youth subcultures were analysed in terms of their cultural attributes – ways of thinking and behaving, modes of dress, hairstyles, musical affiliations, argot, and so on – attributes which, taken as a whole, constituted a particular subcultural *style*. Using ethnographic research, the aim was to penetrate below surface appearances and 'read the signs' in order to 'decode' the symbolic meaning of style for the participants. Importantly, the development of a particular style was seen as an active, creative process, through which the participants resisted or challenged dominant understandings and expectations regarding how young people should conduct themselves. Thus subcultural style, it was argued, should be seen as political in character. The idea that some working-class deviance or crime was not *merely* deviance or crime as normally understood, but represented a form of political action, became a major theme among a number of radical scholars in the 1970s (for a more detailed discussion see Chapter 7). Writers from outside of the BCCCS also explored the notion of subcultural style as resistance, notably Hebdige (1979).

The emphasis placed on creativity, resistance and the symbolic meaning of style by the BCCCS has continued to influence work on transgressive subcultures (in particular that carried out under the rubric of cultural criminology – see Chapter 8). The work of the BCCCS was important in that it highlighted the point that cultural meanings are not fixed, not tied to some essential quality. The BCCCS also illustrated how the various youth subcultures that developed in the post-war period transformed cultural meanings within the wider society: the teddy boy's quiff and drainpipe trousers, and the skinhead's boots and shaven head, came to mean violence; a motor cycle and leather jacket came to mean 'wild ones', rebellion and 'trouble'; more recently, a hood on a sports top came to mean 'hoodie' and 'yob culture'.

However, subcultural studies of the type carried out by the BCCCS have also attracted some criticisms. In particular, attention has focused on the notion of 'decoding' the symbolic meaning of style, with critics arguing that the accounts and interpretations provided by researchers may not correspond with those of the participants. Allied to this are critical issues surrounding the so-called *politics* of subcultural style, for instance, of whether or not the political status of an act is independent from the subjective intent or consciousness of those involved.

Sykes, Matza and the critique of subculture

In the 1950s and 1960s, the Americans Sykes and Matza developed a still influential approach to the study of deviance, an approach that incorporates a critique of subcultural theories. Their central argument is that such theories are wrong to suggest that members of illicit subcultures inhabit different normative and moral worlds to the rest of society where: 'The world of the delinquent is the world of the law-abiding turned upside down' (Sykes and Matza 1957: 664). The cultural criminologist Katz, for instance, takes the view that members of criminal subcultures share a value system that is strongly at variance with that of 'mainstream' society. Sykes and Matza, on the other hand, stress the continuities, rather than discontinuities, between criminal and non-criminal worlds (though their focus is on juvenile delinquency, rather than 'hardened' criminals). They develop this line of argument around two key concepts: *techniques of neutralization* and *subterranean values*.

According to Sykes and Matza, individuals who engage in delinquency interact routinely with conventional society and, because of this, to a large extent share the same values. They are, therefore, no different to anyone else in terms of accepting the norms and laws of that society. Techniques of neutralization are seen as a device for 'neutralizing', at a psychological level, the wrongfulness of a delinquent act, so that in the mind of the offender it becomes morally acceptable. An example would be fighting someone who has 'insulted my girlfriend'. Thus these techniques are seen as being used by offenders *prior* to engaging in delinquent acts (though they may also be used afterwards). For Sykes and Matza, offenders typically use these kinds of justification, which in effect allow them to go ahead with the delinquent act with a clear conscience. They facilitate a suspension of generally accepted social and legal rules, thereby weakening an offender's bond to conventional society. If the typical delinquent was part of a separate subculture, guided by norms and values different to those of conventional society, why, ask Sykes and Matza, would they bother employing techniques of neutralization? Why not simply go ahead with the delinquency anyway? It is important to stress that they see these techniques as being used before a delinquent act and, therefore, as a crucial dimension to delinquent motivations, allowing individuals to 'drift' in and out of delinquency. One difficulty with this though is gathering empirical evidence that offenders do typically use such techniques in this way.

Sykes and Matza argue that the shame or guilt felt by offenders following 'detection and confinement' is evidence of their bond to conventional society. Assuming that the remorse is genuine (no easy thing to establish), it would indicate, they say, that an offender acknowledged that their behaviour was not morally correct. However, while this is plausible, it would only occur when an offender in effect changed their mind; that is, reversed their original justifications based on techniques of neutralization (perhaps after reflecting on what they had done, or being given information about a victim). Otherwise, why would an offender not continue to see their (neutralized) behaviour as acceptable? In fact, a *lack* of remorse could also be seen as evidence that an offender's values are in tune with those of conventional society, in that the lack of remorse may result from them continuing to use the techniques of neutralization that allowed them to commit the offence in the first place.

Humphrey provides a useful summary of the five techniques of neutralization that Sykes and Matza see as being available to offenders:

- *Denial of responsibility:* involves the contention that the blame for one's deviant behavior lies with others who have victimized the offender or adverse living conditions.
- *Denial of injury:* refers to the assertion that (the) victim was not actually harmed or could well afford any monetary loss that was incurred by committing the offense.
- *Denial of the victim:* Means that any wrong-doing is actually justified on the grounds that the 'victim' had been involved in previous injurious acts. Justice has then been served by the act of retribution against the original offender.
- *Condemnation of the condemners:* Is the view that those who would judge the person as deviant are themselves guilty of far worse offenses. Therefore, any attempt to negatively label the person is without merit and should be disregarded.
- *Appeal to higher loyalties:* Means that the deviant rejects the argument of conventional society that he or she is obliged to abide by its laws and moral code. Rather, the offender's loyalties lie with an

oppositional subculture or group that often expect the person to engage in criminal or deviant acts.

(Humphrey 2006: 51)

As already stated, these techniques are conceptualized as a key element of the motivation to offend and are, therefore, seen as employed by an offender prior to the offence. From this perspective, they are not the same as *ex post facto* excuses or justifications put forward by an offender, say in a court, in an attempt to be given a more lenient sentence. One of the problems with this formulation though is separating the first of these uses from the second. However, these problems do not invalidate the twin claims made by Sykes and Matza: first, that delinquent subcultures do not constitute separate moral universes to those of conventional society and, second, that delinquents typically employ techniques of neutralization in order to suspend their commitment to conventional norms and values.

Sykes and Matza's argument that there are significant similarities between the value systems of delinquent subcultures and those of conventional society is developed further through their concept of subterranean values (Matza and Sykes 1961). From their perspective, society contains a subculture of delinquency, rather than a number of delinquent subcultures. In other words, the values that subcultural theorists associate with delinquent subcultures – for example, machismo, hedonism, excitement and daring – are found everywhere, among all classes and ethnicities. In this respect, therefore, what is described as 'mainstream' society does not differ from so-called delinquent subcultures. Those considered to be 'typical' delinquents (because of class, neighbourhood, style of dress), however, are much more likely to be apprehended and sanctioned when they engage in activities that express these values. Members of mainstream society, on the other hand, are in a better position to avoid scrutiny from agents of social control, or to cover their tracks, or to disguise their activities in such a way that they are judged to be acceptable (e.g. on the rugby field), or regrettable, but 'normal' (e.g. because those involved were having a celebratory night on the town).

Further reading

As always, the reader is encouraged to return to original sources. In particular, for examples of subcultural strain theory, see Cohen, A.K. (1955) *Delinquent Boys*. London: Free Press; and Cloward, R. and Ohlin, L. (1961) *Delinquency and Opportunity*. London: Routledge. And for an example of cultural diversity theory, see Downes, D. (1966) *The Delinquent Solution*. London: Routledge & Kegan Paul. An excellent collection of readings on early British work that draws on the concept of subculture is: Carson, W.G.

and Wiles, P. (eds) (1971) *The Sociology of Crime and Delinquency in Britain: Vol. 1, The British Tradition.* Oxford: Martin Robertson.

Highly regarded British studies of youth and subcultures are Parker, H. (1974) *View From the Boys.* Newton Abbot: David & Charles; and Willis, P. (1978) *Profane Culture.* London: Routledge & Kegan Paul.

The classic discussions of techniques of neutralization and subterranean values are Sykes, G.M. and Matza, D. (1957) Techniques of neutralization: a theory of delinquency, *American Sociological Review*, 22: 664–70; and Matza, D. and Sykes, G.M. (1961) Juvenile delinquency and subterranean values, *American Sociological Review*, 26: 712–19. A further influential critique of subcultural approaches is provided by Matza, D. (1964) *Delinquency and Drift.* New York: Wiley.

A number of criminologists have since then drawn on the concept of 'neutralization'. Rumgay, J. (1998) *Crime, Punishment and the Drinking Offender.* Basingstoke: Macmillan Press/New York: St. Martin's Press, for instance, illustrates how offenders who have been drinking, actively and creatively make use of commonsense understandings within the courtroom in order to neutralize their behaviour. Cohen, S. (1993) Human rights and crimes of the state: the culture of denial, *Australian and New Zealand Journal of Criminology*: 26(1): 87–115, examines the 'denials' and techniques of neutralization used by those involved in the violation of human rights on behalf of the state. An extract of this article is reproduced in Muncie, J., McLaughlin, E. and Langan, M. (eds) (2005) *Criminological Perspectives: A Reader.* 2nd edn. London: Sage Publications.

Good examples of the work of the Birmingham Centre for Contemporary Cultural Studies are Cohen, P. (1972) Subcultural conflict in working-class community, *Working Papers in Cultural Studies*, No. 2, Centre for Contemporary Cultural Studies, University of Birmingham; and Hall, S. and Jefferson, T. (eds) (1976) *Resistance through Rituals: Youth Subcultures in Post-war Britain.* London: Hutchinson. On the issue of youth subcultures and 'style', see Hebdige, D. (1979) *Subculture: The Meaning of Style.* London: Methuen.

References

Adler, F. (1975) *Sisters in Crime*. New York: McGraw-Hill.

Agnew, R. (1985) Social control theory and delinquency: a longitudinal test, *Criminology*, 23: 47–61.

Agnew, R. (1987) On testing structural strain theories, *Journal of Research in Crime and Delinquency*, 24(4): 281–6.

Agnew, R. (1992) Foundation for a general strain theory of crime and delinquency, *Criminology*, 30(1): 47–87.

Ahmed, E., Harris, N., Braithwaite, J. and Braithwaite, V. (2001) *Shame Management Through Reintegration*. Cambridge: Cambridge University Press.

Akers, R.L. (1967) Problems in the sociology of deviance: social definitions and behavior, *Social Forces*, 46(4): 455–65.

Alihan, M.A. (1938) *Social Ecology: A Critical Analysis*. New York: Columbia University Press.

Allen, J. (1989) Men crime and criminology: recasting the questions, *International Journal of the Sociology of Law*, 17: 19–39.

Althusser, L. (1971) *Lenin and Philosophy and Other Essays*. London: New Left Books.

Alvesalo, A., Tombs, S., Virta, E. and Whyte, D. (2006) Re-imagining crime prevention: controlling corporate crime?, *Crime, Law and Social Change*, 45: 1–25.

Anderson, H. (1931) *Enforcement of the Prohibition Laws of the United States*. Chicago, IL: National Commission on Law Observance and Enforcement.

Anderson, N. ([1927] 1975) *The Hobo: The Story of Chicago's Prohibition Era*, London: Hutchinson.

Bankowski, Z. and Mungham, G. (1975) *Images of Law*. London: Routledge & Kegan Paul.

Barak, G. (1999) Constituting O.J.: mass-mediated trails and newsmaking criminology, in S. Henry and D. Milovanovic (eds) *Constitutive Criminology at Work: Applications to Crime and Justice*. New York: State University of New York Press.

Barr, R. and Pease, K. (1990) Crime placement, displacement and deflection, *Crime and Justice*, 12: 277–318.

Barton, A., Corteen, K., Scott, D. and Whyte, D. (eds) (2007) *Expanding the Criminological Imagination: Critical Readings in Criminology*. Cullompton: Willan Publishing.

Baudrillard, J. (1988) *Selected Writings*. Cambridge: Polity Press.

Bauman, Z. and Tester, K. (2001) *Conversations with Zymunt Bauman*. Cambridge: Cambridge University Press.

Baumer, E.P. (2007) Untangling research puzzles in Merton's multilevel anomie theory, *Theoretical Criminology*, 11(1): 63–93.

Beccaria, C. (1963) *An Essay On Crimes and Punishments* tr. H. Paolucci, Indianapolis, IN: Bobbs-Merrill (first published in 1764 as *Dei Delitti e Delle Pene*).

Becker, H.S. (1963) *Outsiders: Studies in the Sociology of Deviance*. London: Macmillan.

Becker, H.S. (1967) Whose side are we on? *Social Problems*, 14(3): 239–47.

Becker, H.S. (1974) Labelling theory reconsidered, in P. Rock and M. McIntosh (eds) *Deviance and Social Control*. London: Tavistock.

Beirne, P. (1993) *Inventing Criminology: Essays on the Rise of 'Homo Criminalis'*, Albany, NY: State University of New York Press.

Bell, D. (1960) *The End of Ideology*. Glencoe, IL: Free Press.

Bell, D. (1973) *The Coming of Post-industrial Society: A Venture in Social Forecasting*. London: Heinemann.

Bellamy, R. (ed.) (1995) *Beccaria: On Crime and Punishments and Other Writings*. Cambridge: Cambridge University Press.

Bentham, J. ([1791] 1843) *Collected Works of Jeremy Bentham*. London: J. Bowring.

Bergalli, R. and Sumner, C.S. (eds) (1997) *Social Control and Political Order: European Perspectives at the End of the Century*, London: Sage Publications.

Bernard, T.J. (1987) Testing structural strain theories, *Journal of Research in Crime and Delinquency*, 24(4): 262–80.

Bianchi, H. and van Swaaningen, R. (eds) (1986) *Abolitionism: Towards a Non-repressive Approach to Crime*. Amsterdam: Free University Press.

Black, E. (2003) *War Against the Weak: Eugenics and America's Campaign to Create a Master Race*. New York: Four Walls Eight Windows.

Booth, C. ([1902] 1967) *Life and Labour of People in London*. London: Macmillan.

Bottoms, A.E. (2007) Place, space, crime, and disorder, in M. Maguire, R. Morgan and R. Reiner (eds) *The Oxford Handbook of Criminology*, 4th edn. Oxford: Oxford University Press.

Box, S. (1981) *Deviance, Reality and Society*, 2nd edn. Eastbourne: Holt, Rinehart & Winston.

Box, S. (1983) *Power, Crime and Mystification*. London: Tavistock.

Braithwaite, J. (1989) *Crime, Shame and Reintegration*. Cambridge: Cambridge University Press.

Brown, B. (1986) Women and crime: the dark figure of criminology, *Economy and Society*, 15: 355–402.

Brownmiller, S. (1975) *Against Our Will*, Harmondsworth: Penguin.

Burgess, E.W. (1925) The growth of the city, in R.E. Park, E.W. Burgess and R.D. McKenzie (eds) *The City*. Chicago, IL: University of Chicago Press.

Cain, M. (1989) *Growing Up Good*. London: Sage Publications.

Cain, M. (1990) Towards transgression: new directions in feminist criminology, *International Journal of the Sociology of Law*. 19: 1–18.

Callinicos, A. (1989) *Against Postmodernism: A Marxist Critique*. Cambridge: Polity Press.

Carlen, P. (1992) Criminal women and criminal justice, in R. Matthews and J. Young (eds) *Issues in Realist Criminology*, London: Sage Publications.

Carlen, P. and Collison, M. (eds) (1980) *Radical Issues in Criminology*. Oxford: Martin Robertson.

Carlen, P. (1990) *Alternatives to Women's Imprisonment*. Buckingham: Open University Press.

Carrington, K. and Hogg, R. (eds) (2002) *Critical Criminology: Issues, Debates and Challenges*. Cullompton: Willan Publishing.

Carson, W.G. (1982) *The Other Price of Britain's Oil*. Oxford: Martin Robertson.

Carson, W.G. and Wiles, P. (eds) (1971) *The Sociology of Crime and Delinquency in Britain: Vol. 1, The British Tradition*, Oxford: Martin Robertson.

Carter, M.P. and Jephcott, P. (1954) The social background of delinquency, unpublished manuscript, University of Nottingham.

Carty, A. (ed.) (1990) *Post-modern Law: Enlightenment, Revolution and the Death of Man*. Edinburgh: Edinburgh University Press.

Caudill, H.M. (1977) Dead leaves and dead men, *Nation*, 226: 492–97.

Chadwick, K. and Scraton, P. (2006) Critical criminology, in E. McLaughlin and J. Muncie (eds) *The Sage Dictionary of Criminology*, 2nd edn. London: Sage Publications.

Chambliss, W.J. (1964) A sociological analysis of the law of vagrancy, *Social Problems*, 12(1): 67–77, reprinted in W.G. Carson and P. Wiles (eds) (1971) *The Sociology of Crime and Delinquency in Britain: Vol. 1, The British Tradition*. Oxford: Martin Robertson.

Chambliss, W.J. (1969) *Crime and Legal Process*. New York: McGraw-Hill.

Chambliss, W.J. (1975) Towards a political economy of crime, *Theory and Society*, 2: 152–53.

Chambliss, W.J. (1978) *On the Take: From Petty Crooks to Presidents*. Bloomington, IN: Indiana University Press.

Chamlin, M.B. and Cochran, J.K. (2007) An evaluation of the assumptions that underlie institutional anomie theory, *Theoretical Criminology*, 11(1): 39–61.

Chapman, C.R. and Harris, A.W. (2002) A skeptical look at September 11th: how we can defeat terrorism by reacting to it more rationally, electronic version, *Skeptical Inquirer*. www.csicop.org/si/2002-09/9-11.html.

Christie, N. (1993) *Crime Control as Industry: Towards Gulags Western Style*. London: Routledge.

Clarke, J. and Jefferson, T. (1976) Working-class youth cultures, in G. Mungham and G. Pearson (eds) *Working-class Youth Culture*. London: Routledge & Kegan Paul.

Clarke, J., Hall, S., Jefferson, T. and Roberts, B. (1976) Subcultures, cultures and class: a theoretical overview, in S. Hall and T. Jefferson (eds) *Resistance through Rituals: Youth Subcultures in Post-war Britain*. London: Hutchinson.

Clarke, L. (2003) Conceptualizing responses to extreme events: the problem of panic and failing gracefully, *Research in Social Problems and Public Policy*, 11: 123–41.

Clarke, R.V. (1995) Situational crime prevention, *Crime and Justice*, 19: 91–150.

Clinard, M.B. and Yeager, P.C. (1981) *Corporate Crime*. New York: Free Press.

Cloward, R. and Ohlin, L. (1960) *Delinquency and Opportunity: A Theory of Delinquent Gangs*. London: Collier Macmillan.

Cohen, A.K. (1955) *Delinquent Boys*. London: Free Press.

Cohen, L.E. and Felson, M. (1979) Social change and crime rate trends: a routine activities approach, *American Sociological Review*, 44: 588–608.

Cohen, P. (1972) Subcultural conflict in working-class community, Working Papers in Cultural Studies, No. 2, Centre for Contemporary Cultural Studies, University of Birmingham.

Cohen, S. (1972) *Folk Devils and Moral Panics*. London: MacGibbon and Kee.

Cohen, S. (1985) *Visions of Social Control*. Cambridge: Polity Press.

Cohen, S. (1993) Human rights and crimes of the state: the culture of denial, *Australian and New Zealand Journal of Criminology*, 26(1): 87–115.

Cohen, S. (1998) Intellectual scepticism and political commitment: the case for radical criminology, in P. Walton and J. Young (eds) *The New Criminology Revisited*. Basingstoke: Macmillan.

Cohen, S. (2001) *States of Denial: Knowing about Atrocities and Suffering*. Cambridge: Polity Press.

Coleman, R. (2004) *Reclaiming the Streets: Surveillance, Social Control and the City*. Cullompton: Willan Publishing.

Collier, R. (1998) *Masculinities, Crime and Criminology*. London: Sage Publications.

Collier, R. (2004) Masculinities and crime: rethinking the 'man question', in C. Sumner (ed.) *The Blackwell Companion to Criminology*. Oxford: Blackwell Publishing.

Colvin, M. (2000) *Crime and Coercion: An Integrated Theory of Chronic Criminality*. New York: St. Martin's.

Connell, R.W. (1987) *Gender and Power*. Cambridge: Polity Press.

Connell, R.W. (1995) *Masculinities*. Berkeley, CA: University of California Press.

Connell, R.W. and Messerschmidt, J.W. (2005) Hegemonic masculinity: rethinking the concept, *Gender and Society*, 19(6): 829–59.

Cooley, C.H. (1902) *Human Nature and the Social Order*. New York: Schriber's.

Cornish, D.B. and Clarke, R.V. (eds) (1986) *The Reasoning Criminal: Rational Choice Perspectives on Offending*. New York: Springer-Verlag.

Cornish, D.B. and Clarke, R.V. (2003) Opportunities, precipitators and criminal decision, *Crime Prevention Studies*, 16: 41–96.

Corrigan, P. and Frith, S. (1976) The politics of youth culture, in S. Hall and T. Jefferson (eds) *Resistance through Rituals*. London: Hutchinson.

Cousins, M. (1980) Mens rea: a note on sexual difference, criminology and the law, in P. Carlen and M. Collison (eds) *Radical Issues in Criminology*. Oxford: Martin Robertson.

Cowie, J., Cowie, V. and Slater, E. (1968) *Delinquent Girls in London*. London: Heinemann.

Crawford, A. (1998) *Crime Prevention and Community Safety: Politics, Policies and Practice*. London: Longman.

Crawford, A. (2007) Crime prevention and community safety, in M. Maguire, R. Morgan and R. Reiner (eds) *The Oxford Handbook of Criminology*, 4th edn. Oxford: Oxford University Press.

Crawford, A. and Newburn, T. (2002) Recent developments in restorative justice for young people in England and Wales: community participation and restoration, *British Journal of Criminology*, 42(2): 476–95.

Crawford, A., Jones, T., Woodhouse, T. and Young, J. (1990) *Second Islington Crime Survey*. London: Middlesex Polytechnic.

Criticher, C. (2003) *Moral Panics and the Media*. Buckingham: Open University Press.

Cullen, F.T. and Messner, S.F. (2007) The making of criminology revisited: an oral history of Merton's anomie paradigm, *Theoretical Criminology*, 11(1): 5–37.

Daly, K. (1997) Different ways of conceptualising sex/gender in feminist theory and the implications for criminology, *Theoretical Criminology*, 1(1): 25–51.

Daly, K. (2006) Feminist criminologies, in E. McLaughlin and J. Muncie (eds) *The Sage Dictionary of Criminology*. London: Sage Publications.

Davis, M. (1990) *City of Quartz*. London: Verson.

Derrida, J. (1976) *Of Grammatology*, tr. G.C. Spivak. London and Baltimore, MD: Johns Hopkins University Press.

Ditton, J. (1979) *Contrology: Beyond the New Criminology*. London: Macmillan.

Downes, D. (1966) *The Delinquent Solution*. London: Routledge & Kegan Paul.

Downes, D. and Rock, P. (2007) *Understanding Deviance*, 5th edn. Oxford: Oxford University Press.

Dugdale, R.L. (1887) *The Jukes*. New York: Putnam.

Durkheim, E. ([1893] 1964) *The Division of Labour in Society*. New York: Free Press.

Durkheim, E. ([1897] 1970) *Suicide: A Study in Sociology*. London: Routledge & Kegan Paul.

Durkheim, E. (1982) *Durkheim: The Rules of Sociological Method*, ed. S. Lukes. London: Macmillan.

Eagleton, T. (1996) *The Illusions of Postmodernism*. Oxford: Blackwell.

Eck, J. and Maguire, E. (2000) Have changes in policing reduced violent crime? An assessment of the evidence, in A. Blumstein and J. Wallman (eds) *The Crime Drop in America*. Cambridge: Cambridge University Press.

Einstadter, W.J. (1984) Citizen patrols: prevention or control?, *Crime and Social Justice*: 199–212.

Ekblom, P. (1997) Gearing up against crime: a dynamic framework to help designers keep up with the adaptive criminal in a changing world, *International Journal of Risk, Security and Crime Prevention*, 2(4): 249–65.

Elliot, D., Ageton, S. and Canter, J. (1979) An integrated theoretical perspective on delinquent behavior, *Journal of Research in Crime and Delinquency*, 16: 126–49.

Ellis, L. and Coontz, P.D. (1990) Androgens, brain functioning and criminality: the neurohormonal foundations in antisociability, in L. Ellis and H. Hoffman (eds) *Crime in Biological, Social and Moral Contexts*. New York: Praeger.

Erikson, K.T. (1962) Notes on the sociology of deviance, *Social Problems*, 9, reprinted in H.S. Becker (ed.) (1964) *The Other Side: Perspectives on Deviance*. New York: Free Press.

Felson, M. (1986) Routine activities, social controls, rational decisions and criminal outcomes, in D.B. Cornish and R.V. Clarke (eds) *The Reasoning Criminal*. New York: Springer-Verlag.

Felson, M. (1987) Routine activities and crime prevention in the developing metropolis, *Criminology*, 25: 911–31.

Felson, M. (1998) *Crime and Everyday Life*, 2nd edn. Thousand Oaks, CA: Pine Forge Press.

Felson, M. (2000) The routine activity approach as a general social theory, in S.S. Simpson (ed.) *Of Crime and Criminality: The Use of Theory in Everyday Life*. Thousand Oaks, CA: Pine Forge Press.

Ferrell, J. (1996) *Crimes of Style: Urban Graffiti and the Politics of Criminality*. Boston, MA: Northeastern University Press.

Ferrell, J. (2001) *Tearing Down the Streets*. New York: Palgrave Macmillan.

Ferrell, J. (2004) Boredom, crime and criminology, *Theoretical Criminology*, 8(3): 287–302.

Ferrell, J., Hayward, K., Morrison, W. and Presdee, M. (2004) *Cultural Criminology Unleashed*. London: Glasshouse.

Ferrell, J., Hayward, K. and Young, J. (2008), *Cultural Criminology*, London: Sage.

Ferrell, J. and Sanders, C.R. (eds) (1995) *Cultural Criminology*. Boston, MA: Northeastern University Press.

Ferri, E. (1901) *Criminal Sociology*. Boston, MA: Little Brown.

Fine, B. (ed.) (1979) *Capitalism and the Rule of Law: From Deviancy Theory to Marxism*. London: Hutchinson.

Foucault, M. (1977) *Discipline and Punish: The Birth of the Prison*. London: Penguin.

Gardiner, M. (1996) Alterity and ethics, *Theory, Culture and Society*. 13: 120–43.

Garland, D. (2006) Concepts of culture in the sociology of punishment, *Theoretical Criminology*, 10(4): 419–47.

Garofalo, J. (1987) Reassessing the lifestyle model of criminal victimization, in M.R. Gottfredson and T. Hirschi (eds) *Positive Criminology*. Newbury Park, CA: Sage Publications.

Gelsthorpe, L. (2002) Feminism and criminology, in M. Maguire, R. Morgan and R. Reiner (eds) *The Oxford Handbook of Criminology*, 3rd edn. Oxford: Oxford University Press.

Gelsthorpe, L. and Morris, A. (eds) (1990) *Feminist Perspectives in Criminology*. Buckingham: Open University Press.

Gibbs, J.P. (1966) Conception of deviant behaviour: the old and the new, *Pacific Sociological Review*, 14(1): 20–37.

Glueck, S. and Glueck, E. (1950) *Unraveling Juvenile Delinquency*. New York: Commonwealth Fund.

Goddard, H.H. (1914) *Feeblemindedness: Its Causes and Consequences*. New York: Macmillan.

Goode, E. and Ben-Yehuda, N. (1994) *Moral Panics: The Social Construction of Deviance*. Oxford: Blackwell.

Gordon, D.M. (1971) Class and the economics of crime, *Review of Radical Political Economy*, 3: 51–75.

Gouldner, A.W. (1968) The sociologist as partisan: sociology and the welfare state, *American Sociologist*, 3: 103–16.

Green, P. and Ward, T. (2004) *State Crime: Governments, Violence and Corruption*. London: Pluto Press.

Greenwood, V. (1981) The myths of female crime, in A.M. Morris and L.R. Gelsthorpe (eds) *Women and Crime*. Cropwood Conference Series, No. 13, Cambridge: Cambridge Institute of Criminology.

Gross, B. (1982) Some anti-crime proposals for progressives, *Crime and Social Justice*, 17: 51–4.

Hakim, S. and Rengert, G.F. (1981) *Crime Spillover*. Beverly Hills, CA: Sage Publications.

Hall, S. and Jefferson, T. (eds) (1976) *Resistance through Rituals: Youth Subcultures in Post-war Britain*. London: Hutchinson.

Hall, S., Critcher, C., Jefferson, T., Clarke, J. and Roberts, B. (1978) *Policing the Crisis: Mugging, the State and Law and Order.* London: Macmillan.

Hamm, M.S. (2004) Apocalyptic violence: the seduction of terrorist subcultures, *Theoretical Criminology*, 8(3): 323–39.

Harcourt, B.E. (2001) *Illusions of Order: The False Promise of Broken Windows Policing.* Cambridge, MA: Harvard University Press.

Harding, S. (1991) *Whose Science, Whose Knowledge?* Buckingham: Open University Press.

Hartmann, P. and Husband, C. (1974) *Racism and the Mass Media.* London: Davis-Poynter.

Hartsock, N. (1983) The feminist standpoint: developing the ground for a specifically feminist historical materialism, in S. Harding and M.B. Hintikka (eds) *Discovering Reality.* Dordrecht: Reidel.

Hayward, K. and Young, J. (2007) Cultural criminology, in M. Maguire, R. Morgan and R. Reiner (eds) *The Oxford Handbook of Criminology*, 4th edn. Oxford: Oxford University Press.

Hebdige, D. (1979) *Subculture: The Meaning of Style.* London: Methuen.

Heidensohn, F.M. (1985) *Women and Crime.* London: Macmillan.

Heidensohn, F.M. (1989) *Crime and Society.* Basingstoke: Macmillan.

Heidensohn, F.M. (1994) Gender and crime, in M. Maguire, R. Morgan and R. Reiner (eds) *The Oxford Handbook of Criminology*, 2nd edn. Oxford: Clarendon Press.

Heidensohn, F.M. and Gelsthorpe, L. (2007) Gender and crime, in M. Maguire, R. Morgan and R. Reiner (eds) *The Oxford Handbook of Criminology*, 4th edn. Oxford: Oxford University Press.

Henry, S. and Milovanovic, D. (1994) The constitution of constitutive criminology, in D. Nelken (ed.) *The Futures of Criminology.* London: Sage Publications.

Henry, S. and Milovanovic, D. (1996) *Constitutive Criminology: Beyond Postmodernism.* London: Sage Publications.

Henry, S. and Milovanovic, D. (eds) (1999) *Constitutive Criminology at Work: Applications to Crime and Punishment.* New York: State University of New York Press.

Henry, S. and Milovanovic, D. (2006) Constitutive criminology, in E. McLaughlin and J. Muncie (eds) *The Sage Dictionary of Criminology.* 2nd edn. London: Sage Publications.

Herrnstein, R.J. and Murray, C. (1994) *The Bell Curve: Intelligence and Class Structure in American Life.* New York: Free Press.

Hester, S. and Eglin, P. (1992) *A Sociology of Crime.* London: Routledge.

Hillyard, P., Tombs, S., Pantazis, C. and Gordon, D. (eds) (2004) *Beyond Criminology: Taking Harm Seriously.* London: Pluto.

Hinch, R. (1983) Marxist criminology in the 1970s: clarifying the clutter, *Crime and Social Justice*, 19: 65–73.

Hinsliff, G. (2008) Children's tsar seeks to ban sonic weapon used on hoodies, *The Observer*, 10 February, p. 5.

Hirschi, T. (1969) *Causes of Delinquency*. Berkeley, CA: University of California Press.

Hirschi, T. and Gottfredson, M.R. (1995) Control theory and the life course perspective, *Studies on Crime and Crime Prevention*. 4: 131–42.

Hirschi, T. and Gottfredson, M.R. (2000) In defence of self control, *Theoretical Criminology*, 4(1): 55–69.

Hirst, P.Q. (1975) Radical deviance theory and Marxism: a reply to Taylor, Walton and Young, in I. Taylor, P. Walton and J. Young (eds) *Critical Criminology*. London: Routledge & Kegan Paul.

Hood-Williams, J. (2001) Gender, masculinities and crime: from structures to psyches, *Theoretical Criminology*, 5(1): 37–60.

Hooks, B. (1988) *Talking Back, Thinking Feminist, Thinking Black*. Boston, MA: South End Press.

Hooton, E.A. (1939) *Crime and the Man*. Cambridge, MA: Harvard University Press.

Hope, T. (2006) Review of: M.J. Smith and N. Tilley (eds) (2005) *Crime Science: New Approaches to Preventing and Detecting Crime*. Cullompton: Willan Publishing, in *Theoretical Criminology*, 10(2): 245–50.

Hopkins Burke, R. (2001) *An Introduction to Criminological Theory*. Cullompton: Willan Publishing.

Howe, A. (2004) Managing 'men's violence' in the criminological arena, in C. Sumner (ed.) *The Blackwell Companion to Criminology*. Oxford: Blackwell Publishing.

Hughes, G. (1998) *Understanding Crime Prevention*. Buckingham: Open University Press.

Hulsman, L. (1986) Critical criminology and the concept of crime, *Contemporary Crises*, 10: 63–80.

Humphrey, J.A. (2006) *Deviant Behavior*. Upper Saddle River, NJ: Pearson/ Prentice Hall.

Hunt, A. (1997) Moral panic and moral language, *British Journal of Sociology*, 48(4): 629–48.

Jefferson, T. (1996) From 'little fairy boy' to the 'compleat destroyer': subjectivity and transformation in the biography of Mike Tyson, in M. Mac an Ghaill (ed.) *Understanding Masculinities*. Buckingham: Open University Press.

Jefferson, T. (1997) Masculinities and crime, in M. Maguire, R. Morgan and R. Reiner (eds) *The Oxford Handbook of Criminology*, 2nd edn. Oxford: Oxford University Press.

Jefferson, T. (2002) Subordinating hegemonic masculinity, *Theoretical Criminology*. 6(1): 63–88.

Jeffery, C.R. (1977) *Crime Prevention Through Environmental Design*. Beverly Hills, CA: Sage Publications.

Jewkes, Y. (2004) *Media and Crime*. London: Sage Publications.

Johnson, R.E. (1979) *Juvenile Delinquency and its Origins*. Cambridge: Cambridge University Press.

Jones, S. (1993) *The Language of Genes*. London: Harper Collins.

Jones, T., Maclean, B. and Young, J. (1986) *The Islington Crime Survey*. Aldershot: Gower.

Katz, J. (1988) *Seductions of Crime*. New York: Basic Books.

Kelling, G.L. (1999) Broken windows, zero tolerance and crime control, in P. Francis and F. Penny (eds) *Building Safer Communities*. London: Centre for Crime and Justice Studies.

Kelling, G.L. and Coles, C.M. (1996) *Fixing Broken Windows: Restoring Order and Reducing Crime in Our Communities*. New York: Simon & Schuster.

Kitsuse, J.I. (1962) Societal reaction to deviant behavior: problems of theory and method, *Social Problems*, 9: 247–56, reprinted in E. Rubington and M.S. Weinberg (eds) (1968) *Deviance: The Interactionist Perspective*. Basingstoke: Macmillan.

Kornhauser, R. (1978) *Social Sources of Delinquency*. Chicago, IL: University of Chicago Press.

Lacan, J. (1981) *The Four Fundamental Concepts of Psycho-analysis*. New York: W.W. Norton.

Lanier, M.M. and Henry, S. (1998) *Essential Criminology*. Oxford: Westview Press.

Lea, J. (1998) Criminology and postmodernity, in P. Walton and J. Young (eds) *The New Criminology Revisited*. Basingstoke: Macmillan.

Lea, J. and Young, J. (1984) *What is to be Done about Law and Order?* Harmondsworth: Penguin.

Lemert, E.M. (1951) *Social Pathology*. New York: McGraw-Hill.

Lemert, E.M. (1967) *Human Deviance, Social Problems and Social Control*. Englewood Cliffs, NJ: Prentice-Hall.

Liazos, A. (1972) The poverty of the sociology of deviance: nuts, sluts and preverts [sic], *Social Problems*, 20: 103–20.

Lilly, J.R., Cullen, F.T. and Ball, R.A. (2007) *Criminological Theory: Context and Consequences*, 4th edn. Thousand Oaks, CA: Sage Publications.

Lombroso, C. (1911) *Criminal Man*. New York: G.P. Putnam.

Lombroso, C. (1913) *Crime: Its Causes and Remedies*. Boston, MA: Little Brown.

Lombroso, C. and Ferrero, W. (1885) *The Female Offender*. London: Unwin.

London, J. ([1903] 1995) *The People of the Abyss*. London: Lawrence Hill Books.

Lyng, S. (1990) Edgework: a social psychological analysis of voluntary risk-taking, *American Journal of Sociology*, 95(4): 876–921.

Lyng, S. (1998) Dangerous methods: risk-taking and the research process, in J. Ferrell and M. Hamm (eds) *Ethnography at the Edge*. Boston, MA: Northeastern University Press.

Lyotard, J.F. (1984) *The Postmodern Condition: A Report on Knowledge*. Minneapolis, MN: University of Minnesota Press.

Mathiesen, T. (1990) *Prison on Trial*. London: Sage Publications.

Matthews, R. (1992a) Replacing 'broken windows': crime, incivilities and urban change', in R. Matthews and J. Young (eds) *Issues in Realist Criminology*. London: Sage Publications.

Matthews, R. (1992b) Developing more effective strategies for curbing prostitution, in R.V. Clarke (ed.) *Situational Crime Prevention: Successful Case Studies*. Albany, NY: Harrow and Heston.

Matza, D. (1964) *Delinquency and Drift*. New York: Wiley.

Matza, D. and Sykes, G.M. (1961) Juvenile delinquency and subterranean values, *American Sociological Review*, 26: 712–19.

Mayhew, H. ([1861] 1967) *London Labour and the London Poor: A Cyclopaedia of the Condition and Earnings of Those that will Work, those that Cannot Work, and those that will not Work*. New York: H.M. Kelley. A small section, 'A visit to the rookery of St. Giles and its neighbourhood', is reproduced in M. Fitzgerald, G. McLennan and J. Pawson (eds) (1981) *Crime and Society: Readings in History and Society*. London: Routledge & Kegan Paul.

Mays, J.B. (1954) *Growing Up in the City: A Study of Juvenile Delinquency in an Urban Neighbourhood*. Liverpool: Liverpool University Press.

McLaughlin, E. and Langan, M. (eds) (2005) *Criminological Perspectives: A Reader*, 2nd edn. London: Sage Publications.

McMullan, J.L. (1986) The 'law and order' problem in socialist criminology, *Studies in Political Economy*, 21: 175–92.

McRobbie, A. and Thornton, S. (1995) Re-thinking 'moral panic' for multi-mediated social worlds, *British Journal of Sociology*, 46(4): 559–74.

Mead, G.H. (1934) *Mind, Self and Society*. Chicago, IL: University of Chicago Press.

Mednick, S.A. and Christiansen, K.O. (eds) (1977) *Biosocial Bases of Criminal Behavior*. New York: Gardner.

Mednick, S.A., Moffit, T.E. and Stack, S. (eds) (1987) *The Causes of Crime: New Biological Approaches*. Cambridge: Cambridge University Press.

Menard, S. (1995) A developmental test of Mertonian anomie theory, *Journal of Research in Crime and Delinquency*, 31: 136–74.

Merton, R.K. (1957) Priorities in scientific discoveries: a chapter in the sociology of science, *American Sociological Review*, 22(6): 635–9.

Merton, R.K. (1993) Social structure and anomie, in C. Lemert (ed.) *Social Theory: The Multicultural Readings*, Boulder, CO: Westview Press.

Messerschmidt, J.W. (1993) *Masculinities and Crime*. Lanham, MD: Rowman & Littlefield.

Messerschmidt, J.W. (1997) *Crime as Structured Action: Gender. Race, Class and Crime.* Thousand Oaks, CA: Sage Publications.

Messner, S.F. and Rosenfeld, R. (2001) *Crime and the American Dream*, 3rd edn. Belmont, CA: Wadsworth.

Miller, W.B. (1958) Lower class culture as a generating milieu of gang delinquency, *Journal of Social Issues*, 14(3): 5–19.

Mills, C.W. (1959) *The Sociological Imagination*. Oxford: Oxford University Press.

Morris, T.P. (1957) *The Criminal Area: A Study in Social Ecology*. London: Routledge & Kegan Paul.

Morrison, W. (1995) *Theoretical Criminology: From Modernity to Postmodernism*. London: Cavendish Publishing.

Mullins, C.W. (2006) *Holding Your Square: Masculinities, Streetlife and Violence*, Cullompton: Willan Publishing.

Naffine, N. (1997) *Feminism and Criminology*. Sydney: Allen & Unwin.

Nuttall, J. (1970) *Bomb Culture*. St. Albans: Paladin.

Nye, I.F. (1958) *Family Relationships and Delinquent Behavior*. New York: John Wiley.

O'Brien, M. (2005) What is *cultural* about cultural criminology? *British Journal of Criminology*, 45(5): 599–612.

Park, R.E. (1926) The urban community as a special pattern and a moral order, in E.W. Burgess (ed.) *The Urban Community*, Chicago, IL: University of Chicago Press.

Park, R.E., Burgess, E.W. and McKenzie, R.D. (1925) *The City*. Chicago, IL: University of Chicago Press.

Parker, H. (1974) *View From the Boys*. Newton Abbot: David & Charles.

Parnaby, P.F. and Sacco, V.F. (2004) Fame and strain: the contributions of Mertonian deviance theory to an understanding of the relationship between celebrity and deviant behavior, *Deviant Behavior*, 25: 1–26.

Passas, N. and Agnew, R. (eds) (1997) *The Future of Anomie Theory*, Boston, MA: Northeastern University Press.

Pavlich, G. (2005) *Governing Paradoxes of Restorative Justice*. London: Rouledge-Cavendish.

Pearce, F. (1976) *Crimes of the Powerful*. London: Pluto Press.

Pearce, F. and Tombs, S. (1998) *Toxic Capitalism: Corporate Crime and the Chemical Industry*. Aldershot: Dartmouth.

Pearson, G. (1975) *The Deviant Imagination*. London: Macmillan.

Pearson, G. (1976) Cotton town: a case study and its history, in G. Mungham and G. Pearson (eds) *Working Class Youth Culture*. London: Routledge & Kegan Paul.

Pease, K. (2002) Crime reduction, in M. Maguire, R. Morgan and R. Reiner (eds) *The Oxford Handbook of Criminology*, 3rd edn. Oxford: Oxford University Press.

Pepinsky, H.E. and Quinney, R. (eds) (1991) *Criminology as Peacemaking.* Bloomington, IN: Indiana University Press.

Phillipson, M. (1971) *Sociological Aspects of Crime and Delinquency.* London: Routledge & Kegan Paul.

Pollak, O. (1950) *The Criminality of Women.* New York: Barnes/Perpetuo.

Pollner, M. (1974) Mundane reasoning, *Philosophy of Social Sciences*, 4(1): 35–54.

Poole, E.D. and Regoli, R.M. (1979) Parental support, delinquent friends and delinquency, *Journal of Criminal Law and Criminology*, 70: 188–93.

Porter, R. (2000) *Enlightenment: Britain and the Creation of the Modern World*, London: Penguin.

Poulantzas, N. (1973) The problem of the capitalist state, in J. Urry and J. Wakeford (eds) *Power in Britain*. London: Heinemann.

Pratt, J.C. and Cullen, F.T. (2005) Assessing macro-level predictors and theories of crime: a meta-analysis, in M. Tonry (ed.) *Crime and Justice, Vol. 32*, pp. 373–450. Chicago. IL: University of Chicago Press.

Presdee, M. (2000) *Cultural Criminology and the Carnival of Crime.* London: Routledge.

Price, W.H. and Whatmore, P.B. (1967) Behaviour disorders and patterns of crime among XYY males identified at a maximum security hospital, *British Medical Journal*, 1: 533–46.

Quinney, R. (1969) *Criminal Justice in American Society.* Boston, MA: Little, Brown.

Quinney, R. (1977) *Class, State and Crime: On the Theory and Practice of Criminal Justice.* New York: McKay.

Rafter, N.H. and Heidensohn, F.M. (eds) (1995) *International Feminist Perspectives in Criminology.* Buckingham: Open University Press.

Reckless, W.C. ([1950] 1973) *The Crime Problem.* Englewood Cliffs, NJ: Prentice Hall.

Rock, P. (2007) Sociological theories of crime, in M. Maguire, R. Morgan and R. Reiner (eds) *The Oxford Handbook of Criminology*, 4th edn. Oxford: Oxford University Press.

Roshier, B. (1989) *Controlling Crime.* Buckingham: Open University Press.

Ruggiero, V. (2000) *Crime and Markets: Essays in Anti-criminology.* Oxford: Clarendon Press.

Ruggiero, V., South, N. and Taylor, I. (eds) (1998) *The New European Criminology: Crime and Social Order in Europe.* London: Routledge.

Rumgay, J. (1998) *Crime, Punishment and the Drinking Offender.* Basingstoke: Macmillan Press/New York: St Martin's Press.

Sacco, V.F. (2005) *When Crime Waves.* Thousand Oaks, CA: Sage Publications.

Sampson, J.R. (2006) Collective efficacy: lessons learned and directions for future inquiry, in F.T. Cullen, J.P. Wright and K.R. Blevins (eds) *Taking*

Stock: The Status of Criminological Theory, Advances in Criminological Theory, Vol. 15. New Brunswick, NJ: Transaction Publishing.

Sampson, R.J. and Groves, W.B. (1989) Community structure and crime: testing social-disorganization theory, *American Journal of Sociology*, 94: 774–802.

Samuel, L.R. (2001) *Brought to You By*. Austin, TX: Texas University Press.

Schutz, A. (1972) *The Phenomenology of the Social World*. London: Heinemann.

Schwartz, M. and Friedrichs, D. (1994) Postmodern thought and criminological discontent: new metaphors for understanding violence, *Criminology*, 32(2): 221–46.

Scott, J. (1996) *Only Paradoxes to Offer: French Feminists and the Rights of Man*. Cambridge, MA: Harvard University Press.

Scraton, P. (2002) Defining 'power' and challenging 'knowledge': critical analysis as resistance in the UK, in K. Carrington and R. Hogg (eds) *Critical Criminology: Issues, Debates, Challenges*. Cullompton: Willan Publishing.

Shacklady Smith, L. (1978) Sexist assumptions and female delinquency: an empirical investigation, in C. Smart and B. Smart (eds) *Women, Sexuality and Social Control*. London: Routledge & Kegan Paul.

Shah, S.A. and Roth, L.H. (1974) Biological and psychophysiological factors in criminality, in D. Glaser (ed.) *Handbook of Criminology*. London: Rand McNally.

Shaw, C.R. (1929) *Delinquency Areas*. Chicago, IL: University of Chicago Press.

Shaw, C.R. (1930) *The Jack-roller: A Delinquent Boy's Own Story*. Chicago, IL: University of Chicago Press.

Shaw, C.R. and McKay, H.D. (1931) *Social Factors in Juvenile Delinquency: Report of the Causes of Crime*. National Commission on Law Observance and Enforcement, Report No. 13, Washington, DC: Government Printing Office.

Shaw, C.R. and McKay, H.D. (1942) *Juvenile Delinquency and Urban Areas: A Study of Delinquents in Relation to Differential Characteristics of Local Communities in American Cities*. Chicago, IL: University of Chicago Press.

Shaw, C.R. and Moore, M.E. (1931) *The Natural History of a Delinquent Career*. Chicago, IL: University of Chicago Press.

Sheldon, W.H. (1949) *Varieties of Delinquent Youth: An Introduction to Constitutional Psychiatry*. New York: Harper.

Sheptycki, J.W.E. (1995) Transnational policing and the makings of a postmodern state, *British Journal of Criminology*, 35(4): 613–35.

Sheptycki, J.W.E. (1997) Transnationalism, crime control and the European state system: a review of the scholarly literature, *International Criminal Justice Review*, 7: 130–40.

Short J.F. and Strodtbeck, F. (1965) *Group Process and Delinquency*. Chicago, IL: University of Chicago Press.

Silvestri, M. and Crowther-Dowey, C. (2008) *Gender and Crime*. London: Sage Publications.

Sim, J. (1994) The abolitionist approach: a British perspective, in A. Duff, S. Marshall, R.E. Dobash and R.P. Dobash (eds) *Penal Theory and Practice: Tradition and Innovation in Criminal Justice*. Manchester: Manchester University Press.

Simon, R.J. (1975) *Women and Crime*. Toronto: Lexington Books.

Sinclair, U. (1905) *The Jungle*. New York: Signet.

Smart, C. (1976) *Women, Crime and Criminology: A Feminist Critique*. London: Routledge & Kegan Paul.

Smart, C. (1979) The new female criminal: reality or myth, *British Journal of Criminology*, 19(1): 50–9.

Smart, C. (1981) Response to Greenwood, in A.M. Morris and L.R. Gelsthorpe (eds) *Women and Crime*. Cropwood Conference Series, No. 13, Cambridge: Cambridge Institute of Criminology.

Smart, C. (1990) Feminist approaches to criminology, or postmodern woman meets atavistic man, in L.R. Gelsthorpe and A.M. Morris (eds) *Feminist Perspectives in Criminology*. London: Routledge & Kegan Paul.

Smart, C. (1995) *Law, Crime and Sexuality: Essays in Feminism*. London: Sage Publications.

Smith, M.J. and Tilley, N. (eds) (2005) *Crime Science: New Approaches to Preventing and Detecting Crime*. Cullompton: Willan Publishing.

Snider, L. (2004) Female punishment: from patriarchy to backlash? in C. Sumner (ed.) *The Blackwell Companion to Criminology*. Oxford: Blackwell Publishing.

Stinchcombe, A.L. (1975) Merton's theory of social structure, in L.A. Coser (ed.) *The Idea of Social Structure*. New York: Harcourt Brace Jovanovich.

Sumner, C.S. (1976) Marxism and deviancy theory, in P. Wiles (ed.) *The Sociology of Crime and Delinquency in Britain: Vol. 2, The New Criminologies*. Oxford: Martin Robertson.

Sumner, C.S. (ed.) (1990) *Censure, Politics and Criminal Justice*. Buckingham: Open University Press.

Sumner, C.S. (1994) *The Sociology of Deviance: An Obituary*. Buckingham: Open University Press.

Sumner, C.S. (2004) The social nature of crime and deviance, in C.S. Sumner (ed.) *The Blackwell Companion to Criminology*. Oxford: Blackwell Publishing.

Sutherland, E.H. (1937) *The Professional Thief: By a Professional Thief*. Chicago, IL: University of Chicago Press.

Sutherland, E.H. ([1949] 1983) *White-collar Crime*. New York: Holt, Rinehart & Winston.

Sutherland, E.H. and Cressey, D.R. (1970) *Criminology*, 8th edn. Philadelphia, PA: J.B. Lippincolt.

Sykes, G.M. and Matza, D. (1957) Techniques of neutralization: a theory of delinquency, *American Sociological Review*, 22: 664–70.

Taylor, I. (1971) Soccer consciousness and soccer hooliganism, in S. Cohen (ed.) *Images of Deviance*. Harmondsworth: Penguin.

Taylor, I. (1981) *Law and Order: Arguments for Socialism*. London: Macmillan.

Taylor, I. (1999) *Crime in Context*. Cambridge: Polity Press.

Taylor, I., Walton, P. and Young, J. (1973) *The New Criminology: For a Social Theory of Deviance*. London: Routledge & Kegan Paul.

Thio, A. (1973) Class bias in the sociology of deviance, *American Sociologist*, 8: 1–12.

Thompson, K. (1998) *Moral Panics*. London: Routledge.

Thrasher, F.M. ([1927] 1963) *The Gang*. Chicago, IL: Phoenix Press.

Tierney, J. (1980) Political deviance: a critical commentary on a case study, *Sociological Review*, 28(4): 829–50.

Tierney, J. (1988) Viewpoint: romantic fictions: the re-emergence of the crime as politics debate, *Sociological Review*, 36(1): 133–45.

Tierney, J. (2006) *Criminology: Theory and Context*, 2nd edn. Harlow: Pearson Longman.

Tilley, N. (ed.) (2005) *Handbook of Crime Prevention and Community Safety*. Cullompton: Willan Publishing.

Tittle, C.R. (1995) *Control Balance: Toward a General Theory of Deviance*. Boulder, CO: Westview.

Tittle, C.R. (1997) Thoughts stimulated by Braithwaite's analysis of control balance theory, *Theoretical Criminology*, 1(1): 99–110.

Tittle, C.R. (2000) Control balance, in R. Paternoster and R. Bachman (eds) *Explaining Criminals and Crime: Essays in Contemporary Theory*. Los Angeles, CA: Roxbury.

Tittle, C.R. (2004) Refining control balance theory, *Theoretical Criminology*, 8(4): 395–428.

Toby J. (1957) Social disorganization and stake in conformity: complementary factors in the predatory behaviour of hoodlums, *Journal of Criminal Law, Criminology and Police Science*, 48: 12-17.

Turk, A.T. (1969) *Criminality and the Legal Order*. Chicago, IL: Rand McNally.

Unnever, J.D., Colvin, M. and Cullen, F.T. (2004) Crime and coercion: a test of core theoretical propositions, *Journal of Research in Crime and Delinquency*, 41: 244–68.

Valier, C. (2002) *Theories of Crime and Punishment*. Harlow: Longman.

Van Swaaningen, R. (1997) *Critical Criminology: Visions from Europe*. London: Sage Publications.

Vaneigem, R. (2001) *The Revolution of Everyday Life*. London: Rebel Press.

Virkkunen, M. (1987) Metabolic disfunctions amongst habitually violent offenders: reactive hypoglycaemia and cholesterol levels, in S.A. Mednick,

T.E. Moffit and S.A. Stack (eds) *The Causes of Crime: New Biological Approaches*. Cambridge: Cambridge University Press.

Vold, G.B. (1958) *Theoretical Criminology*. New York: Oxford University Press.

Vold, G.B., Bernard, T.J. and Snipes, J.B. (2002) *Theoretical Criminology*, 5th edn. Oxford: Oxford University Press.

Waddington, P.A.J. (1986) Mugging as a moral panic: a question of proportion, *British Journal of Sociology*, 32(2): 245–59.

Walklate, S. (2003) *Understanding Criminology: Current Theoretical Debates*, 2nd edn. Buckingham: Open University Press.

Walters, R. (2007) Critical criminology and the intensification of the authoritarian state, in A. Barton, K. Corteen, D. Scott and D. Whyte (eds) *Expanding the Criminological Imagination: Critical Readings in Criminology*. Cullompton: Willan Publishing.

Whyte, W.F. ([1943] 1955) *Street Corner Society*, 2nd edn. Chicago, IL: University of Chicago Press.

Wilkins, L. (1964) *Social Deviance: Social Policy, Action and Research*. London: Tavistock.

Williams, K.S. (2004) *Textbook on Criminology*, 5th edn. Oxford: Oxford University Press.

Willis, P. (1978) *Profane Culture*. London: Routledge & Kegan Paul.

Willmott, P. (1966) *Adolescent Boys of East London*. London: Routledge & Kegan Paul.

Wilson, H. (1980) Parental supervision: a neglected aspect of delinquency, *British Journal of Criminology*, 20: 203–35.

Wilson, J.Q. and Herrnstein, R.J. (1985) *Crime and Human Nature: The Definitive Study of the Causes of Crime*. New York: Simon & Schuster.

Wilson, J.Q. and Kelling, G.L. (1982) Broken windows: the police and neighborhood safety, *Atlantic Monthly*, 249(3): 29–38.

Wilson, J.Q. and Kelling, G. (1989) Making neighborhoods safe, *Atlantic Monthly*, March, p. 29.

Wright, R.A. and Decker, S. (1994) *Burglars on the Job: Streetlife and Residential Break-ins*. Boston, MA: Northeastern University Press.

Young, J. (1971) *The Drugtakers: The Social Meaning of Drug Use*. London: MacGibbon and Kee/Paladin.

Young, J. (1975) Working class criminology, in I. Taylor, P. Walton and J. Young (eds) *Critical Criminology*. London: Routledge & Kegan Paul.

Young, J. (1986) The failure of criminology: the need for a radical realism, in R. Matthews and J. Young (eds) *Confronting Crime*. London: Sage Publications.

Young, J. (1987) The tasks facing a realist criminology, *Contemporary Crises*, 11: 337–56.

Young, J. (1988) Radical criminology in Britain: the emergence of a competing paradigm, in P. Rock (ed.) *A History of British Criminology*. Oxford: Oxford University Press.

Young, J. (1994) Incessant chatter: recent paradigms in criminology, in M. Maguire, R. Morgan and R. Reiner (eds) *The Oxford Handbook of Criminology*, 1st edn. Oxford: Clarendon Press.

Young, J. (1998) Writing on the cusp of change: a new criminology for an age of late modernity, in P. Walton and J. Young (eds) *The New Criminology Revisited*. Basingstoke: Macmillan.

Young, J. (2002) Critical criminology in the twenty-first century: critique, irony and the always unfinished, in K. Carrington and R. Hogg (eds) *Critical Criminology: Issues, Debates, Challenges*. Cullompton: Willan Publishing.

Young, J. (2003) Merton with energy, Katz with structure, *Theoretical Criminology*, 7(3): 389–414.

Young, J. (2006) Left realism, in E. McLaughlin and J. Muncie (eds) *The Sage Dictionary of Criminology*, 2nd edn. London: Sage Publications.

Young, J. (2007) *The Vertigo of Late Modernity*. London: Sage Publications.

Index

GENDER AND CRIME

A Reader

Karen Evans and Janet Jamieson (eds)

Focusing explicitly on questions of gender and crime, Evans and Jamieson guide the reader through a range of classic and groundbreaking studies, highlighting key contributions and debates and providing an indication of the new directions an engendered criminology may take us in coming years.

This engaging reader is divided into five sections, mapping the theoretical, empirical, and practical developments that have endeavoured to identify the ways in which gender informs criminology. Issues addressed by the readings include:

- Female offending
- Gendered patterns of victimisation
- The gendered nature of social control
- Masculinity and crime
- Placing gender in an international context

Evans and Jamieson's powerful concluding chapter clearly sets out the achievements and the challenges that the gender and crime question has posed for criminology. They argue that unless the question of gender remains at the forefront of criminological endeavours, criminology will fail to offer an agenda informed by an understanding of social justice that strives to be attentive to both victims and offenders, whether they be male or female.

Gender and Crime is key reading for students of criminology, criminal justice and gender studies.

Readings by: *Jon Bannister, Susan Brownmiller, Beatrix Campbell, Pat Carlen, Meda Chesney-Lind, Ruth Chigwada-Bailey, Richard Collier, Jock Collins, Jason Ditton, R. Emerson Dobash, Russell P. Dobash, Stephen Farrall, Lorraine Gelsthorpe, Elizabeth Gilchrist, Annie Hudson, Ruth Jamieson, Nancy Loucks, James W. Messerschmidt, Allison Morris, Greg Noble, Lisa Pasko, Scott Poynting, Lorraine Radford, Marcia Rice, Carol Smart, Laureen Snider, Elizabeth A. Stanko, Paul Tabar, Kaname Tsutsumi, Anne Worrall.*

Contents: *Series editor's foreword – Publisher's acknowledgements – Introduction: Gender and crime – the story – **Part 1: Engendering the agenda** - Introduction - Criminological theory: Its ideology and implications concerning women - Challenging orthodoxies in feminist theory: A black feminist critique – Girls' troubles and "female delinquency" ' - Twisted sisters, ladettes, and the new penology: The social construction of "violent girls" ' – **Part 2: Engendering the victim** - Introduction - Women fight back - Typical violence, normal precaution: Men, women and interpersonal violence in England, Wales, Scotland and the USA - Women and the "fear of crime": Challenging the accepted stereotype - Women's violence to men in intimate relationships: Working on the puzzle – **Part 3: Gender and social control** - Introduction – "Troublesome girls": Towards alternative definitions and policies - Justice in the making: Key influences on decision-making – Black women and the criminal justice system - Women's imprisonment in England and Wales: A penal paradox – **Part 4: Engendering masculinity** - Introduction - Boys will be boys - Structured action and gendered crime - Masculinities and crime: Rethinking the "man question" - Gender, class, racism, and criminal justice: Against global and gender-centric theories, for poststructuralist perspectives – **Part 5: International perspectives** - Introduction - Constituting the punishable woman: Atavistic man incarcerates postmodern woman - Globalization and violence against women: Inequalities in risks, responsibilities and blame in the UK and Japan – "You deserve it because you are Australian": The moral panic over "ethnic gang rape" ' - Genocide and the social production of immorality' – Conclusion: gender and crime – the legacy? - References – Index.*

June 2008 352pp

978-0-335-22523-1 (Paperback) 978-0-335-22522-4 (Hardback)

KEYWORDS IN POLICING

Ian K. Pepper and Helen Pepper

"Language reflects the operating heart and culture of any group of people or organization. The police service is no different except that in England and Wales it uses 43 slightly different 'dialects' as well. This book provides newcomers to British policing with an essential phrasebook that will support them while they learn the language of the profession."

Peter Wright, former Assistant Chief Constable of West Mercia Constabulary

'A valuable reference text for those studying and involved in the field of law enforcement. Easy to use, accurate, understandable and comprehensive and goes a long way to demystify common everyday terminology used in today's criminal justice system.'

Dr Nigel J. Callaghan, Forensic Physician and Barrister at Law

Like any large organization, the police service has developed its own language that may be confusing to those new to its ranks, such as police officers, community support officers, special constables, crime scene investigators or intelligence analysts.

This book is an invaluable reference, providing short, easy to read definitions of the most significant keywords and abbreviations used within contemporary policing and law enforcement.

Presented in alphabetical order, the user-friendly definitions describe the words, terms and abbreviations which are frequently used within 21st century policing.

Keywords in Policing is essential reading for students and professionals studying and working in the fields of policing, law enforcement and criminal justice, particularly those on vocational courses, serving within the police force, community support officers, or working with alternate law enforcement agencies.

Contents: Introduction: The development of law enforcement and policing across the UK – Using this collection of keywords, acronyms, abbreviations and mnemonics – Alphabetical listings – Table of statutes – Appendix 1: Police forces across the UK – Appendix 2: MG forms – Appendix 3: National Occupational Standards – Appendix 4: The phonetic alphabet – References.

2008 144pp

978-0-335-22377-0 (Paperback) 978-0-335-22376-3 (Hardback)

ETHNICITY AND CRIME

A Reader

Basia Spalek (ed)

"Basia Spalek has compiled an excellent reader about a much researched and highly sensitive subject. Crucially, she contextualises ethnicity and crime within broadly defined social and intellectual contexts, avoiding the limitation of all too frequently repeated research based solely on statistical measures and policy evaluations."

Simon Holdaway, Professor of Criminology and Sociology, Sheffield University

Issues in relation to race and ethnicity have generated substantial and ever-growing interest from, and within, a multitude of academic, research and policy contexts. This book brings together important material in race and ethnic studies and provides different ways of thinking about race and ethnicity in relation to crime and the criminal justice system.

Ethnicity and Crime: A Reader consists of a collection of works that capture the main themes that arise from within this vast area of work. It is divided into five sections:

- 'Race and crime', racial discrimination and criminal justice
- The racialisation of crime: Social, political and cultural contexts
- Race, ethnicity and victimisation
- Self and discipline reflexivity: Ethnic identities and crime
- Ethnic identities, institutional reflexivity and crime

Each section contains recurring and overlapping themes and includes many different ways of thinking about race and ethnicity in relation to crime. It spans theoretical approaches that might be labelled as positivist, critical race analyses, left realist approaches, feminist, as well as post-modern perspectives.

This is the first title in the new series Readings in Criminology and Criminal Justice and follows the series format of thematic sections, together with an editor's introduction to the complete volume and an introduction to each section.

Contents: *Series editor's foreword – Publisher's acknowledgements – Introduction – PART 1 'Race and crime', racial discrimination and criminal justice – Ethnic minorities, crime and criminal justice: A study in a provincial city – Some recent approaches to the study of race in criminological research: Race as social process – Discrimination in the Courts? – The Enlightenment and Euro-American theories of the judicial process – PART 2 The racialisation of crime: Social, political and cultural contexts – The race and crime debate – The myth of black criminality – Tolerance, freedom, justice and peace? Britain, Australia and anti-Muslim racism since 11 September 2001 – Introduction to The Asian Gang – PART 3 Race, ethnicity and victimisation – Racist violence in Europe: Challenges for official data collection – Racial victimization: An experiential analysis – Racism and victimization – Woman abuse in London's black communities – PART 4 Self and discipline reflexivity: Ethnic identities and crime – Political Blackness and British Asians – Racism, ethnicity and criminology: Developing minority perspectives – Constructing whiteness: The intersections of race and gender in US white supremacist discourse – Researching black Muslim women's lives: A critical reflection – Criminology and orientalism – PART 5 Ethnic identities, institutional reflexivity and crime – Can Macpherson succeed where Scarman failed? – (In)visible barriers: The experience of Asian employees in the probation service – Conclusion – Bibliography – Glossary – Useful websites – Index.*

2008 488pp

978-0-335-22379-4 (Paperback) 978-0-335-22378-7 (Hardback)

CRIMES OF THE POWERFUL

A Reader

David Whyte

Crimes of the powerful – the crimes committed by state institutions and private business organizations or corporations – are often overlooked by Criminology, or are treated at best as a mildly interesting diversion from the real business of crime and criminal justice. Indeed, academic Criminology in the main tends to reinforce the idea that the real problems of society can be located in the lower strata of society and is yet to come to terms with overwhelming evidence that crimes of the institutionally powerful kill, rip off and steal from more people than crimes committed by individuals.

This exciting Reader introduces debates on crimes of the powerful with a selection of 45 extracts from key authors. Each section of the book is introduced with an original essay to contextualize the readings and explain their importance for rethinking the relationship between crime and power.

The book is organised into the following sections:

- State, Violence and Crime
- Partners in Crime
- Capitalism and Crimes of the Powerful
- Law and the Corporation
- Explanations
- Definitions
- The Problem of Criminalization

If we are to fully understand the crimes of the powerful, it is crucial to recognise that the process of criminalisation is profoundly influenced by state institutions and corporations – and more importantly, by the relationship between them. The readings in this book show how their ability to both make and break the law remains a key source of power for those institutions.

Crimes of the Powerful explores how law and 'crime' provide a framework for configuring and reproducing social relations of power, in doing so, provides criminology, sociology, politics and international relations students with new insights into a subject of growing importance.

Contents: *Section 1: State, Violence, Crime – Section 2: Partners in Crime – Section 3: Capitalism and Crimes of the Powerful – Section 4: Law and the Corporation – Section 5: Explanations – Section 6: Definitions – Section 7: The Problem of Criminalisation.*

2008 280pp

978-0-335-22390-9 (Paperback) 978-0-335-22389-3 (Hardback)